Rumors of Baseball's Demise

Rumors of Baseball's Demise

*How the Balance of Competition
Swung and the Critics Missed*

ROBERT CULL

McFarland & Company, Inc., Publishers
Jefferson, North Carolina, and London

All photographs: Baseball Hall of Fame Library, Cooperstown, New York.

LIBRARY OF CONGRESS CATALOGUING-IN-PUBLICATION DATA

Cull, Robert J.
    Rumors of baseball's demise : how the balance of competition swung and the critics missed / Robert Cull.
       p.   cm.
    Includes bibliographical references and index.

    ISBN 0-7864-2251-3 (softcover : 50# alkaline paper)

    1. Baseball—United States—History. 2. Major League Baseball (Organization)—History. I. Title.
GV863.A1C85   2006
796.357′640973—dc22   2005031456

British Library cataloguing data are available

©2006 Robert Cull. All rights reserved

No part of this book may be reproduced or transmitted in any form or by any means, electronic or mechanical, including photocopying or recording, or by any information storage and retrieval system, without permission in writing from the publisher.

Cover image ©2006 Photodisc

Manufactured in the United States of America

McFarland & Company, Inc., Publishers
  Box 611, Jefferson, North Carolina 28640
    www.mcfarlandpub.com

To Erica

Contents

Acknowledgments	viii
Preface	1
Introduction	5
1. Parity and Payrolls	13
2. Player Movement	42
3. Player Development: The Evolution of the Draft	77
4. Pitching Quality on Championship Teams	106
5. Pitching Variability	127
6. The Wild Card	152
7. Conclusions	202
Epilogue	215
Appendix A. Market Size Population of Metropolitan Statistical Areas	217
Appendix B. Major League Attendance Regressions, 1945–1996	219
Notes	223
Bibliography	231
Index	233

Acknowledgments

I trace my passion for baseball, and sports generally, to my father, Bob Cull Sr., and my uncles Jack, Jerry, Jim and Larry Cull, and Neil Ward. No Cubs-Sox or Bears-Packers argument was ever too inane, and no opportunity to needle someone when his team was down was ever passed up. Thanks, guys. As I see these "values" being handed down to a new generation, I sometimes wonder if it is altogether healthy; but, in the end, we are who we are.

Thanks also to my mother, Kathy Cull, and my siblings, Betsy Cull, Bill Cull, Mark Cull, and Maureen O'Brochta, who offered encouragement during the many years I spent on this project. And thanks to my parents-in-law, Edie and Milt Mintzer, for renewing my subscription to the invaluable *Baseball Weekly* (which evolved into *Sports Weekly*), in each of those years.

I received help from many friends. Kari Labrie assembled player salary data for Chapters 2 and 3, and reformatted earlier drafts of the manuscript. Polly Means created the figures in Chapter 2. A number of economists and friends—some avid baseball fans, some not—offered helpful advice and encouragement, including Mark Bykowsky, George Clarke, Steve Haber, Zorina Khan, Steve Knack, Jeff Prisbrey, Halsey Rogers, Dave Schmidt, Ken Sokoloff, and Colin Xu. George also provided comments on parts of the draft. Special thanks to Mark for putting me in touch with Andy Wirkmaa, who put me in touch with McFarland.

Many friends who are baseball fans have influenced my thinking on competitive balance through casual conversations I am sure they have forgotten. There is no way to include them all, but I wanted to name a handful; Keith Bruch, Bryan Butler, Louis Camphor, Dennis Carolyn, Matt Cash, Matt Farmer, Mike Farmer, Mike Pollino, Tim Sidlow, Frank Urban, and Neil Ward Jr.

Three friends deserve special thanks. Lance Davis and Stan Engerman provided very helpful comments on multiple drafts of the manuscript. Not only has Tim Sloan had to listen to me prattle on about this book for nine years, he provided detailed editorial suggestions on the manuscript. He should really be a coauthor of some of the chapters. I cannot thank him enough.

My wife, Erica, has also listened to me prattle on about baseball for years. She complains only a little bit, and each year buys me the full baseball package on cable television for my birthday, fully realizing the negative impact it is likely to have on her own television viewing. She also provided helpful comments on substantial portions of the manuscript. For all the sacrifices, great and small, that this project has entailed, I say thanks, hon.

Preface

I set out to write a very different book, one describing baseball's ills in the wake of the mid–1990s labor strife. In particular, my motivation stemmed from the fact that 1994 was finally going to be *the* year for my team, the Chicago White Sox. When the strike asphyxiated the season, the Sox were within reach of the Central Division title and showing every sign of washing away several decades of disappointment and futility.

There was much to cleanse. Middle-aged Yankees fans can wax nostalgic about seeing Mickey Mantle and the Bronx Bombers dismantle another opponent in the House that Ruth Built. Older White Sox fans had the 1959 World Series appearance to savor. They could draw on fond memories of Minnie Minoso, Nellie Fox, Billy Pierce, and Luis Aparicio. Fans who cut their teeth on the White Sox teams of the early '70s had somewhat different experiences. Dick Allen, a remarkable hitter, was with the team for a few years, but the offense was generally feeble. As the Sox came to bat I remember my father saying, "We'll score. All we need is a walk, a stolen base, a sacrifice bunt, and a wild pitch." It was the truly awful Sox teams of the '70s that made the 1994 team so much more satisfying, and the strike that much more difficult to bear. Why couldn't they have stopped playing in one of the countless years when my team was 20 games out of first place? How long would Chicago fans suffer for the Black Sox scandal of 1919? (The suffering would end with the Sox' 2005 World Series title; one championship may not be sufficient compensation for 87 years of futility, but it certainly felt good to see the long drought come to an end.)

And thus was my dissatisfaction with major league baseball born. Of course, I didn't lack for company. But, whereas my dissatisfaction was born of a specific opportunity lost, others saw the strike as symptomatic of deep troubles within the game. Just before the strike, Peter Gammons, a baseball writer I had come to enjoy on ESPN's *Baseball Tonight*, published a book that offered a litany of baseball's current deficiencies: spiraling player salaries, soon-to-be plummeting television revenues, a number of teams struggling financially, interminable games, and a shrinking pool of major-league-quality talent made thinner by expansion. As a result of those problems, Gammons wrote, "the future of what was once a leisurely pastime hangs in the balance."[1]

Compounding the disgust and despair over the current state of baseball was a growing sense that the game was better in the past, particularly in the gilded years of the 1950s. Nostalgic longing for a return to a distant Golden Age is as old as Homer, and baseball has never been immune from it. Yet, the "halcyon days of yore" thesis seemed to be gaining currency among baseball fans. That view was typified by David Halberstam's books on the 1949 and 1964 seasons (focusing on the Yankees–Red Sox and Yankees-Cardinals, respectively) and Ken Burns' nine-inning epic on PBS. To their credit, neither man ignored the game's past failings, particularly the segregation that tainted the first five decades of the modern era and the racism that retarded play (especially in the American League) in the late '50s and early '60s. Nevertheless, both men's works strike the reader or viewer as elegies for a bygone era when the times were simpler, the games were purer, and the players were American icons rather than pampered mercenaries.

The refrain has grown so familiar that most fans take it as an article of faith that large-market teams spend so much more on player salaries that their success on the field is all but assured. And I suppose I was no different before researching this book. Having lived in Chicago, Los Angeles and Washington, D.C., I had seen firsthand a number of so-called large-market teams (the Angels, Cubs, Dodgers, Orioles, and White Sox) that had failed to win, so I knew that market size and payroll alone were insufficient to produce victory. At the same time, however, it was impossible not to notice that the big-market Yankees and Red Sox were gobbling up free agents, while the small-market Expos and Pirates were losing the services of players like Moises Alou, Barry Bonds, Larry Walker, and Pedro Martinez just as they hit the prime of their careers. Seeing Jason Giambi in a Yankees uniform or Pedro Martinez in a Red Sox uniform does give me an uneasy feeling, as it should any fan worried about competitive balance. Such moves contributed to a growing sense among fans that the economics of the game were tilting the playing field inexorably toward the large-market teams.

In my day job as a research economist I conduct statistical analysis, and so I thought I would apply those techniques to study the evolution of competitive balance in baseball since World War II. I gathered data on attendance, winning percentages, pitching performance, player development — anything that might shed light on the relative degree of competition in the major leagues over the last 60 years. And I fully expected those data to reveal the most recent era as less balanced than others, or at least less balanced than the late 1970s and 1980s. But it didn't work out that way. By most measures, the 1990s were the most competitively balanced decade since World War II.[2] That trend has continued into the new millennium, with a few notable exceptions, such as the 2003 Detroit Tigers, with their woeful .265 winning percentage.

I should have known better. When I began researching the book in the mid–1990s, there were ample signs of competitive balance, but I was too focused on the White Sox to notice. Prior to the strike and the lead-up to it, the game's appeal was as broad as ever. In 1992, attendance was 55,870,466, ranking just below 1991's then all-time high of 56,813,760. Although some small-market teams were reported to be struggling financially, the 1992 Pittsburgh Pirates made the National League playoffs and the Milwaukee Brewers finished just four games behind the division winner and eventual world champion Toronto Blue Jays. In 1993, with the introduction of the Florida Marlins and the Colorado Rockies, total attendance hit 70,257,938, a figure that would not be eclipsed until 1998. In 1994, the Montreal Expos were leading their division when the strike hit.

As my results came dribbling in, I was forced to rethink my views on competitive balance in the 1990s. I would discuss them with family and friends to gauge the plausibility of my arguments, often failing to convince fans who viewed competitive balance through the prism of their own team's fortunes. And in 1996, the New York Yankees—the team that perennially has posed the greatest threat to competitive balance in the minds of most fans—won the first of four World Series titles in a five-year span. What had already been an uphill struggle grew even more arduous.

As the 1990s wound down, however, some friends started to be convinced, offering words of encouragement such as, "Doesn't the Padres' appearance in the World Series help out your book?" And the recent successes of the Oakland A's, Seattle Mariners, and Minnesota Twins, coupled with the 2003 World Series championship of the Florida Marlins, has elicited even more comment. Michael Lewis's book *Moneyball*, which describes the Oakland A's highly successful use of statistical analysis in drafting and acquiring players, also appeared in 2003. His explanation for the A's success offered additional reasons to be somewhat more sanguine about the future of small-market teams, although I would point out that a number of teams from such markets have been successful and not all of them follow the A's methods. In short, recent anecdotal evidence and the empirical analyses offered here lead to the same conclusions. To paraphrase Mark Twain, the reports of baseball's death have been greatly exaggerated. Let me convince you.

Introduction

If baseball's perceived ills are undermining competitive balance — if they are creating leagues divided between large-market haves and small-market have-nots — it should be easy to point to a number of truly awful teams. In fact, if terrible teams are defined as having winning percentages under .400, a record of 64–98, there were fewer terrible teams in the last 18 years than there were in any other period since World War II. About 15% of all major league teams finished below .400 between 1946 and 1965 (Table 1). In no five-year period prior to 1965 did the percentage of awful teams dip below 10 (column 2). The lowest figure is 11.3% for 1956–60, and that figure derives largely from the fact that there were no bad teams in 1959, the only time this occurred. It was a strange year, and until 2005, the last year in which the White Sox won the American League pennant.

Ten to 15% awful teams per year might not seem large, that is, until the pre–1965 experience is compared with later years. From 1966 to 1985 only 9 to 10% of all teams were sub–.400.[1] After 1985, the share of sub–.400 teams dipped even further, to about 5%. Not only the percentage but also the absolute number of awful teams reached its lowest levels after 1985, which is surprising given that there were almost twice as many teams in the major leagues in the '90s than in the '50s. The last period in the table comprises 1996–2003, an eight-year period, so the number of sub–.400 teams (16) is larger than for the other periods. However, those 16 sub–.400 teams represent 6.8% of the total, a figure similar to those for 1986–1990 and 1991–1995.

Shares of sub–.400 teams for some periods are inflated by expansion years. It may be a bit unreasonable to expect a new organization to win 65 games in its inaugural season. Table 1 also presents shares of sub–.400 teams that exclude all expansion years (1961, 1962, 1969, 1977, 1993, and 1998). The revised figures only reinforce the original conclusions. The share of sub–.400 teams in 1961–65 excluding expansion years declined to 13.3%, but revised figures for 1966–70, 1976–1980, 1991–95, and 1996–2003 are all below 9%, and, as before, the figures tend to be lower after 1985.

The data suggest that all this talk of small market versus large market, of baseball's "haves" and "have-nots," is overdone. Fewer teams are truly over-

Table 1—Sub-.400 Teams

Period	Sub-.400 Teams (1)	% League (2)	Lowest Win Pct. (3)	% League Excluding Expansion Years (4)
1946–1950	13	16.3%	.318	16.3%
1951–1955	13	16.3%	.273	16.3%
1956–1960	9	11.3%	.338	11.3%
1961–1965	14	14.3%	.250	13.3%
1966–1970	10	9.3%	.321	6.0%
1971–1975	11	9.2%	.351	9.2%
1976–1980	14	10.9%	.327	8.8%
1981–1985	13	10.0%	.349	10.0%
1986–1990	6	4.6%	.335	4.6%
1991–1995	8	5.9%	.352	4.6%
1996–2003	16	6.8%	.265	6.8%

matched now than at any point since World War II. Contrary to the alarmists, the steady decline of sub-.400 teams in recent years indicates that competitive balance in baseball is waxing rather than waning. The goal of this book is to describe the factors that have led to increased competitive balance and to explain why so few fans and writers are aware of that fact.

There are some obvious reasons why such balance has gone unnoticed, or at least under-emphasized. From 1996 to 2000, the New York Yankees won four of five World Series titles. In his 2003 book *May the Best Team Win*, economist Andrew Zimbalist documented an increasingly strong statistical association between team payrolls and winning percentages during this period, which seemed to reinforce the conventional wisdom arising from the period of Yankees hegemony.[2] Moreover, had the last period in Table 1 been split, the share of sub-.400 teams from 2001 to 2003 would have been 11.1%, a figure similar to those for the pre–1980 periods.[3]

Within Table 1 itself, there is some evidence of growing imbalance in the late 1990s. For example, the lowest winning percentage in each period (column 3) is not only another indicator of competitive balance, but also an indication of how disadvantaged expansion teams were in their first years of existence. Looking only at those five-year periods that contained expansion years, the lowest winning percentage in 1961–65 was the 1962 Mets' .250; for 1966–70 it was the 1969 Expos and Padres, both at .321; for 1976–80, the 1979 Blue Jays (.327); and for 1991–95, the 1991 Indians (.352).[4] Similar comparisons hold for five-year periods that contain no expansion years—the very worst teams in baseball had higher winning percentages after 1965. However, the 2003 Detroit Tigers (.265) buck that trend. There is no simple explanation for the Tigers' futility in that year, but it should be noted that Detroit is a major market and the team plays in a relatively new ballpark, both factors purported to assist teams. Their problems would not appear to be typical of those characterizing the small-market teams that are the focus of so many worries among writers and fans.

The data indicate that, contrary to the views of many pundits and commentators, competitive balance is not in decline. Indeed, there appear to be as many reasons for satisfaction about the current level of play in the major leagues as there are to be concerned about it. This book explores the reasons why the current economics of the game have not, and likely will not, adversely affect the quality of the product on the field. At the outset, however, it is fair to consider whether the fans even care about competitive balance.

They might, for example, prefer to have an arch-villain like the Yankees. However, the regression in Table 2 illustrates that greater competitive balance has historically led to greater fan interest. The premise is that fans are more likely to come to the ballpark if (1) they have enough disposable income, and (2) their team is in the race. Income is important because professional sports are entertainment, one of the first things that households forego when times are tough. In economic terms, demand for entertainment is said to be income elastic, meaning baseball attendance should be sensitive to changes in income. In addition, total attendance should increase when there are additional teams added to the league. Finally, if fans are more likely to turn out if their club is in the pennant (now playoff) race, attendance should increase in years when relatively more teams are in the race, controlling for fan income and the number of teams in the league.

Total attendance in any given year (call it year i) is assumed to be a function of the number of teams in the league, the inflation-adjusted level of per capita national disposable income, and the number of teams within 10 games of a playoff berth (a division championship from 1969 to 1993, or a league championship for years prior to 1969):[5]

$Attendance_i = B_0 + B_1 \times Teams\ in\ League_i + B_2 \times Per\ Capita\ Income_i + B_3 \times Teams\ in\ Race_i + e_i$.

Each B indicates the change in attendance associated with a one-unit increase in the associated variable, with B_0 representing a baseline or starting attendance number. For example, B_1 indicates the effect that adding a new team to the league will have on attendance. This simple model won't explain perfectly the yearly variation in attendance from 1945 to 2000. The e at the end of the equation is an error term that measures how much the simple model under predicts or overpredicts attendance in year i. The coefficients (B's) are calculated to minimize the size of these error terms.

The model explains 89% of the variation in attendance (Table 2).[6] The coefficient on "Teams" indicates that adding one to the natural log of teams increases the natural log of attendance by 0.607.[7] In English, suppose there were 14 teams in the league, real per capita income was $4,079 (measured in 1967 dollars), and there were five teams within 10 games of a playoff berth, all of

Table 2 — Major League Attendance Regression (1945–2003) Dependent Variable: Log of Total League Attendance

Independent Variables	Coefficient
Constant	7.331
	(8.86)†
Natural Log of Teams	0.607
	(2.51)*
Natural Log Real Per Capita Income	0.936
	(5.77)†
Teams in Race (i.e., within 10 games of making playoffs at season's end)	0.033
	(3.01)†
R-squared	0.89
Observations	112

t-statistics in parentheses; † indicates significance at the $p < .01$ level; * at the $p < .05$ level.

Notes: Strike-shortened seasons 1981, 1994, and 1995 are excluded from the analysis because total attendance was necessarily lower in those years. R-squared is a measure of the extent to which variation in attendance is explained by variation in the independent variables. It can range from 0 to 1, with one indicating that attendance is perfectly described by the estimated coefficients multiplied by the other variables. Observations are the total number of data points that enter the regression. There were 56 full seasons from 1945 to 2003, and the attendance figure for each league in each year is treated as a separate data point. Very similar results are obtained when the figures for the AL and NL are combined to make one observation per year. Income per capita comes from the U.S. Department of Commerce Bureau of Economic Analysis and is measured in 1967 dollars. The consumer price index used to derive real per capita income comes from the U.S. Bureau of Labor Statistics: http://www.bls.gov/cpi/. Attendance data are from Total Baseball (1997) for 1945–1996, and compiled from team attendance data from http://www.baseballreference.com/ for 1996–2003.

which describes the American League in 1977. If the league had added two new teams, the model predicts that attendance would have increased by 1.8 million. The model also indicates that if real per capita income increased by $100 to $4,179, attendance would have increased by 490,939. Neither the income nor the additional team results are especially interesting, but both factors must be controlled for to isolate the attendance impact of additional teams in the race (the model's measure of competitive balance). That both of these coefficients seem reasonable, however, inspires confidence in the model. The main result is, finally, that for each additional team within 10 games of a division championship at season's end, attendance would have increased by 718,519.

The relationship between attendance and each of these variables is reliable. The t-statistics indicate that if the "true" coefficients were zero (i.e., these variables had no impact on attendance), one would expect the data to produce coefficients this large less than 1% of the time. The evidence is that fans are more inclined to go to games if they have the money and if their team is in the race, which augers well for baseball's immediate future. Despite a recent economic slowdown, real household income in the United States is unlikely to take a dramatic dip any time soon. In addition, the number of teams within 10 games of a championship continues to be greater under the new wild-card format. Of course, it's unclear whether fans respond to potential wild-card champions in the same way that they did to division champions. Chapter 7, therefore, offers data bearing on the nature of the expected races under the new format, and on the fan response to the wild card during 1995, a year when lingering resentment over the strike might have made those races especially unattractive. However, the data suggest that on balance the new format is positive for baseball.

The attendance data, moreover, make it clear that baseball need not be overly concerned that in opinion polls fans no longer consider it their favorite sport. As long as incomes grow, fans are likely to attend more baseball, football, basketball, and hockey games. The idea that the American sports "pie" is of constant size, and that one sport's gain is necessarily another's loss is false. Baseball is insulated from disaster in another important way: America's professional sports are not perfect substitutes for one another. In late June, all of July, and most of August, baseball faces no real competition from other professional sports. Gloom-and-doom forecasts might make good copy, but the attendance data indicate that they are not going to come true any time soon.

To sum things up at this point, the evidence indicates that competitive balance in the major leagues is not in decline. Furthermore, more so than at any time since World War II, more teams have an opportunity to compete for division titles, league pennants, and world championships. That competition, in turn, will attract the spectators and dollars that will sustain the game. As noted above, the remainder of this book examines the evolution and determinants of competitive balance. The analysis focuses on the years after World War II when, among other things, Jackie Robinson and Branch Rickey showed America what major league baseball could be like if all the best players were allowed to play. Summarizing trends over nearly 60 years is an art more than a science, however. For some types of analysis, such as on sub–.400 teams in Table 1.1, five-year periods seemed appropriate. For other types of analysis, data are grouped into four eras, although their demarcation is admittedly subjective.

The first period, which runs from 1946 through 1962, is called the "Mantle era," as the team from the Bronx dominated as none had before or has since. The Yankees won 13 league titles in 17 years, and never finished lower than fourth. In 14 of those years they posted a winning percentage higher than .600. Things weren't much more balanced in the National League. The Dodgers won seven pennants, finished in second six times, in third two times, and fourth once. Their only bad year was 1958 (seventh place), the year they moved to Los Angeles. In nine of 17 years they posted winning percentages above .600. Aside from an occasional flash in the pan ('50 Phillies), and winners at the tail ends of the era ('46 Cardinals, '60 Pirates, and '61 Reds), the remaining six pennants were distributed evenly between the Giants and the Braves.

Yes, the Yankees won AL pennants in 1963 and 1964. They did, however, go on to lose both World Series, getting swept by the Dodgers in 1963. Jim Bouton's book *Ball Four*, moreover, made it clear that the '63–'64 teams were qualitatively different from their predecessors. Free spirits like Bouton and Joe Pepitone played integral roles. In 1963, Whitey Ford was still a dominant force (24–7, 2.74 ERA, 269.1 IP, and 189 strikeouts), but Mantle was a shadow of his former self (65 games, .314 BA, 15 HR, 35 RBI).[8] By '63, the Yankees were a team in transition, and so they are placed in the next era.[9]

The second era runs from 1963 to 1976, and marks the ascendance of the black player. Willie Mays, Willie McCovey, Ernie Banks, Roberto Clemente, Frank Robinson, Henry Aaron, and others dominated the National League. Slower to integrate, the American League took a pounding in the early years of the period. From 1963 to 1969, the NL took five of the seven series. After that, things evened out: from 1970 to 1976 the AL won four series, the NL three. Competitive balance remained a problem, though not as serious as in the Mantle era. Five teams dominated. In the AL, the Orioles appeared in four World Series (winning two),[10] and the A's appeared in three (winning them all). In the NL, the Reds appeared in four (winning two), the Dodgers four (two wins), and the Cardinals appeared in three and won two.

In Hank Aaron's autobiography he reflects, though not too bitterly, on the media attention heaped on Willie Mays. He also details his unjust treatment at the hands of MVP voters.[11] The same won't happen here. The second era is called the Henry Aaron era. He did have some of his greatest years prior to 1963, but he retired in 1976 (fittingly, the end of the era), and had great years throughout. As late as 1973 he hit 40 home runs and batted .301. He is the all-time leader in home runs and RBI, which is reason enough to name an era after him.

The third era marks the emergence of the free agent. Although high-priced free agents were hawking their wares in 1976 — Jim "Catfish" Hunter comes to mind — the era begins with the arrival of Reggie Jackson in New York in 1977 (and the Yankees' first world title since 1962).[12] Players shuffled between teams, salaries skyrocketed, but, as noted above, there was competitive balance. It is tempting to name this era after Reggie, but Mr. October wasn't the man truly responsible for the changes in the game. That man was Marvin Miller, the executive director of the Major League Players Association. Nonplayers rarely receive enough credit (and, in the case of managers, often receive too much blame), and so 1977–1992 is referred to as the Marvin Miller era. That leaves 1993–2003 as the recent era.

Contrary to some pundits and commentators, the research that follows suggests that the prospects for baseball are bright largely because of greater competitive balance. Chapter 1 examines the "large-market–small-market" debate in detail. The key findings are that large-market teams do spend a lot more money on players, but that spending does not, on average, lead to much higher winning percentages. Chapter 2 provides evidence on increased competitive balance and tries to explain when and why it occurred, and why large markets do not enjoy that great an advantage. A large part of the explanation is that large-market teams routinely overpay for veteran players because of the way free agent salaries are negotiated.

Chapter 3 considers the amateur draft, which helped spread the available pool of talent more equitably among all major league teams. It is little surprise, therefore, that the evolution of the draft has coincided with greater competitive balance. The leveling effect of the draft appears to have strengthened over the years as teams have slowly improved their ability to select good players, especially pitchers. Chapter 4 explains why it is important that the draft has become a source of pitching talent, especially for small-market teams. The key finding is that good pitching is necessary to win a title. The same cannot be said of hitting. On numerous occasions, weak-hitting teams have won titles. Pitching isn't, however, sufficient to ensure a title. That is, the best-pitching team doesn't always win the division, but a weak-pitching team *never* (well, almost never) wins. Chapter 5 then presents the evidence on the variability of pitching performance relative to hitting performance, arguing that year-to-year variability in pitching is a driving force behind competitive balance. Attempts to "buy" pennants by buying pitchers may fail because for pitchers, unlike hitters, the past is frequently not prologue.

As noted, Chapter 6 presents the evidence on the effect of the wild-card playoff format on competitive balance. Chapters 1–5 demonstrate that small-market teams weren't and aren't in that bad a competitive situation, even without the wild card. Nevertheless, the new playoff format might provide small-market teams with a better opportunity to compete for baseball's ultimate prize. The chapter explains what the races from 1977 to 1992 would have looked like under the new format and concludes that, on balance, the format would have provided some minor benefits in terms of competitive balance. Finally, Chapter 7 offers concluding comments and speculation about why Commissioner Bud Selig feels the need to fix a game that's not really broken.

1
Parity and Payrolls

The large-market–small-market debate often combines, or confuses, two imperfectly related issues—market size and payroll. The logic seems straightforward. Step one: teams in large-markets can and do pay more for players. Step two: by attracting and paying for better players, large-market teams win more games, so many more that their small-market brethren increasingly cannot afford to compete with them. Step three: small-market teams lose fans, suffer a loss of revenues that further impairs their ability to compete, and so on to oblivion. The evidence in this chapter will provide some support for step one, large-market teams do spend more on players. The evidence in support of steps two and three, that teams that spend more necessarily win more and that small-market teams are on a path to oblivion, is far less convincing.

Before proceeding with the analysis, it is first necessary to define what is meant by the term large-markets. While one can measure market size in a number of ways, Appendix A offers the most recent data for the two measures relied upon throughout the book: (1) the population of metropolitan statistical areas ("MSAs") as defined in U.S. Census statistics, and (2) MSA population divided by the number of teams in the market. In Chicago, for example, MSA population is divided by two to indicate that the White Sox and Cubs share the market.

So why is large-market advantage so ingrained in most fans' heads? Largely because the most readily available, though misleading, statistics offer support for that proposition. On November 23, 1999, *Baseball Weekly* (*BW*) noted that the eight playoff teams in that year were all among the top 10 spenders on player salaries:

> The World Series champion Yankees had a record payroll of $91.99 million, about $18 million more than the previous high set by Baltimore in 1998. Among playoff teams they were followed by Texas ($80.8 million), NL pennant winner Atlanta ($79.3 million), Cleveland ($73.5 million), Boston ($72.3 million), the New York Mets ($71.5 million), Arizona ($70 million) and Houston ($56.4 million).... [T]he Top Five included baseball's most notorious underachievers of 1999: Los Angeles was fourth at $76.6 million, followed by Baltimore at $75.4 million.

The article went on to note that from 1995 to 1999, only one team ranked in the bottom half by payroll reached the playoffs (the 1997 Astros, 18th of 28 teams). All 10 of the World Series participants over that period were among the Top 10 in payroll. To their credit, the writers at *BW* did mention that paying a lot doesn't ensure success. But the basic message is that if a team spends bundles and doesn't choose its players too badly, it is going to win. That message is wrong, or at least far too simplistic. The presumed demarcation between the haves and the have-nots is simply not that sharp.

For starters, the *BW* information implies that, from 1995 to 1999, one playoff team typically ranked about 13th in salary, which is near the median, in a league of 30 teams. That statistic itself is misleading because, as demonstrated below, salary data is a lagging indicator rather than a leading indicator of success. Put another way, teams commonly pay high salaries for past performance, not future performance. At this point, however, just note that some teams in the middle of the pack in terms of end-of-year payroll made it to the playoffs during this period. Those teams typically spent only about 60% to 70% of the figure for the highest spending team. And one of them—the 1998 San Diego Padres—made it to the World Series. The Padres spent just over $50 million in that year, while the Orioles and the Yankees (the eventual World Series champions) spent about $75 million each.[1] Moreover, *BW* wrote this article in 1999, before the Oakland A's made the playoffs in four consecutive years (2000–2003) while ranked in the bottom quartile in team payroll. Similarly, the Minnesota Twins made the playoffs in both 2002 and 2003 with a payroll slightly higher than that of the A's and well below the major league median.

One would expect the growing inequality in payrolls to be reflected in greater dispersion in winning percentages. But since World War II, winning percentages have actually narrowed. The first chapter presented some evidence on this topic, namely the declining share of teams with winning percentages below .400. Chapter 2 will demonstrate that free agency has coincided with slightly more, rather than less, competitive balance. In Chapter 3, the evidence will suggest that most of the credit for narrowing winning percentages should go to the amateur draft.

SALARIES

However, it is possible that huge spending disparities between teams are a recent phenomenon, and that this book's focus on the long sweep of baseball history obscures the current problems. All the preceding talk about continued competitive balance doesn't change the fact that in 1998 the Orioles spent nine times more on player salaries than did the Expos. If the established veteran players are even *slightly* better than younger players, spending *nine* times the level that "small-market" teams do should ensure that, position by position, the small-market team is slightly overmatched. All of those slight mismatches should make certain that a small-market team simply cannot beat a high-spending large-market team over a 162-game season.

Many people associated with the game have looked at the data on salaries and come to a similar conclusion. Pete Williams of *BW* noted that the 1998 data (Table 1.1) prompted Commissioner Bud Selig, at baseball's November 1999 meeting in Naples, Florida, to make sure that general managers "realized that the growing disparity between baseball's haves and have-nots continues to pace the game on a track toward Armageddon." Williams continued:

> Selig asked that only the 30 general managers stay in the meeting room.... Not that he needed to make such a dramatic show of things. The annual salary figures compiled by the Player Relations Committee, presented earlier in the week told the entire grim story. Of the 15 teams with payrolls below $44 million, only the Toronto Blue Jays, with a record of 88–74, finished the year above the .500 mark.[2]

As in 1997, the Houston Astros were the lowest spending team to reach the playoffs in 1998, ranking 12th with a $48.3 million payroll. Again, the underlying logic seems almost unassailable — good teams get to the postseason by spending money, and teams that can't or won't spend don't win. While the argument has intuitive appeal, it is flawed. At the very least, salary data are routinely misanalyzed and a large disparity in salaries between two teams in one year is not sufficient evidence to argue that competitive balance is threatened over the longer term.

Note that even if the information in Table 1.1 is taken at face value, the link between high salaries and winning isn't as direct as some would have you believe. While the simple correlation between payroll and winning percentage is high (.74), it isn't a perfect association. Notable breaks in the pattern are evident throughout the list. Four of the teams in the top 10 in terms of payroll didn't make the playoffs. Their combined winning percentage was only .517. The Orioles, the team with the highest payroll, had a winning percentage of only .488. As noted throughout the book, there is ample evidence that spending money on players does not ensure success on the field, and 1998 was no exception.

The flip side of the money-success proposition — that *not* spending money on players ensures failure — is, at first glance, better supported by the evidence in Table 1.1. As Williams noted, with but one exception, teams in the lower half in terms of payroll did have losing seasons. In that same table, however, is evidence that lower-spending teams were able to produce wins much more cheaply than the teams that spent a lot. The $/win column indicates that teams with lower payrolls tended to produce their wins for about one-third to one-half the cost of their high-spending competitors. Cincinnati, for example, finished with a record only two games worse than the Orioles, but did so at a cost per win only 29% as large. This has a lot to do with evidence in Chapter 2 that veteran players tend to receive compensation greater than their on-field performance should warrant.

So, even if Table 1.1 is interpreted as indicating that teams have to spend money to win (which is simplistic), the $/win figures indicate that those wins

Table 1.1—1998 Team Payrolls

Team	Payroll Millions ($)	W-L	Win. Pct.	$/Win
Baltimore	74.0	79–83	.488	936,657
NY Yankees*	73.8	114–48	.704	647,489
Texas*	62.2	88–74	.543	706,311
Atlanta*	61.7	106–56	.654	582,455
Los Angeles	60.7	83–79	.512	731,707
Boston*	59.3	92–70	.568	645,076
NY Mets	58.7	88–74	.543	666,598
Cleveland*	56.6	89–73	.549	636,443
Anaheim	54.2	85–77	.525	637,518
San Diego*	53.0	98–64	.605	540,777
Chi Cubs*	50.7	90–73	.552	563,178
Houston*	48.3	102–60	.630	473,471
San Francisco	47.9	89–74	.546	538,368
Colorado	47.9	77–85	.475	621,879
St. Louis	47.6	83–79	.512	573,602
Seattle	44.7	76–85	.472	588,619
Chi White Sox	37.8	80–82	.494	472,875
Toronto	37.3	88–74	.543	423,506
Milwaukee	36.9	74–88	.457	498,028
Kansas City	35.6	72–89	.447	494,583
Arizona	32.8	65–97	.401	504,838
Philadelphia	29.2	75–87	.463	398,967
Tampa Bay	27.6	63–99	.389	438,413
Detroit	23.3	65–97	.401	358,754
Minnesota	22.0	70–92	.432	314,679
Cincinnati	20.7	77–85	.475	268,926
Florida	19.1	54–108	.333	354,463
Oakland	18.6	74–88	.457	251,150
Pittsburgh	13.7	69–93	.426	198,478
Montreal	8.3	65–97	.401	127,962

Correlation between Payroll and Winning Percentage: .74

Source: MLB Player Relations Committee. Does not include postseason award bonuses. Totals are based on Aug. 31 rosters and include prorated shares of signing bonuses and earned incentive bonuses.
* indicates playoff team. $/win = payroll/wins.

wouldn't come cheaply. Even an owner like Peter Angelos of the Orioles eventually proved unwilling to incur these costs to achieve average success, and thus near the end of the 2000 season he unloaded many of the veterans that had contributed to the team's success in the mid–1990s.

In general, the more successful teams will find it very costly to keep their lineups intact. Just ask George Steinbrenner of the Yankees. This all bodes well for the game.

TEAM SALARIES AND
WINNING PERCENTAGE: 1985–2003

The data in Table 1.1, data that Major League Baseball often puts forth in discussing payrolls and competitive balance, are also misleading in important respects. For one thing, the payroll data include incentive bonuses.[3] When do players receive their incentive bonuses? When they are playing well, which is after they have achieved goals specified in their contracts. It comes as little surprise, therefore, that teams in the playoffs, teams with players that are performing well on an individual basis, experience a salary boost at the end of the season. Note that the salary boost does not cause improved performance; it results from good performance.

Another reason why the salary data in Table 1.1 are misleading is that teams make mid- and late-season personnel decisions based on their current performance. Which teams are most likely to increase their payrolls? Those in the midst of a pennant race. It happens every year. The teams that are in the race look to get that one player who will put them into the playoffs. And teams that are out of the race are willing to give up good players. Why? Teams in the race are teams in need, and are therefore willing to offer a better deal than they might otherwise be willing to offer. Also, these mid- to late-season deals are an opportunity to dump large salaries, especially salaries of players that will be coming up for free agency in the next year. It is better to get something for such players now, rather than lose them to free agency, or face the pressure of trying to re-sign them at a much higher salary next year. And it's not only the large-market contenders that acquire players this way. In 1999, the small-market Cincinnati Reds (96–66) acquired the large-market Orioles' starting pitcher Juan Guzman for the stretch drive. Like performance bonuses, these late-season acquisitions are a consequence of rather than a cause of good performance. By relying on the data in Table 1.1, Major League Baseball muddles the lines of causation between payroll and team performance.

To get a more accurate assessment of how much teams can improve their winning percentages by spending money on players, one should look at salary data from the beginning of the season, before incentive bonuses are paid and late-season personnel moves are made. Such data, or something close to them, were available at an Internet Web site maintained by the Business of Baseball (BOB) Research Committee of the Society for American Baseball Research (SABR). Doug Pappas, the chairman of the BOB committee, was instrumental in making available in computerized form yearly salaries from 1985 to 1999 for each player paid by a major league team, even players that were injured or later cut. Team salary estimates by year are derived by adding up the individual salaries.[4]

One drawback to the pre-bonus, beginning of season Pappas data is that they extend only through 1999. Similar estimates for 2000 to 2003 were not posted, and the original pre–2000 data is no longer available via the SABR website.[5] What is available appears to be the post-bonus data, but there is no documentation to substantiate that guess (see *www.businessofbaseball.com*). Sadly, Doug Pappas passed away in May 2004 before he could help clear up these questions.

The following analysis uses both the Pappas salary data and the currently available SABR payroll data. As further checks on the quality of those data, results are also derived using payroll data reported in the press (Associated Press, *USA Today*, or *New York Times*) that are also available via the BOB Web site. In most years, those payrolls appeared in or very near April and November, thus providing estimates for the beginning and end of each season. The April payroll data should produce results similar to the Pappas data, since no bonuses had been paid and no players had changed teams at the start of the season. The Pappas data are probably somewhat superior in that they come from the same source and are constructed from individual player salaries, whereas the mainstream media presumably took the team payroll estimates provided by MLB. However, to the extent that the two series produce similar results, it is less troubling to rely on the April payroll data after 1999, when the Pappas data are no longer available. Finally, the November data should indicate the extent to which using the estimates after performance bonuses are paid and high-salaried players have migrated to winning teams can overstate the statistical relationship between winning percentages and payrolls.

The correlations between the Pappas payrolls and winning percentages appear in the first column of Table 1.2. Prior to the last half of the 1990s, there was a positive, statistically significant correlation between those payrolls and winning percentages for only two of the 10 years listed in the table (1989 and 1994). By contrast, in four of the five years from 1995 to 1999, there was a positive link between Pappas payroll data and winning percentage. However, with the exception of 1998, those correlations are in the .4 to .6 range, somewhat less than the .74 correlation for the 1998 MLB data reported above in Table 1.1, or the .725 correlation for that year reported in Table 1.2, column 1.

At least two things stand out about the MLB and Pappas figures for 1998. First, the winning percentage correlations that the two series produce are almost identical, which indicates that purging the incentive bonuses and the end-of-season player movement from the payroll data weakens only slightly their positive association with winning percentages for that one year. Second, 1998 was a strange year because so few large-market teams played poorly. Both New York teams, both Los Angeles area teams, both Texas teams, the Boston Red Sox and the Chicago Cubs all had winning percentages above .500. The only large-market teams with losing records were the Baltimore Orioles, Chicago White Sox, Detroit Tigers, and Philadelphia Phillies; and the Orioles and White Sox were just a smidgen below .500. Thus the high correlation for 1998 is not driven principally by the Yankees' remarkable 114–48 season. If the Yankees are dropped

Table 1.2 — Correlation Between Winning Percentage and Team Payrolls 1985–2003

Year	Correlation with Payroll (Pappas, No Bonuses, Beginning of Season) (1)	Correlation with Payroll (SABR, No Adjustments) (2)	Correlation with April Payroll (3)	Correlation with Nov. Payroll (4)	Number of Teams in Calculation (5)
1985	.313	.346*	—	—	26
1986	.307	.202	.258	.224	26
1987	-.081	-.078	—	.150	26
1988	.155	.216	.152	.421†	26
1989	.484†	.396†	—	.483†	26
1990	-.011	.018	—	.188	26
1991	.221	.215	.277	.379*	26
1992	.034	.033	-.017	.156	26
1993	.308	.357*	.301	.433†	28
1994	.387†	.417†	.393†	.490§	28
1995	.273	.323*	.271	.563§	28
1996	.578§	.547§	.576§	.639§	28
1997	.441†	.444†	.448†	.672§	28
1998	.725§	.655§	.688§	.764§	30
1999	.565§	.568§	.578§	.687§	30
2000	—	.318*	.327*	.498§	30
2001	—	.312*	.339*	—	30
2002	—	.440†	.443†	.476§	30
2003	—	.421†	.418†	—	30
1985–1994 (number of team years in calculation)	.113* (264)	.119* (264)	.138* (160)	.192§ (238)	
85–94 Payrolls normalized (0 to 1)	.205§ (264)	.214§ (264)	.225§ (160)	.325§ (238)	
1995–2003 (number of team years in calculation)	.500§ (144)	.350§ (264)	.348§ (264)	.489§ (204)	
95–03 Payrolls normalized (0 to 1)	.527§ (144)	.425§ (264)	.440§ (264)	.605§ (204)	

*indicates significantly different from zero at the p = 0.10 level. † at the p=0.05 level. § at the p=0.01 level.

Source for salaries: Doug Pappas, SABR Business of Baseball Committee, salary data was available at: http://www.roadsidephotos.com/baseball/1999.htm. The SABR payrolls, April payrolls, and November payrolls are all available at http://www.businessofbaseball.com.

from the calculation, the correlation drops, but only to .70. When the general pattern is as strong as it is for 1998, one team doesn't make that big a difference. However, when the pattern is a bit weaker, one team can make a substantial difference. For example, if the Yankees data are dropped from the 1997 calculation, the correlation drops from .441 to .378 and is significant at only a 10% level (much weaker than the 5% level when they are included). In short, all the evidence presented here indicates that 1998 was a strange year, so strange that it is misleading to draw inferences about the strength of the relationship between team payroll and winning percentages based solely on that data, or on data from any single year for that matter.

But it might also be misleading to draw inferences based on the data from the late 1980s and early 1990s. For two of those years (1987 and 1990), the estimated relationship is actually negative (though insignificant). To get a better handle on what these correlations mean, observations are plotted for payroll and winning percentages for two years. If the relationship between payroll and winning were a perfect one, teams would be located along a line that begins in the southwest corner of the graph (where the low-payroll losers would be located) and the slopes upward toward the northeast corner of the graph (where the high-payroll winners would reside).

But the data for 1990 show a very different pattern. In that year, the estimated trend line is flat, which is obvious from the correlation for 1990 in Table 1.2 (-.011). It's still somehow more impressive to see it on the graph. The data

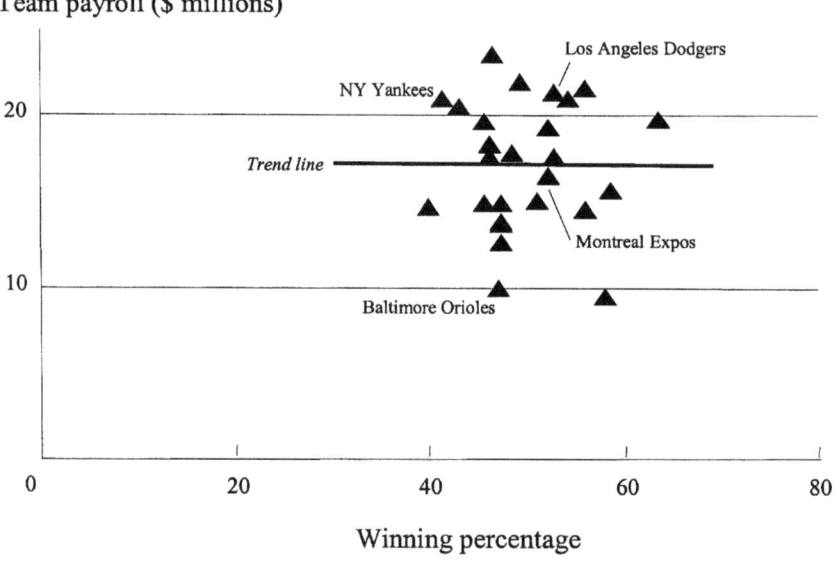

Figure 1—1990 Baseball Season

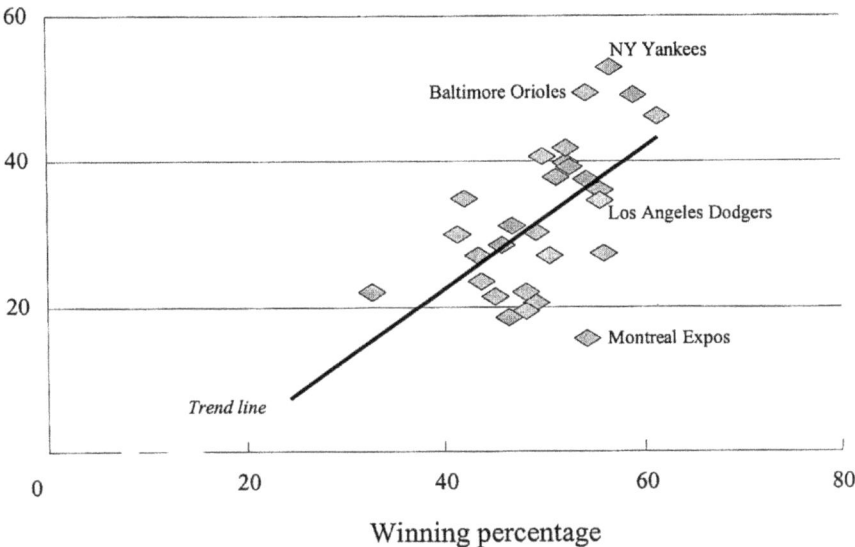

Figure 2 — 1996 Baseball Season

points show no pattern; anomalies abound. The 12 teams that spent anywhere from $8 million to $25 million to win about half their games form a nearly vertical line in the middle of the graph. The Yankees spent like crazy and lost a lot. The Orioles, in a year that was clearly prior to the arrival of owner Peter Angelos and the construction of Oriole Park at Camden Yards, were a lot more frugal. They had the second lowest Pappas payroll in baseball, and yet won about half their games, substantially more than did the Yankees.

The second year plotted is 1996, the one with the highest correlation (.58) between Pappas payrolls and winning percentages, aside from 1998 (see Table 1.2). For that year, the upward sloping relationship is evident. Teams like the Yankees and Orioles are in the upper right portion of the graph; each had a high payroll and won a lot of games. But the relationship isn't a perfect one. The Dodgers paid about $15 million less than the Yankees to achieve about the same winning percentage. And the Expos spent about $35 million less, far less than half the Yankee payroll, to achieve roughly the same winning percentage.

The teams in the middle of the graph hover in a cloud that suggests an upward-sloping relationship. Still, among the eight to 12 teams with winning percentages near .500, payrolls ranged from below $20 million to over $40 million. So, even in a year where the evidence strongly supports those who argue that you have to pay to win, there remain reasons to be skeptical.

However, looking at the evidence from 1985 to 1999, one plausible conclusion that emerges from Table 1.2 and the plots is that paying to win didn't really become important until the late 1990s. And indeed, almost all of the years when there was a positive, statistically significant relationship between the Pappas payroll figures and winning percentage are at the tail end of the period. The same pattern emerges for the April payroll data (column 3), and the SABR payroll data (column 2), except that SABR payrolls are significantly associated with winning percentages for two additional years in the 1980s and early 1990s. Again, this could be because those figures are not a pure estimate of payrolls at the season's inception. The November payrolls, which are clearly not an accurate reflection of preseason spending, are more strongly linked with winning than the other series, both before and after 1995. But, looking at the correlations for any of the four payroll series, one could reasonably conclude that the relation between spending and winning has grown much stronger in recent years. So isn't this some sort of sign? Aren't the doomsayers right?

Well, not really. Figure 5 presents the data from 1995 to 1999, and it does display the upward tilt that one would expect, but that is largely because of the three data points in the northeast corner. Those three teams—the Atlanta Braves, Cleveland Indians, and the New York Yankees—all had average Pappas payrolls in the $50 million to $60 million range and average winning percentages near .600.[6] Eliminate those three observations, and you get something resembling a cloud, with rumors spending wildly varying amounts of money to achieve winning percentages near .500. For example, the Baltimore Orioles had an average Pappas payroll just under $60 million and won 49.7% of their games from 1995 to 1999. By contrast, the Cincinnati Reds won 50.8% of their games while spending $36 million per year; and the Oakland A's won 50.5% of their games and spent only $24 million per year, roughly 40% what the Orioles spent.

For the whole decade, no team had an average winning percentage below .400 or above .600, and the only team really close to .400 was the Tampa Bay Devil Rays, an expansion team for which there were only two seasons of data (1998 and 1999). The only team near a .600 winning percentage was the Braves. If the Braves and the two 1998 expansion teams (Devil Rays and Arizona Diamondbacks) are eliminated from the calculations, all the teams had average winning percentages between .451 and .553. The bottom line is that the data through 1999 do suggest that big spenders enjoy an advantage over other teams, but viewed over longer periods the range of winning percentages remains quite compressed.

And there are reasons to think that the strong link between payrolls and winning percentages from 1995 to 1999 was a bit of an aberration. The first is that the post–1999 data show a weaker relation (.3-.45), and in 2000 and 2001 the correlation is significant only at a 10% level. While the Pappas data were not available after 1999, by the late 1990s the Pappas, April and SABR payrolls were all producing very similar correlations with winning percentages, so it should not cause concern that the recent years rely on the latter two data

Team payroll ($ millions)

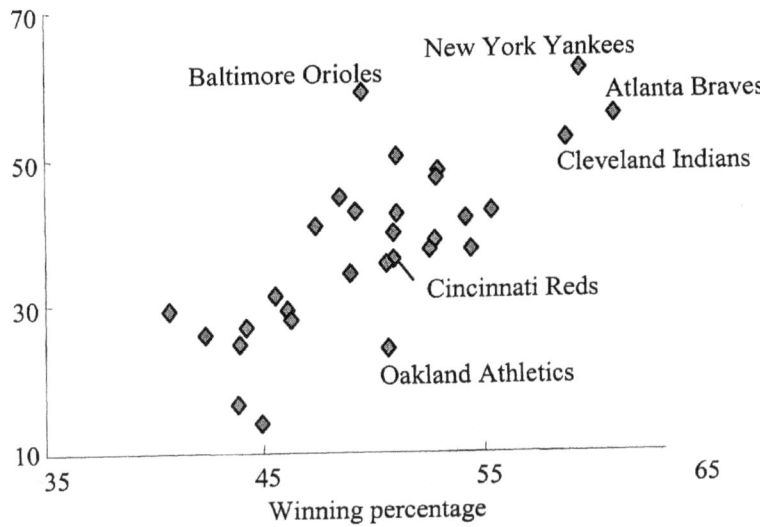

Figure 3 — Baseball Seasons 1995–99

sources. Other authors, most notably Zimbalist (2003), did not have the benefit of the two most recent years of data, and thus their conclusions were somewhat more pessimistic than those presented here.

A second reason to doubt the validity of the correlations from 1995 to 1999 is that they are so heavily influenced by the Yankees. While it is not generally acceptable research practice to drop one team from the calculations, this is a team that raised its payroll from nearly $20 million in 1990 to almost $200 million in 2004. They have also won a lot of games since 1995. It can be argued that their recent winning percentages cannot be maintained forever, and thus the correlations for the recent period are likely to come down. On the other hand, given their vast resources and the proven ability of their general manager, Brian Cashman, to assemble teams, they might not have a losing year for a long time to come. In any event, at the least the correlations that exclude the Yankees do provide an indication of the relation between spending and winning for other teams.

Table 1.3 presents the correlations between Pappas and April payrolls for all teams except the Yankees. Again, the Pappas and April payrolls are preferred because they are the best estimates of salaries prior to the start of the season. While the exclusion of the Yankees results in slight but noticeable reductions in those correlations from 1995 to 1999, the effect is more noticeable for 2000 to 2003. In 2000 and 2001, the exclusion of the Yankees renders the relation statistically insignificant. In 2002 and 2003, the correlations decline substantially (by .08 and .09), and drop in significance from the 5% level to the 10% level. Looking only at the correlations for April payrolls that exclude the Yankees (column 4), one could reasonably conclude that the 1995–1999 period was an aberration, and that there has been no strong link between spending and payrolls before or since for teams other than the Yankees.

However, given the limited number of observations in a season (one for each team), the yearly correlations are not likely to be the most accurate reflection of the underlying relationship between spending and winning because they are too prone to statistical flukes. More reliable indicators are the correlations calculated by pooling observations over multiple years. Some of those calculations appear at the bottom of Tables 1.2 and 1.3. For the April payroll data from 1985 to 1994 the estimated correlation is .138, which is statistically significant at a 10% level. For 1995–2003 the estimate is .348, significant at a 5% level, and, as noted, if the Yankees are excluded it falls to .301. Similar comparisons hold for all four sources of payroll data, although the correlation is especially high for the Pappas payrolls after 1995 because those data are not available for the most recent years. So, there's been a strengthening of the positive relationship between spending and winning, but it's just not that big an increase when the data are analyzed over sufficiently long time periods. And correlations around .30-.35 are a far cry from the .74 calculated from the MLB payroll data for 1998.

Yankees owner George Steinbrenner: His team's four World Series Championships from 1996 to 2000, coupled with a payroll increase from nearly $20 million in 1991 to nearly $200 million in 2004, are important reasons why fans and commentators fret about competitive balance.

There is a slight statistical problem with the multiyear correlations that needs to be addressed. During this period, payrolls were increasing rapidly, much faster than the rate of inflation, while the average winning percentage remained at .500, as it must when one team's win is always another's loss. Thus, there is no way that the winning percentages can match the escalation that is

Table 1.3 — Correlation Between Winning Percentage and Team Payrolls, 1985–2003, Excluding the Yankees from the Calculations

Year	Correlation with Payroll (No Bonuses, Beginning of Season)	Correlation with Payroll (No Bonuses, Beginning of Season) Yankees Excluded	Correlation with April Payroll	Correlation with April Payroll Yankees Excluded	Number of Teams in Calculation (with Yankees)
	(1)	(2)	(3)	(4)	(5)
1985	.313	.256	—	—	26
1986	.307	.259	.258	.208	26
1987	-.081	-.147	—	—	26
1988	.155	.135	.152	.132	26
1989	.484**	.499**	—	—	26
1990	-.011	.059	—	—	26
1991	.221	.234	.277	.308	26
1992	.034	.048	-.017	-.006	26
1993	.308	.292	.301	.285	28
1994	.387**	.314	.393**	.323	28
1995	.273	.244	.271	.242	28
1996	.578***	.549***	.576***	.547***	28
1997	.441**	.378*	.448**	.389**	28
1998	.725***	.697***	.688***	.653***	30
1999	.565***	.524***	.578***	.538***	30
2000	—	—	.327*	.306	30
2001	—	—	.339*	.287	30
2002	—	—	.443**	.367*	30
2003	—	—	.418**	.328*	30
1985–1994 (number of team years in calculation)	.113* (264)	.105* (254)	.138* (160)	.125 (154)	
85–94 Payrolls normalized (0 to 1)	.205*** (264)	.187*** (254)	.225*** (160)	.201** (154)	
1995–2003 (number of team years in calculation)	.500*** (144)	.456*** (139)	.348*** (264)	.301*** (255)	
95–03 Payrolls normalized (0 to 1)	.527*** (144)	.488*** (139)	.440*** (264)	.390*** (255)	

*indicates significantly different from zero at the $p = 0.10$ level. ** at the $p=0.05$ level. *** at the $p=0.01$ level.

Source for Salaries: Doug Pappas, SABR Business of Baseball Committee, salary data available at: http://www.roadsidephotos.com/baseball/1999.htm. The SABR payrolls, April payrolls, and November payrolls are all available at http://www.businessofbaseball.com.

hidden in the salary data, which could result in a downward bias for those correlations. What is needed is a payroll measure with a scale that does not change over time.[7] Just below the simple multiyear correlations are ones with payrolls expressed as a fraction of the highest team salary in that year. The process ensures that all payrolls are normalized to lie in the interval zero to one.

As expected, the correlations using normalized payrolls are higher than the simple calculations, although those from the early period (1985–94) are most strengthened. For example, the correlation between winning and SABR payrolls jumps from .119 to .214 for the normalized data, and its significance level increases from 10% to 1% (Table 1.2, column 2). The jump for the 1995–2003 period is a bit smaller (from .35 to .425), and the significance level remains at 1%. Similar comparisons hold for the other sources of payroll data. Excluding the Yankees, the normalized correlations for the April payroll data are .201 for the early period, and .390 for the latter (Table 1.3, column 4). Based on the normalized payroll data, one would also conclude that the relation between spending and winning has grown a bit stronger. However, the relation was also evident early in the period, which indicates that that this is not just a recent phenomenon.

And the data presented here, while better than the MLB data, are themselves misleading. An upper bound estimate of the true positive relationship between spending and winning is likely to be around .3. The key problem with the Pappas or SABR data, or any other salary data for that matter, is that current salaries tend to summarize past performance. And this blurs the lines of causation between payroll and winning percentage. Does anybody really believe that a player performs well *because* he receives a high salary in a given year? No, of course not. We expect the player to perform well now because he did so in the past, and his salary is high *because* of his past performance. As described in the next chapter, player compensation is, in most respects, a backward-looking rather than a forward-looking exercise. Players are rewarded for their past exploits.

So what does this mean in the context of team payrolls? Most winning teams go through a similar process. They start out lousy. Because they are lousy, they have a low payroll, and most of their players are unproven. Some of those young players pan out, and their team starts winning, but the payroll remains relatively low at first. As the team keeps winning, and the young players mature into stars, the payroll keeps creeping up until, by the time the team is perennially in the playoffs, its payroll ranks among the top 10 in the game. Teams that win for a little while also have higher attendance, and thus can afford a high-salaried free agent or two. This, too, tends to contribute to a top 10 payroll by the time that team "has arrived."

There are exceptions like the Yankees, Red Sox, and Dodgers, teams that always have high payrolls, whether they are winning or not. But, for the rest of the league, the general pattern holds. Look at the Braves of the '90s. They were atrocious at the start of the decade and, as a result, had a low payroll. They acquired young pitchers Tom Glavine, John Smoltz, and Steve Avery, and all proved to be pretty good. The team started winning in the early 1990s, and the payroll started creeping up. As the winning continued, the Braves had enough dollars to afford some free agents, and they made a great move in signing free agent pitcher Greg Maddux, who became the most dominant pitcher of the 1990s.[8] Since that acquisition, the Braves maintained their position at the top of the league in terms of payroll and winning percentage. Note that the high payroll did not cause their success. Rather, the payroll was a consequence of their success. Granted, however, a high payroll enabled them to maintain their dominance.

One could argue that the Braves are a bad example because almost all of their games are televised on TBS, a cable station that former team owner Ted Turner also owned during this period. The result was a much greater fan following and higher revenues for the Braves relative to most other teams. Those others just don't have the financial resources to follow the Braves' example. But the small-market San Diego Padres went through the same evolution. In 1994, they were a weak team, and their Pappas payroll ranked them 28th in the league. In 1995, they ranked 22nd; by 1996 it was 18th. As the team improved, their payroll crept up the rankings. They always had Tony Gwynn. Young players like Ken Caminiti and Steve Finley came into their own, and by 1998 the Padres went 98–64 and made it all the way to the World Series. They ranked 10th in the league in payroll according to the MLB data. They also had enough money to acquire veteran slugger Greg Vaughn, who hit more than 50 home runs that year.

It's the same pattern as for the Braves, except that the Padres were unable to maintain their success. The Braves and Padres are two clear examples of how team payrolls lag team performance. The team becomes good, then it gets paid. And this is a big part of what underlies the positive relationship between payrolls and winning percentages.

What is needed is a measure of salaries that leads rather than lags performance. One crude way to do this is to calculate the correlation between current winning percentage and past payrolls. Presumably, last year's payroll is less influenced by current success, certainly with regard to the midseason acquisitions that often inflate the current payrolls of winning teams. Perhaps more importantly, last year's salaries reflect one less year of winning. As a result, they are a more accurate prediction of what these teams were expected to do before anyone really knew how good they were, rather than a reward for what they had already accomplished. In short, if the correlation between winning percentage and lagged payroll is a strong one, it is easier to believe that high payrolls cause more wins.

But the relationship isn't a strong one. Indeed, there is not a statistically significant correlation between the lagged Pappas payrolls and winning percentage for any year between 1986 and 1996 (Table 1.4, column 1). Similar results hold for the April payrolls (column 3). In other words, on average, knowing a team's payroll in a given year provided little or no reliable information about its winning percentage in the next year during that period, which is pretty amazing. Lineups, payrolls, and winning percentages can change pretty quickly. But no significant relationship between lagged payroll and current winning percentage is surprising. When payrolls are lagged two years (columns 2 and 4), not only are there no positive significant correlations, but both the April and Pappas payrolls produce *negative* significant correlations for two years. This means that higher spending teams in a given year were likely to have below average winning percentages two years hence, which is also a remarkable indication of the extent to which winning percentages even out over time despite the vast sums that some teams pay to their players.

Similar to the figures for contemporaneous payrolls, the lagged payroll correlations indicate that big spenders appear to enjoy a bigger advantage starting in 1997. From 1997 to 1999, there was a positive, statistically significant relationship between the lagged Pappas payrolls and winning percentages, the only three years for which this is true. The same holds for the lagged April payrolls. These correlations ranged from about .4 to about .6. However, the lagged April payroll correlations for 2000 to 2003 are significant in only one year (2003), and at only a 10% level. Coupled with the results for 1986 to 1996, those figures suggest that the three years from 1997 to 1999 are the exception rather than the rule.

The argument here is not that there really is *no* relationship between spending and winning. The lagged payroll test is, however, another indication that the link isn't nearly as strong as most pundits and baseball executives suggest. And the basic point is that winning causes high payrolls to a much greater extent than spending causes wins. Once salary data are purged of incentive bonuses and late-season acquisitions, the correlation between payroll and winning percentage declines to .20–.40. After taking the next logical step and lagging the salary data by one or two years, the correlation is rarely significant.

Contrast the correlations in Table 1.4 with those between lagged winning percentages and current payrolls in Table 1.5. If a higher payroll really caused a higher winning percentage, we would expect the correlations between lagged salaries and winning to be stronger than those between lagged winning percentages and current salaries. But the reverse is true — the lagged winning percentage correlations in Table 1.5 are much stronger than the lagged payroll correlations in Table 1.4. And the link between past winning and current payrolls appears to be growing stronger, which helps account for the increase in the correlation between current winning percentages and payrolls in Table 1.2.

Nor is it the case that 1997 to 1999 stand out as exceptional years, as was the case for correlations between winning percentage and lagged payrolls. Correlations of .560 or higher are found between either April or Pappas payrolls

Table 1.4 — Correlation Between Winning Percentage and Lagged Team Payrolls, 1986–2003

Year	Correlation Between Current Winning Percentage and Payroll in (Pappas) prior year (1)	Correlation Between Current Winning Percentage and Payroll two years prior (2)	Correlation Between Current Winning Percentage and April Payroll in prior year (3)	Correlation Between Current Winning Percentage and April Payroll two years prior (4)	Number of Teams in Calculation
1986	.221	—	—	—	26
1987	.043	-.043	.065	—	26
1988	-.043	.029	—	.044	26
1989	.121	.070	.085	—	26
1990	.114	-.376*	—	-.363*	26
1991	.066	.192	—	—	26
1992	-.244	-.288	-.190	—	26
1993	-.171	-.426**	-.149	-.298	26
1994	.087	-.310	.084	-.356*	28
1995	.141	.011	.141	-.002	28
1996	.167	-.090	.142	-.117	28
1997	.613***	.323*	.601***	.303	28
1998	.429**	.536***	.470**	.530***	28
1999	.418**	.399**	.388**	.400**	30
2000	.258	.332*	.269	.354*	30
2001	—	.265	.243	.270	30
2002	—	—	.300	.191	30
2003	—	—	.337*	.191	30
1986–1994 (number of team years used in calculation)	.005 (236)	-.086 (208)	-.007 (132)	-.123 (104)	
86–94 Lagged Payrolls normalized (0 to 1)	.010 (236)	-.145** (208)	-.024 (132)	-.232** (104)	
1995–2003 (number of team years used in calculation)	.304** (172)	.242*** (200)	.238*** (262)	.182*** (260)	
95–03 Lagged Payrolls normalized (0 to 1)	.331*** (172)	.257*** (200)	.312*** (262)	.235*** (260)	

*indicates significantly different from zero at the p = 0.10 level. ** at the p=0.05 level. *** at the p=0.01 level.

Source for Salaries: Doug Pappas, SABR Business of Baseball Committee, salary data available at: http://www.roadsidephotos.com/baseball/1999.htm. The SABR payrolls, April payrolls, and November payrolls are all available at http://www.businessofbaseball.com.

Salary data lagged one (two) year(s). For example, 1986 winning percentages are paired with 1985 team salaries in calculating the correlations.

(or both) and winning percentages in the prior season for 1986, 1989, 1992, 1994, 1996, 1997, 1999, 2000, and 2003. All are significant at the 5% level, most at 1%. And unlike the lagged payroll correlations, those for winning percentages also hold when the data are lagged two years (columns 2 and 4, Table 1.5). These correlations provide a strong indication that the feedback mechanism from winning to higher salaries continues to be a defining feature of modern major league baseball. And they suggest strongly that winning causes payrolls to grow to a far greater extent than high payrolls cause teams to win.

Based on all of this evidence, one would conclude that the correct estimate of a positive causal correlation from spending to winning percentage is between 0 and .25. Spending more than their competitors gives teams an advantage, but that advantage is far from insurmountable. To illustrate, the following regression is run using winning percentage and SABR payroll data (in $ millions) from 1985 to 2003:

$$Winning\ Pct_{it} = .479 + .00059 \times SABR\ payroll_{it}$$
$$(4.83)^{***}\ (90.61)^{***}$$
$$r\text{-}squared = .04$$

where i represents team i, and t stands for year t. T-statistics are in parentheses below the estimated coefficients and the stars indicate that both of them are significant at the 1% level. The SABR payrolls were chosen because they were available for all years and produced correlations with winning percentages in the 0-.25 range (.119 for 1985 to 1994, .350 for 1995 to 2003). The model implies that teams start out with a .479 winning percentage, which increases by .00059 for every million dollars of SABR payroll.

If a team with the median payroll in 2003 ($68.2 million) increased its payroll by about $15 million, so that it now ranked at the 75th percentile (83.15 million), the model implies that its winning percentage would change from .516 to .528. That is a change from an 84–78 record to an 86–76 record. If the model is estimated on only the data since 1995, the SABR payroll coefficient doubles, which would imply about a four-game swing for a team moving from the 50th to 75th percentile in payroll. Again, however, the post–1994 model corresponds to a correlation between winning percentages and SABR payrolls of .35, which is outside the 0-.25 plausible range. The main point is that for plausible increases in payrolls, the implied change in a team's record is no more than a handful of games. This is not to ignore the impact of spending, because a handful of games can be quite important in a season. But the models do imply that the effect of payrolls on winning percentages is hardly determinative.

In an influential book, Zimbalist (2003) concludes that since the mid-1990s there has been a much stronger relationship between payroll size and the likelihood of on-field success based on data from 1980 to 2001. There are at least three reasons for the difference between Zimbalist's results and those presented here. First, as noted above, Zimbalist lacked data for 2002–2003, which suggest

Table 1.5 — Correlation Between Team Payrolls and Lagged Winning Percentages, 1985–2003

Year	Correlation Between Current Payroll and Winning Percentage in (Pappas) prior year (1)	Correlation Between Current Payroll and Winning Percentage two years prior (2)	Correlation Between Current April Payroll and Winning Percentage in prior year (3)	Correlation Between Current April Payroll and Winning Percentage two years prior (4)	Number of Teams in Calculation
1985	.357*	.292	—	—	26
1986	.449**	.532***	.578***	.617***	26
1987	.316	.398**	—	—	26
1988	.196	.334*	.219	.354*	26
1989	.612***	.315	—	—	26
1990	.407**	.625***	—	—	26
1991	.378*	.287	.408**	.360*	26
1992	.572***	.406**	.609***	.353*	26
1993	-.073	.282	-.077	.295	26
1994	.569***	-.063	.575***	-.076	28
1995	.244	.432**	.211	.451**	28
1996	.639***	.351*	.628***	.338*	28
1997	.581***	.478**	.591***	.522***	28
1998	.511***	.497***	.530***	.508***	28
1999	.644***	.580***	.659***	.574***	30
2000	—	—	.598***	.551***	30
2001	—	—	.471***	.636***	30
2002	—	—	.464***	.428**	30
2003	—	—	.568***	.460**	30
1985–1994 (number of team years used in calculation)	.188*** (262)	.145** (260)	.220*** (158)	.145* (156)	
85–94 Payrolls normalized (0 to 1)	.373*** (262)	.330*** (260)	.392*** (158)	.297*** (156)	
1995–2003 (number of team years used in calculation)	.500*** (142)	.417*** (140)	.418*** (262)	.387*** (260)	
95–03 Payrolls normalized (0 to 1)	.530*** (142)	.455*** (140)	.512*** (262)	.482*** (260)	

*indicates significantly different from zero at the p = 0.10 level. ** at the p=0.05 level. *** at the p=0.01 level.

Source for salaries: Doug Pappas, SABR Business of Baseball Committee, salary data available at: http://www.roadsidephotos.com/baseball/1999.htm. The SABR payrolls, April payrolls, and November payrolls are all available at http://www.businessofbaseball.com.

Winning percentage data lagged one (or two) year(s). For example, 1985 winning percentages are paired with 1986 team salaries in calculating the correlations.

a return to a more normal relationship between winning and payrolls. Second, although the notes to his tables do not explicitly state it, it appears that he used end-of-year payrolls for his calculations.[9] This is because he finds a positive, significant association between payroll and winning in exactly the same years as in column 4 of Table 1.2, which relied on November payrolls. Third and finally, although he tests for the possibility that causation runs from winning percentages to payrolls (which is more than most analysts have done), he cannot come to a strong conclusion using contemporaneous data. Based on a standard statistical test developed by Clive Granger, Zimbalist concludes that from 1980 to 1994 there is no evidence of causality from payroll to performance. Since 1995, the evidence indicates that causality runs in both directions. He does not state whether there was causality from performance to payrolls prior to 1995, which is strongly supported by the results presented here. And he does not indicate whether causality runs more strongly in one direction than the other since 1995. The results here in which one variable is lagged indicate that causality runs from winning to payrolls much more than the reverse.

This is not to denigrate Zimbalist's research, which is cited approvingly throughout this book. It is, however, to point out that a more thorough analysis of the data supports more nuanced conclusions regarding payrolls and the likelihood of winning. Zimbalist (2004), an updated and revised version of his book, anticipates some of these criticisms in light of the recent success of teams like the Oakland A's and Minnesota Twins. In its foreword Bob Costas notes that:

> How is it that the selective results of one season *prove* a point, but the overwhelming evidence of the preceding seven years is a mirage? ... Zimbalist never said, I never said, and no one with enough common sense to fill a thimble ever said that a low-payroll team couldn't *ever* succeed or that high-payroll teams couldn't fail. What Zimbalist does say is that the *opportunities* for success are very significantly diminished by a smaller payroll, especially over the longer term.

The italics are Costas's. The results here indicate that the likelihood of winning improves with spending, but the effects are not a large as Costas seems to suggest, and clearly winning has the much larger effect on spending. These conclusions are not based on only a single year's outcomes, nor only seven. Only time will tell for certain, but the available evidence is consistent with the last half of the 1990s being a slight aberration rather than the beginning of an irreversible trend.

This chapter and the next focus on the relationships between three key variables—market size, winning percentages, and team payrolls. The evidence in the next chapter will demonstrate that there is no discernible link between market size and winning percentages. In this chapter, the evidence so far indicates that the oft-repeated link between team payrolls and winning percentages is largely a product of incomplete data analysis—there is only a weak causal link from spending to winning. That leaves only one relationship to explore, the link between market size and team payroll. It could be that the large-market teams spend more, get insufficient value in return, and have winning percentages a lot like their small-market competitors. Or it could be that payrolls don't have a lot to do with market size. Some large-market teams spend, some small-market teams spend, but it doesn't do either group a tremendous amount of good in terms of winning percentage.

To help choose between these two hypotheses, Table 1.6 presents correlations between market size (as measured by the population of the Metropolitan Statistical Area) and payrolls.[10] The correlations are positive in each of the 19 years, and statistically significant in 15 of them. Again, the yearly correlations are probably less reliable than those averaged over longer periods, but those, too, tell the same story. For 1985 to 1989, the correlation is .430; for 1990 to 1999, the figure is .247; and for 2000 to 2003 it is .512. All three multiyear correlations are highly significant. The evidence strongly indicates that large-market teams do, in fact, have higher payrolls. Coupled with the weak relationship between payrolls and winning percentages, this indicates that large-market teams do not get much in return for the extra dollars that they spend. These results are, to a large extent, a consequence of a market that over-rewards its veteran players, which is discussed in the next chapter.

The most surprising thing about Table 1.6 is that the relation between market size and payroll was stronger in the 1980s than in the 1990s, although it has returned to its previous level since 1999. The smallest yearly correlations are for 1994 to 1997, and none are significant. At the very least, no one can say that no small-market teams were spending during this period. To cite two examples, from 1994 to 1996 Atlanta and Cincinnati both ranked in the top 10 in payroll in each year, and neither ranked in the top half of the league in MSA population.

The Atlanta-Cincinnati experience from 1994 to 1996 brings us back to the question of whether a small-market team can sustain winning over multiple years. The Braves' experience suggests yes, but they enjoy some special advantages. The Padres' experience suggests no. Which one is typical? To help address that issue, Table 1.7 presents the Pappas payroll data and team rankings for 1994–96. The Cincinnati Reds provide an example of a team from one of the smallest markets sustaining a high payroll over multiple years, and without enjoying spectacular success on the field. They did make the playoffs in one of those years, but the key point is that they were able to pay what rivals from larger cities did for an extended period. And they didn't have the television advantages that the Braves did.

Although the recent escalation in salaries by a handful of large-market teams is worrisome, it still seems likely that all of the major league markets can generate revenues sufficient to pay a winning team. The small-markets do have to pick their spots. But, when they get some young talent to gel, and their record begins to improve, they can and do spend to keep those players together and

Table 1.6 — Correlation Between Metropolitan Statistical Area Population and Team Payrolls, 1985–2003

Year	Correlation	Teams in the Calculation
1985	.467**	26
1986	.560***	26
1987	.467**	26
1988	.579***	26
1989	.356*	26
1990	.332*	26
1991	.446**	26
1992	.464**	26
1993	.393**	28
1994	.262	28
1995	.198	28
1996	.182	28
1997	190	28
1998	.349*	30
1999	.448**	30
2000	.443**	30
2001	.451**	30
2002	.507***	30
2003	.680***	30
1985–1989	.430***	130
1990–1999	.247***	278
2000–2003	.512***	120

*indicates significantly different from zero at the p = 0.10 level. ** at the p=0.05 level. *** at the p=0.01 level.

From 1985 to 1999 payroll data from Doug Pappas are used. From 2000 on, the April payroll data from businessofbaseball.com is used. MSA population data are taken from http://www.uscensus.gov for US cities. The 1990 census figures are used for the first half of the sample (1985 to 1994); 1997 figures are used for the second half (1995 to 2003). Population figures for the Census Metropolitan Areas of Montreal and Toronto are taken from http://www12.statcan.ca. For those two cities, 1996 figures are used for the first half of the sample; 2001 figures for the second half.

to attract others. By contrast, teams like the Yankees don't need to wait for young talent to gel. When they lose, they just reload with a new cast of high-priced veteran players, who might or might not play well enough to win a championship. But the key thing is that, despite an inability to reload in every year, the small-markets often compete effectively.

Examples from Table 1.7 abound. Look at Seattle and Cleveland, two MSAs with populations near 3 million, well below the median for the league's 30 teams. Seattle, one of the weakest franchises in baseball since its inception in 1977, finally put together a talented nucleus of relatively young players by the early 1990s. Centered around Ken Griffey Jr. (.308 BA, 27 HR, 103 RBI in 1992), the cast featured pitcher Randy Johnson (12–14, 210.3 IP, 3.77 ERA, 241 K), outfielder Jay Buhner (.243 BA, 18 HR, 73 RBI), and first baseman Tino Martinez (.257 BA, 16 HR, 66 RBI). In 1992, despite the early signs of success

Table 1.7 — Team Salary Rankings, 1994–1996

Team	1996 Rank	1996 Payroll ($ mil)	MSA Popul. (mil.)	1995 Rank	1994 Rank
NY Yankees	1	53.0	19.6	2	1
Baltimore	2	49.4	2.4	4	9
Atlanta	3	49.2	3.0	3	3
Cleveland	4	46.2	2.9	9	20
Chi White Sox	5	41.9	8.3	5	8
Cincinnati	6	40.7	1.8	6	7
Boston	7	39.7	5.5	18	11
Seattle	8	39.2	3.0	12	21
Colorado	9	37.9	2.0	15	23
St. Louis	10	37.4	2.5	10	19
Texas	11	35.9	4.0	13	14
San Francisco	12	34.8	6.3	11	5
Los Angeles	13	34.6	14.5	16	10
Chi Cubs	14	31.0	8.2	20	12
Florida	15	30.1	3.2	24	25
Philadelphia	16	29.7	5.9	19	15
Toronto	17	28.5	3.9	1	2
San Diego	18	27.2	2.5	22	28
Houston	19	26.9	3.7	14	18
California	20	26.9	14.5	17	24
NY Mets	21	23.5	19.6	23	16
Minnesota	22	22.0	2.5	25	17
Detroit	23	21.9	5.2	8	6
Pittsburgh	24	21.3	2.4	26	26
Milwaukee	25	20.5	1.6	27	22
Oakland	26	19.4	6.3	7	13
Kansas City	27	18.5	1.6	21	4
Montreal	28	15.4	3.1	28	27

Source for payroll data: Doug Pappas, SABR Business of Baseball Committee, salary data available at http://www.roadsidephotos.com/baseball/1999.htm.

reflected in their individual statistics, they finished 64–98, the worst record in the American League. By 1995, they won the AL West and beat the Yankees in the first round of the playoffs. Their payroll crept from 21st in 1994, to 12th in 1995, to eighth in 1996. The team develops, then it gets paid, and the small-market can foot the bill, at least for a while.

Cleveland's experience is equally instructive. A talented nucleus comes together, including youngsters Albert Belle (OF, .290 BA, 38 HR, 129 RBI in 1993), Kenny Lofton (OF, .325 BA, .410 OBP, 116 R, 66 SB), Jim Thome (1B, .266 BA, .396 OBP, 7 HR, 22 RBI), Sandy Alomar (C, .270 BA, 6 HR, 32 RBI), and Manny Ramirez (OF/DH, 22 G, 53 AB, .170 BA, 2 HR, 5 RBI). They still were not quite as good as the Chicago White Sox in the AL Central in 1994, but they were gaining ground. By 1995, they took over first place in the division and appeared in the World Series against the Braves. In 1997, they were in the World Series against the Florida Marlins (another small-market team).[11] The Indians retained the top spot in the division from 1995 to 1999. All of the players mentioned appeared in the all-star game at least once. The Indians' payroll went from 20th in 1994, to ninth in 1995, to fourth in 1996.

So yes, large-market teams do tend to spend more than small-market teams. But no, small-market teams don't *always* spend less. When the situation requires it, that is, when their team becomes a proven winner, they spend. So the question is, for how long can they do it? Can they keep something good going as long as their large-market competitors? This is where the evidence is mixed. Atlanta and Cleveland are both mid- to small-market teams that were the doormats of their respective leagues throughout the 1970s and 1980s. They got their acts together, and then maintained dynasties in recent years. Cleveland won five straight division crowns from 1995 to 1999. Atlanta has won 13 consecutive division titles since 1991.[12] But perhaps they are the exception. Atlanta has the aforementioned cable television advantages and newly built Turner Field, and Cleveland has Jacobs Field, arguably the best place to watch a game in baseball. What would have happened had Ted Turner not been the Braves' owner? What if the Indians hadn't built a new ballpark, or their new park had been as unappealing as the one built by their rivals, the White Sox?

And this is where you have to look at teams like the San Diego Padres and Minnesota Twins and wonder. Neither of those teams had the television revenues of Atlanta or the sexy new ballpark (although San Diego did open one in 2004), and neither maintained a dynasty. Only the Twins reached the pinnacle, a World Series title, and that was in 1991, at the start of the decade, when team salaries were a lot lower. The Padres did reach the series in 1998, but they were swept by the Yankees, lost key veterans Greg Vaughn and Ken Caminiti, and didn't even contend in 1999. On the other hand, despite losing Griffey and the earlier departures of Tino Martinez and Randy Johnson, the Seattle Mariners made it to the ALCS in 2000. In 2001 they lost Alex Rodriguez to the Rangers, and yet they recorded the most wins in major league history, tying the 1906 Cubs. While some of their success is likely attributable to the increased revenues associated with their new ballpark, Safeco Field, the Mariners were among the best teams in baseball since their first playoff appearance in 1995 until 2004, despite playing in a small market.

But how about small-market teams that don't have a new ballpark? The Reds are an instructive case. They won a World Series in 1990, and the lingering effects of that success are reflected in their top seven ranking in payroll from 1994 to 1996 — as demonstrated, you win, and then you pay. By 1998, their decline was complete, and their payroll was ranked 26th. But in 1999, they picked up Greg Vaughn, young players like Pokey Reese and Sean Casey had fine years, veteran Barry Larkin maintained his high level of performance, and the Reds were 96–66. They lost in a one-game playoff with the New York Mets to determine the wild-card entry in NL playoffs. And in the off-season they acquired Ken Griffey Jr., an acquisition that wasn't cheap. They looked poised to contend again, and even built a new ballpark, but Griffey's injuries have made it difficult for them to capitalize on their opportunity. Despite playing in an old and relatively unattractive ballpark (the Metrodome), the Twins made the playoffs three years in a row. The 1990s Reds and the post–2000 Twins indicate that, even without special advantages, small-market teams can maintain success for an extended period, or, like the Reds, they can bring young talent along quickly enough to establish two separate winning stints within the same decade. Their inherent disadvantages are overstated.

Before leaving Table 1.7, note that it's not just the small-market teams that pick their spots when it comes to spending. The Chicago Cubs, Philadelphia Phillies, Houston Astros, California (now Anaheim) Angels, and New York Mets— all large-market teams— never cracked the top 10 in payroll from 1994 to 1996. Other large-market teams that had enjoyed success came to the end of the line with a particular group of players. The great Detroit Tigers teams of the '80s— Alan Trammel, Lou Whitaker, Kirk Gibson, Jack Morris, etc.— drifted from contention. Their payroll dropped from sixth in 1994 to eighth in 1995 to 23rd in 1996. The Toronto Blue Jays teams that won the 1992 and 1993 World Series went from the second highest payroll in 1994 to the 17th highest in 1996. Granted, Toronto is a borderline large-market. But if you'd rather call it a small-market, their two World Series championships further underscore the points about how well small-market teams performed in the 1990s.

The point is that teams like the Dodgers and Yankees, those that spend like crazy all the time, are the exception rather than the rule. Even the Dodgers stayed near the middle of the pack in payroll from 1994 to 1996. So even if spending did give a team a big advantage, and the evidence here suggests that any such advantage is probably modest, most large-market teams tend not to exploit it. They seem to follow the same formula as all other teams— they wait to get a talented nucleus of young players, develop them while acquiring a free agent or two, and then pay through the nose to maintain their success. The chapter closes with a partial explanation of why some large-market teams don't always exploit their ability to spend.

DIFFERENT FANS, DIFFERENT INCENTIVES?

Based on the figures in Table 1.7, it seemed plausible that there were some large-market teams that didn't fully avail themselves of the advantages that a high payroll could convey. For example, if Cubs fans are going to show up to Wrigley Field no matter what, their owners, the Tribune Company, who have a fiduciary responsibility to their shareholders, probably have little incentive to establish a high enough payroll to compete at the upper echelons.

And there might be more teams like the Cubs, large-market teams with little incentive to spend, teams like the Red Sox, or maybe the Dodgers. If this were true, then maybe the small-market teams aren't at as great a disadvantage as the simple population statistics would suggest. This idea is tested using the following regression for each team from 1945 until 1996:

Attendance = B_0 + B_1**Current Winning Percentage* + $B2$**Last Year's Winning Percentage* + B_3**Real Per Capita Income* + $B4$**MSA Population*

The basic idea is that teams with higher current winning percentages that are located in larger cities whose residents have higher per capita income should have higher attendance. The analysis follows Scully (1989) by including last year's winning percentage in the regressions. He found that variable to be a significant determinant of attendance, and argued that it was a reasonable proxy for season ticket sales—a high winning percentage in year *t* meant more season ticket sales in year *t+1*, and thus higher attendance.

Tables 1.8 and 1.9 summarize the highlights of this regression.[13] Table 1.8, which summarizes the results for the American League franchises, indicates how much attendance would increase for each franchise under three different scenarios: (1) their winning percentage in the current year went from .000 to 1.000 (i.e., they won all their games), (2) their winning percentage in the *prior* year went from .000 to 1.000, and (3) real per capita income in their market increased by $1,000. These scenarios are not intended to be depictions of reality. They are simply a means of translating the regression results in the appendix into terms that are easier to understand. The main idea is to summarize differences across franchises in the sensitivity of attendance to winning and changes in income. Table 1.9 provides the results for the National League.

While team attendance differs in some interesting ways, the patterns are more similar than one might have expected. For all but two American League teams, the Baltimore Orioles and the Kansas City Royals, there is a statistically significant positive relationship between either the current year's or the past year's winning percentage (or both) and attendance. National League results are even more pronounced. For every team there is a positive significant link between winning and attendance. Fans respond to winners throughout the league, which is no big surprise.

The Orioles' results are a bit interesting as they indicate that their fans show up whether the team is winning or not. Having gone to a lot of Orioles games in the past 10 years, the statistical result seems plausible. But that's the only large-market team that doesn't seem to have to win to draw fans, and who knows how long that will last, especially now that Washington, DC, has finally got a team.[14] So the data don't provide much support for the proposition that some large-market teams get a free ride from their fans, and thus don't really have to pursue winning as seriously as other teams. Thus there was little point in updating these regressions through 2003.

That said, there is some variation across franchises in the attendance boosts associated with current winning percentage, and it does suggest somewhat

Table 1.8 — Regression Results, Attendance Characteristics by American League Franchise, 1945–96

Team	Attendance Boost, Perfect Record Current Year (millions)	Attendance Boost, Perfect Record Prior Year (millions)	Attendance Boost, $1,000 Increase in Local Real Income Per Capita (thousands)
AL East			
New York Yankees	3.34	Not signif.	Not signif.
Boston Red Sox	3.31	2.58	68.9
Milwaukee Brewers	Not signif.	3.99	95.4
Baltimore Orioles	Not signif.	Not signif.	Not signif.
Toronto Blue Jays	Insufficient data		
AL Central			
Minnesota Twins	5.46	Not signif.	Not signif.
Cleveland Indians	4.91	2.55	68.9
Detroit Tigers	2.94	Not signif.	78.8
Chicago White Sox	1.83	Not signif.	Not signif.
Kansas City Royals	Not signif.	Not signif.	127.5
AL West			
Anaheim Angels	4.35	4.25	130.7
Seattle Mariners	4.28	Not signif.	Not signif.
Oakland A's	3.04	2.03	Not signif.
Texas Rangers	2.44	Not signif.	Not signif.

The numbers in the table are derived from the regression models in part 1 of the Appendix. "Not signif." indicates that the estimated coefficient was statistically insignificant.

greater attendance sensitivity in smaller markets. For the typical team, a perfect winning percentage translates into 3 million or maybe 4 million additional fans. The New York Yankees, Boston Red Sox, Detroit Tigers, Chicago White Sox, Texas Rangers, New York Mets, Chicago Cubs, and Houston Astros, all large-market teams, would each receive fewer than 3.5 million additional fans for a perfect season.

The Minnesota Twins, Cleveland Indians, Seattle Mariners, Atlanta Braves, San Francisco Giants, and San Diego Padres would attract 4 million to 6 million additional fans during a perfect season. Now not all of those six are prototypical small-market teams. The Braves have their aforementioned advantages from cable television, and the Giants are a medium market team rather than a small-market team. Still, these results suggest that small-market teams get a bigger attendance boost from winning than large-market teams. The results also suggest that both of the truly small-market teams that made it to the World Series in the 1990s, the Padres and Twins, were richly rewarded by their fans. These markets appear to be big enough to support adequately a winning team.

The estimated attendance boosts associated with a perfect record in the

Table 1.9 — Regression Results, Attendance Characteristics by National League Franchise, 1945–96

Team	Attendance Boost, Perfect Record Current Year (millions)	Attendance Boost, Perfect Record Prior Year (millions)	Attendance Boost, $1,000 Increase in Local Real Income Per Capita (thousands)
AL East			
Atlanta Braves	5.88	2.56	Not signif.
Philadelphia Phillies	3.99	Not signif.	159.7
New York Mets	2.39	Not signif.	111.6
Montreal Expos	Insufficient data		
NL Central			
Chicago Cubs	3.44	2.34	Not signif.
St. Louis Cardinals	3.37	Not signif.	308.2
Houston Astros	2.96	Not signif.	Not signif.
Pittsburgh Pirates	2.74	Not signif.	77.6
Cincinnati Reds	2.00	Not signif.	180.1
NL West			
San Francisco Giants	5.06	Not signif.	Not signif.
San Diego Padres	4.83	3.08	Not signif.
Los Angeles Dodgers	3.84	Not signif.	66.8

The numbers in the table are derived from the regression models in part 2 of the Appendix. "Not signif." indicates that the estimated coefficient was statistically insignificant.

prior year provide somewhat less support for the proposition that large-market attendance is less responsive to winning. In the American League, the estimated coefficient for prior winning percentage is positive and significant for the Milwaukee Brewers, Cleveland Indians, and Oakland A's, all small- or medium-market teams, and for the Anaheim Angels and Boston Red Sox, both large-market teams.[15] In the National League, that coefficient is positive for small-market San Diego, medium-market Atlanta, and large-market Chicago. For the eight teams mentioned, a perfect season would mean 2 million to 4 million additional fans in the subsequent season, although there is no obvious relationship between market size and the size of the attendance boost. For example, the biggest effects, 4 million additional fans, are estimated for the small-market Brewers and the large-market Angels.

Like the effects of past winning percentage, those for increases in real per capita income are not well explained by market size. Local market conditions, as reflected in real per capita income, drive attendance for some teams but not others. The small-market Pittsburgh Pirates, Cincinnati Reds, Milwaukee Brewers, and Kansas City Royals all get attendance boosts when incomes rise. The small-market San Diego Padres and Minnesota Twins do not. The large-market New York Mets, Detroit Tigers, Anaheim Angels, and Los Angeles Dodgers appear to benefit from increases in market income, but the New York Yankees and both Chicago teams do not. Nor is there any obvious relationship between the size of the income effect and the size of the market.

Overall, these results provide some evidence that the attendance of large-market teams is less responsive to current winning percentage than is small-market attendance, controlling for past winning percentage and market incomes, both of which may or may not play an important role in attendance in a given market. Does this mean that large-market teams have less incentive to win? Well, maybe a little less, but the results in Table 1.6 still indicate a strong link between market size and team payroll. Therefore, large-market incentives to win have been sufficient to produce some large disparities in payrolls between large- and small-market teams.

There is also a flip side to the attendance sensitivity results. They imply that small-market teams lose more in attendance when their winning percentages are low than do their large-market competitors. This does mean that small-market lean years may be a little more lean than for other teams. However, despite that possible disadvantage, there is no relationship between market size and winning percentage, as will be demonstrated in Chapter 2. Moreover, as shown in the first chapter, the share of teams with winning percentages below .400 is about as low as it's ever been, and the link between payrolls and winning percentage is not nearly as strong as most people think it is. Taken together, these results suggest that although small-market attendance patterns are slightly different than those for large-market teams, those differences do not put them at an insurmountable disadvantage. It would be difficult, even wrongheaded, to conclude that these markets are too small to compete effectively.

CONCLUSION

The evidence in this chapter, and the prior one, should help lay to rest a couple of myths about competitive balance in baseball. First, there is much less dispersion in winning percentages now than there was in the past. Indeed, both the share and the absolute number of teams with winning percentages below .400 are as low as they have ever been. Almost every team in baseball wins at least four of every 10 games it plays. That's a pretty remarkable fact, especially in comparison with other major professional sports leagues like the NBA (six of 29 teams had winning percentages below .400 in 2003–2004) or the NFL (13 of 32 teams were sub-.400 in 2003).[16] Second, there is not a strong causal relation between team payrolls and winning percentages. In fact, it is winning that causes high payrolls much more than it is the reverse. So, while a small-market team may eventually lose its stars due to budget constraints, there is a period early in these stars' careers when that team can enjoy on-field success without paying a lot for it. And, based on the evidence, it is not certain that small-market teams can't keep a good team together over a multiyear period. The next chapter takes the analysis further by examining the movement of players between teams.

2
Player Movement

Teams that can afford free agents do have an advantage, but how great an advantage is it? To help answer that question, this chapter links data since 1945 on player movements to the size of markets. The results indicate that teams in larger cities are more likely to acquire free agents than small-market teams. Large-market clubs are also more likely to acquire veterans in exchange for prospects. However, these tendencies are not strong, and the prospects often outperform the veterans. In addition, existing research on major league salaries indicates that most players are underpaid relative to their productivity level early in their careers but overpaid later on (Zimbalist 1992). The chapter's ultimate conclusions are, first, that all major league cities are probably of sufficient size to permit their teams a few free agents, but that some need to be more selective than others because they have a smaller margin for error. Second, large-market teams that horde free agents are probably going to substantially overpay for the productivity they receive. Third, and most importantly, with the addition of the amateur draft, the present market for players puts teams from small cities at less disadvantage than did the player market of the '40s and '50s. All the talk of large-markets eclipsing small-markets is overdone.

THE DATA

There were about 4,500 transactions between 1945 and January 1, 1993, in which at least one player went from one team to another. The *Baseball Encyclopedia* (*BE*) was good enough to list all of these transactions in one place. The initial goal for this book was to incorporate all of them into one database that included the statistics of the players involved in each transaction, and data both on the two teams' performance and their cities' demographic characteristics. In this way, it would be possible to explain a team's personnel decisions in the context of where it was in the standings and its city's population base. The players' statistics would then indicate which team got the better end of the deal, both in the first year after a trade and over the long haul. That goal (all 4,500 transactions) proved too ambitious, but it was possible to create a database of the first 1,500 transactions as listed alphabetically in the *BE*, and that should be adequate for the analysis that follows.

Of course, a number of aspects of player movement might have changed since 1993, and so more recent data were also collected. Unfortunately, subsequent editions of the *BE* don't provide a transactions list. The post–1993 analysis therefore relies on a database of all free agent signings from 1998 to 2003 that was drawn from a number of sources. Because trades and acquisitions through waivers comprise a much smaller share of player movements today, a detailed study of free agents seemed the more sensible way to approach the most recent period.

MARKET SIZE

Table 2.1 presents the simple correlation between winning percentage and market population. Column (1) presents results for the population of metropolitan statistical areas ("MSAs") as defined in U.S. Census statistics. Column (2) presents results for adjusted MSA population figures—MSA population divided by the number of teams in the market. Of course, some people in a market might attend the games and watch the telecasts of both teams. The adjusted MSA population figures, therefore, might understate the advantage that teams in some large-markets have.

On the other hand, because they ignore competition from the cross-town franchise, the unadjusted MSA population figures likely overstate that advantage. Using either measure, however, the qualitative results of the analysis are similar.

Table 2.1—Correlation Between Winning Percentage and Market Population

	MSA Population	MSA Population Divided by Number of Teams in Market	MSA Population (Calculations Exclude Yankees)	MSA Population Divided by Number of Teams in Market (Calculations Exclude Yankees)
	(1)	(2)	(3)	(4)
1946–1950	0.320***	0.283**	0.184	0.151
1951–1960	0.405***	0.217***	0.271***	0.107
1961–1970	-0.054	-0.018	-0.159**	-0.101
1971–1980	0.047	0.057	-0.042	-0.014
1981–1990	0.167***	0.174***	0.152**	0.160**
1991–2000	0.081	0.074	-0.016	-0.020
2001–2003	0.229**	0.159	0.113	0.042

*indicates significantly different from zero at the p = 0.10 level. ** at the p=0.05 level. *** at the p=0.01 level.

MSA is Metropolitan Statistical Area as reported by the U.S. Census.

The correlation between market size and winning percentage was largest prior to 1960. Throughout the '60s and '70s there was little relationship between market size and winning percentages. In the 1980s, the correlation jumped a bit but still remained below its pre–1960 level, less than half the pre–1960 levels for market size as measured by MSA population. These results are in line with evidence in other chapters—in terms of competitive balance, things have gotten better, not worse. That conclusion is further underscored by the statistically insignificant relationship between winning percentage and market size in the 1990s. Given all the talk about small-markets, one would have expected a pronounced positive relationship between size and wins, but it's not there.

There is, however, a positive and significant correlation between MSA population and winning percentages post–2000. And this is what is troubling to many commentators and fans. They should relax a bit. First, the correlation is smaller than those prior to 1960. Second, only three years of data enter the calculations, so it is uncertain whether the relationship will hold throughout the decade. Third, the relationship is not robust to the way population is measured. When MSA population is divided by the number of teams in a market (column 2), the relationship is no longer significant. Fourth and finally, the calculation is heavily influenced by one team, the Yankees. When they are excluded from the calculations, the correlation is not significant using either population measure (columns 3 and 4). By and large, there is little evidence that teams from large metropolitan areas have enjoyed more success on the field than others since 1990.

One might argue that these measures of market size are too simple—there's a lot more to it than the number of people in an area. Rich franchises enjoy huge advantages because of their cable television rights, concessions, and parking. But each of those advantages is an indication that there is higher demand for the product being offered in one market than another. Higher demand could be attributable not only to the number of people in a market, but also to how much money they have, or, perhaps, to an unusual passion for baseball. To control for potential income effects, MSA population was multiplied by per capita income in each community to create a new measure of market size. The correlations in Table 2.1 were re-computed and yielded similar conclusions.[1] So, using multiple sensible measures, there is no strong connection between winning and market size since 1990.

Perhaps then large (small) markets are simply places where fans have an unusually strong (weak) passion for baseball. Proponents of these "good" baseball town, "bad" baseball town arguments tend not to be folks who are concerned about sorting out causation. One is often left wondering whether a place is a good baseball town because the team is winning, or whether the team is winning because it's located in a good baseball town. The analysis of the attendance patterns of individual franchises in Chapter 1 indicated, however, that fans respond to winning pretty similarly across markets. Be skeptical of any definition that relies on "good" baseball town arguments to define large-markets, especially in light of the results in Table 2.1.

A refined version of the large-market–small-market argument might be that, while there are a number of cities large enough to support a winning franchise, there are some that are just too small to ever win a championship. To assess that proposition, markets were ranked by their MSA population to determine the percentage of league champions ranked in the bottom half (or the bottom quarter). The results (presented in Table 2.2) indicate that, since the inception of the amateur draft in 1965, nearly half of league champions (47.2%) ranked in the bottom half of the population rankings. Had the adjusted MSA population figures been used, San Francisco and Oakland would have ranked below the median, which would have lifted the share of small-market champs to 70% from 1971 to 1975 and 1986 to 1990. That would have pushed the post–1965 figure from 47% to 58%. By contrast, prior to 1965, less than a third of the league champions hailed from cities of below-median size. While it seems unlikely that the draft is entirely responsible for this result, it is interesting that since its inception, only half of the league champions have come from larger markets.

Table 2.2 — Frequency of League Champions from Small Markets

	% Below Median MSA Population	% Below 25th Percentile in MSA Population
1946–1950	30.0	10.0
1951–1955	10.0	0.0
1956–1960	30.0	20.0
1961–1965	30.0	20.0
1966–1970	60.0	10.0
1971–1975	40.0	20.0
1976–1980	40.0	20.0
1981–1985	60.0	30.0
1986–1990	30.0	20.0
1991–1995*	62.5	0.0
1996–2000	50.0	0.0
2001–2003	33.3	0.0

*Excludes strike-shortened 1994 season.
MSA is Metropolitan Statistical Area as reported by the U.S. Census.

Many recent champions have come from cities that weren't particularly populous, but have any come from really tiny cities? Cincinnati, Kansas City, and Minnesota all won league (and World Series) championships while ranked in the bottom quartile of major league cities. Prior to 1965, 12.5 percent of the league champions were from cities ranked in the bottom quartile. Since 1965, 13.5 percent of the champions were from the bottom quartile, so the situation has improved, albeit slightly. If market size played no role in determining league champions, over long periods of time about one-fourth of the champions would come from the bottom quartile, and so 14% is low. However, aside from Milwaukee (MSA population 1.6 million), Kansas City (1.7 million), and Cincinnati (1.9 million), the below-median markets range in population from 2.2 to 3.6 million. Because these markets are much more similar to one another than they are to large-markets like New York (19.9 million) or Los Angeles (15.6 million), the distinction between the third and fourth quartiles is not particularly meaningful. Thus the share of champions with populations below the median seems to be the more telling statistic.

The figures on teams from the lowest quartile after 1990 distort the post–1965 figure, but those are a little misleading because Minneapolis–St. Paul and San Diego crept just above the 25th percentile in MSA population according to 1990 census data. In the early 1990s, both would have been in the lowest quartile, except that Baltimore occupied one of the spaces. The population of the Baltimore metropolitan area was used in these calculations because early in the sample Washington, DC, and Baltimore each had a team. Once the Senators left DC, that was no longer true, and thus the Orioles found it easier to draw fans from both cities. Had the population of the Baltimore-Washington metropolitan area been used, the Orioles would have moved to the first quartile, and Minnesota would have ranked in the fourth quartile at the time of their 1991 league championship. San Diego also would have ranked in the lowest quartile in 1998 if the Baltimore-Washington population figures had been used, and two new teams not been introduced (Tampa Bay and Arizona). If the 1998 San Diego Padres are added to the list, the fourth quartile produced 10 percent of the champions from 1996 to 2000. If the 1991 Minnesota Twins are also included, the lowest quartile produced 12.5 percent of the champions from 1991 to 1995, and the share since 1965 becomes 16%. Yet, even without the Minnesota and San Diego championships, the figure has increased over time. The evidence indicates that the teams in the smallest markets may be at a slight competitive disadvantage, but it is a disadvantage that has been overstated in the popular press.

All of this evidence on market size and winning frames the discussion on player movement, especially free agency. The popular perception is that the large-market teams use their superior resources to acquire all the best veteran talent. Indeed, the evidence that follows indicates that they are more likely to acquire established stars through free agency than are small-market teams. However, the winning percentage data and the championship data indicate that, with or without high-priced free agents, the large-market teams are not enjoying an excessive share of success. The logical conclusion is that free agency is not the boon that some profess it to be. And the data that follow support that conclusion, largely because the future performance of free agents is more erratic than expected, and because teams routinely overpay for players in the last half of their careers.[2]

FREE AGENTS

The analysis begins with free agency rather than trades because that seems to have people most upset these days. The first question to examine is whether large-market teams are more likely to sign free agents. Table 2.3 indicates that they are, but that this is a relatively recent development. The average size of the cities to which free agents were signed was slightly larger than the average size of all cities in the league, no matter whether MSA population is used or MSA population divided by the number of teams in the market. That disparity grew larger over time. Prior to 1981, the average major league MSA contained 3.7 million people, and the average MSA in which there was a free agent signing had 4.2 million. After 1990, the average MSA had 6 million residents; the average free agent MSA had 7.3 million. Results for the MSA population figures that adjust for the number of teams in a market are quite similar.

The average free agent MSA population statistic can be inflated by a few signings by an especially large-market (e.g., New York). A better indicator of the typical franchise that used the free agent market is probably the median MSA size.[3] That statistic makes it even clearer that the dominance of large cities in the free agent market occurred after 1990. Prior to that point, there was very little difference between the median MSA in baseball and the median free agent MSA. After 1990, the median MSA had a population of 3.8 million while the median free agent MSA had 5.3 million.

Table 2.3 — Market Size (in millions) of Teams Signing Free Agents

	Pre–1981: 20 Free Agents	1981–1990: 64 Free Agents	1991–1993: 20 Free Agents
Average MSA population for teams signing a free agent	4.21	5.85	7.25
Divided by number of teams in market	2.66	3.93	4.87
Overall average MSA population	3.67	5.14	5.95
Divided by number of teams in market	2.63	3.62	4.02
Minimum MSA population for teams signging a free agent	1.27	1.43	1.58
Median MSA population for teams signing a free agent	2.82	3.05	5.32
Divided by number of teams in market	2.58	2.96	4.54
Overall median MSA population for teams signing a free agent	2.52	2.96	3.81
Divided by number of teams in market	2.39	2.88	3.13

Notes. Overall population of metropolitan statistical areas calculated in the last year of the period (1980, 1990, or 1993). Average and median calculations for 1993 exclude Denver and Miami because the Colorado Rockies and Florida Marlins joined the league in that year, and thus were not responsible for the free agent signings summarized here.

The results in Table 2.3 are surprising, not so much because free agents were attracted to somewhat larger markets than the major league average, but because the shift to large-market dominance of free agency appears to have occurred so abruptly. Whatever advantages large-markets enjoyed, they had enjoyed them for a long time, and the recent talk about the growing divide between baseball's haves and have-nots was, therefore, likely to be overstated. These figures call that assertion into question. Small-market teams appear to have been abruptly priced out of the free agent market as player salaries escalated, although the situation is more complex than the figures in Table 2.3 indicate.

Because the post–1990 data from *BE* ran through only 1993, the sample is small, and so data on all free agents from 1998 to 2003 were also collected; these appear in Table 2.4. Unlike the data from *BE*, the recent dataset also has information on salaries, making it easier to document the level at which smaller cities are priced out of the player market. The top half of Table 2.4 contains information on average market size versus the average market size to which free agents were signed. As expected, as one slides up the salary scale, the margin between the average "free agent" MSA population and the average MSA population grows wider — for the full sample of free agent signings, the average free agent MSA has 6.4 million people, the overall average MSA 6 million; players with contracts larger than $2.5 million toil in cities populated by 7.8 million people, on average; those with contracts larger than $10 million land in cities with 8.8 million.[4] It's also interesting to note that the average market size for free agents signed to minor league contracts was only 5.7 million, below the average MSA, which suggests that small-market teams are more likely to rely on unproven talents or over-the-hill veterans making a last-gasp attempt to stay in baseball.

While the figures for the average free agent MSA in the top half of Table 2.4 suggest that small-markets are rapidly and progressively priced out of the player market as salaries escalate, there is evidence for the median free agent MSAs in the bottom half of the table which suggests that the relationship is a bit more gradual. Again, the median figures are preferable because the average figures are too heavily influenced by free agents signed by teams in New York, Los Angeles, and Chicago. There also is a distinction between the figures for MSA population and those that are adjusted for the number of teams in the market. The adjusted figures shift Oakland and San Francisco from the eighth largest MSA to 18th. Because both of those teams were very active in the market for free agents during this period, the adjusted population figures indicate that small-markets were more active in the free agent market than the unadjusted figures do. For players signing contracts less than or equal to $10 million, the adjusted median free agent MSA is 3.6 million which is nearly the same as for the adjusted median MSA overall (3.5 million). So, it's not that small-market teams aren't active on the free agent market. They appear to be

Greg Maddux went from the large market Chicago Cubs to the medium-market Atlanta Braves via free agency, bucking the trend toward superstar signings by large-market teams. Maddux led major league pitchers in the 1990s in wins (157) and ERA (2.44), and the Braves won the division title in every full season that he was a member of the team.

every bit as active as large-market teams, except when it comes to a select group of players. Notice also that the disparity between the adjusted median free agent MSA and adjusted median MSA overall is pretty small for contracts between $1 million and $10 million (4.3 million versus 3.5 million). If all markets competed for free agents on equal footing, the adjusted free agent MSA would be between the 15th and 16th most populous MSAs, the same as for the sample overall. The 4.3 million figure for Houston ranks 13th, which is not far off.

It is when contracts rise above $10 million, which accounts for 89 of the 704 signings (13%), that small-markets find it more difficult to compete. The adjusted median free agent MSA for contracts more than $10 million is 4.7 million (for Texas), which ranks ninth overall. Ninth might not seem that high, but consider that if the ninth-ranked team is the median, the remaining 21 teams are responsible for only half of the free agent signings. To summarize, small-markets are gradually priced out of the market for free agents as salaries rise, and dramatically so once contracts surpass $10 million. For contracts below the $10 million level, the effects are much less pronounced. The numbers indi-

Table 2.4 — Market Size of Teams Signing Free Agents 1998–2003, in millions

	#	Average Population where Free Agents were signed	Overall Average Population	Adjusted* Average Population where Free Agents were signed	Adjusted* Overall Average Population
All Free Agents	704	6.41	5.99	4.47	4.30
Signed to minor league contract	238	5.72	5.99	4.12	4.30
Signed to major league contract	466	6.76	5.99	4.65	4.30
Free agents with contracts >$1,000,000	297	7.37	5.99	4.97	4.30
Free agents with contracts >$2,500,000	207	7.82	5.99	5.18	4.30
Free agents with contracts >$5,000,000	152	8.23	5.99	5.38	4.30
Free agents with contracts >$10,000,000	89	8.81	5.99	5.58	4.30
Free agents with contracts >$20,000,000	50	9.23	5.99	5.73	4.30

	#	Median Population where Free Agents were signed	Overall Median Population	Adjusted* Median Population where Free Agents were signed	Adjusted* Overall Median Population
All Free Agents	704	4.32	3.97	3.63	3.47
Signed to minor league contract	238	3.47	3.97	3.36	3.47
Signed to major league contract	466	4.68	3.97	3.63	3.47
Free agents with contracts >$1,000,000	297	5.44	3.97	4.32	3.47
Free agents with contracts >$2,500,000	207	5.83	3.97	4.32	3.47
Free agents with contracts >$5,000,000	152	5.83	3.97	4.32	3.47

(table continued on page 51)

(Table 2.4 — Market Size of Teams Signing Free Agents 1998–2003, in millions—*continued*)

	#	Median Population where Free Agents were signed	Overall Median Population	Adjusted* Median Population where Free Agents were signed	Adjusted* Overall Median Population
Free agents with contracts >$10,000,000	89	5.97	3.97	4.68	3.47
Free agents with contracts >$20,000,000	50	6.34	3.97	4.68	3.47

Notes. *Adjusted population figures divide MSA population by the number of teams in the market.

Sources: http://ourworld.compuserve.com/homepages/m_n_hbumbaco/roster/00agency.html
http://www.canoe.ca/BaseballMoneyMatters/freeagents_signings.html
http://www.gobi.com/shared/sports/mlb/stats/signings.html
http://totalsports.aol.com/stats/bbo/mlb/mlb.fasign.html
http://sportinggreen/SG/bbo/mlb/stats/98.mlb.fasign.html
http ://sportsillustrated.cnn.com/baseball/news/2002/12/06/free_agent_signings/

Ken Griffey Jr., a superstar who didn't end up playing for a large-market team. When it became clear that he would not re-sign with the Seattle Mariners, they orchestrated a trade, but with the small-market Cincinnati Reds. The Reds then signed him to a long-term contract. Despite losing Griffey and the earlier departures of Tino Martinez and Randy Johnson, the Mariners made it to the ALCS in 2000. In 2001 they lost Alex Rodriguez to the Rangers, and yet they recorded the most wins in major league history, tying the 1906 Cubs.

cate that they can and do participate in the player market, no matter what Bud Selig and the small-market owners might tell you.

Moreover, a comparison of the sheer number of signings in Tables 2.3 and 2.4 indicates growing participation on the part of all teams in this market. Table 2.3 contains 20 signings from 1990 to 1992. Recall that data were collected for only a third of the transactions listed in BE, so let's assume that there would have been 60 had all of them been collected. The post–1990 data in Table 2.3 cover three years, the data in Table 2.4 cover six, so multiplying by two would imply 120 signings had the earlier period been of the same length. In addition, an adjustment is necessary because major league baseball has grown from 26 to 30 teams (about 15%), which makes the total 138 transactions. For 1998–2003, there were 466 signings of players to major league contracts. The BE counts a free agent signing as a transaction only if a player moves from one team to another, while the data in Table 2.4 include cases where a player re-signed with his team, which occurred in 147 of 466 cases. So, a fair comparison would be 138 free agent signings for the early 1990s versus 319 for 1998 to 2003. Teams are much more active on the free agent market than they were, and the market size figures in Table 2.4 indicate that it's not just the Yankees that account for the change.

On the basis of Tables 2.3 and 2.4, the large-market teams do have a substantial advantage in attracting a select subset of players, but aside from that group the large-market advantage is not very pronounced. And the advantage becomes even smaller if one considers what large-market teams are getting for their money. Let us first establish where free agents are in their careers when they arrive in a new city. Because most of the free agents in Table 2.4 haven't yet completed their careers, it is more accurate to use the BE data from Table 2.3 for these calculations. Free agents tend to be about two-thirds of the way through careers that average roughly 14 years. Of the four to five years remaining in their careers, free agents spend a little more than two with the team that signs them. This suggests that free agents do not, on average, provide long-term solutions to teams' personnel problems. And teams that play the free agent game need to constantly readjust, which is difficult to do. Table 2.5 indicates that free agents don't hang around long in either large or small-markets, so it does not appear that large-market teams are better able to lock their free agents into longer contracts, or at least they weren't as of the early 1990s.

Many free agents play only one year (or sometimes not at all) after signing their contracts. Four free agents from the late '70s, 10 from the '80s, and two from the '90s did not play beyond the year they signed their free agent contract. That's about 15% of the whole BE sample of free agents. This group includes a number of well-known veterans taking one last shot, one often doomed to failure. There was Al Bumbry's 1985 season with San Diego (95 AB, .200 BA, 1 HR, 10 RBI), Dick Allen's 1977 swan song with Oakland (171 AB, .240 BA, 5 HR, 31 RBI), Jose Cruz's 1988 season with the Yankees (80 AB, .200

Table 2.5 — Length of Career of Free Agent Signees, by Market Size

Signed by Teams in MSAs Below Median Size

	Career Average	Years Left in Career Average	Years Left with Team Average
Prior to 1981 (n*=9)	14.0	5.1	2.9
1981–1990 (n=29)	14.2	2.8	1.6
Post 1990 (n=7)	15.3	4.9	2.1

Signed by Teams in MSAs Above Median Size

	Career Average	Years Left in Career Average	Years Left with Team Average
Prior to 1981 (n=11)	12.1	4.0	2.2
1981–1990 (n=35)	15.1	4.0	1.8
Post 1990 (n=13)	14.2	4.7	3.0

Notes. *"n" represents the number of free agent signees in the period.

BA, 1 HR, 7 RBI), or Joaquin Andujar's last gasp with Houston in 1988 (2–5, 4.00 ERA, 78.7 IP). The point is that a sizable share of free agents are players who are well past their primes.

While Table 2.5 indicates that no team gets a lot of years out of its free agents on average, large-market teams might enjoy an advantage if their free agents outproduce those signed by small-market teams. Table 2.6, which provides data from *BE* for free agent pitchers, indicates that such concerns are unwarranted. Free agent pitchers have had about the same immediate impact on both large- and small-market teams. In fact, in the year of their signing, free agent pitchers signed by small-market teams prior to 1981 had better average ERAs (3.60 vs. 6.00), more innings pitched (177.0 vs. 118.8), and a better record (12–9 vs. 8–7) than pitchers signed by large-market teams. The small-market free agents did, however, have fewer saves, on average (0.3 vs. 10.3), than their large-market counterparts, but that was due to one player, Bill Campbell, who had 31 saves for the Red Sox in 1977. The median number of saves for free agents from both small- and large-market teams was zero.

From 1981 to 1990, free agent pitchers signed by small-market teams had average ERAs and innings pitched almost identical to those for large-market signees. The small-market pitchers actually held a slight edge in average number of saves (3.3 vs. 1.3) and average records (6–5 vs. 6–7). The post–1990 results were mixed. Small-market signees held an advantage in innings pitched (145.1 vs. 111.5) and saves (3.2 vs. 1.2); but they trailed in ERA (4.70 vs. 4.10) and record (6–10 vs. 5–7). There is no way that an unbiased observer could look at this evidence and conclude that the average quality of free agent pitchers signed by large-market teams was higher than that of small-market teams, at least in the year in which these players were signed.

Of course, the number of observations in Table 2.6 is small, and there is no information from the most recent past, so this could be a misleading picture. However, the data in table 2.7 on all free agent pitchers signed from 1998

Table 2.6 — Performance of Free Agent Pitchers in Year of Signing, by Market Size

	No.	Avg.	Min.	Max.
Prior to 1981				
Small-market				
ERA	3	3.6	3.5	3.7
Innings Pitched	3	177.0	107.0	237.0
Saves	3	0.3	0	1
Wins	3	11.7	8	17
Losses	3	8.7	7	11
Large-market				
ERA	3	6.0	3.0	10.7
Innings Pitched	3	118.8	19.3	197.0
Saves	3	10.3	0	31
Wins	3	7.7	0	13
Losses	3	7.0	0	12
1981–1990				
Small-market				
ERA	12	4.2	2.3	8.5
Innings Pitched	12	96.2	16.3	190.7
Saves	12	3.3	0	14
Wins	12	6.3	0	12
Losses	12	5.0	0	12
Large-market				
ERA	12	4.2	2.8	6.2
Innings Pitched	12	102.1	4.3	217.3
Saves	12	1.3	0	8
Wins	12	5.7	0	16
Losses	12	6.7	0	16
Post–1990				
Small-market				
ERA	6	4.7	2.2	8.2
Innings Pitched	6	145.1	19.7	254.0
Saves	6	3.2	0	17
Wins	6	5.8	0	11
Losses	6	9.8	3	18
Large-market				
ERA	5	4.1	3.0	5.1
Innings Pitched	5	111.5	64.3	203.7
Saves	5	1.2	0	4
Wins	5	4.8	2	11
Losses	5	7.2	1	15

Note: All cities with MSA population below the MLB median are considered small-markets; those above the median are large-markets.

to 2003 yield similar conclusions. In the year of their signing, large-market pitchers averaged slightly more innings pitched than small-market pitchers (93.6 vs. 85.6) and had lower average ERAs (5.43 vs. 5.65). Those numbers are heavily influenced by one or two pitchers, unlike the median figures. The median large-market pitcher had a 4.43 ERA in 72 innings pitched; the median small-market pitcher had a 4.83 in 68.7 innings pitched. Moreover, the average small-market pitcher had a record the same as his large-market counterpart (5–5, with two saves). The bottom line is that, on average, the free agent pitchers signed by small-market teams in the last six years have been just about as productive as those signed by large-market teams.

Table 2.7 — Performance of Free Agent Pitchers in Year of Signing, by Market Size, 1998–2003

	Average	Median	Min.	Max.
Small-market (109 Free Agents)				
ERA	5.65	4.83	0.00	43.20
Innings Pitched	85.6	68.7	1.0	271.7
Saves	2.4	0	0	46
Wins	4.6	3	0	21
Losses	4.9	4	0	19
Large-market (145 Free Agents)				
ERA	5.43	4.43	2.34	81.00
Innings Pitched	93.6	72.0	0.3	303.2
Saves	2.2	0	0	55
Wins	5.3	4	0	21
Losses	5.3	5	0	14

Notes: All cities with MSA population (adjusted for the number of teams in the market) below the MLB median are considered small-markets; those above the median are large-markets. Only those pitchers that appeared in a major league game in the year of their acquisition (and for the team that they signed with) are included in the calculations.

As noted, large-market teams in Tables 2.6 and 2.7 are defined as having MSA populations above the league median. The number of free agents signed by teams in small- and large-markets is itself a telling statistic. Prior to 1981, there were three free agent pitchers signed by small-market teams, three by large-market teams; from 1981 to 1990, 12 were signed by small-market teams, 12 by large-market teams; after 1990, the figures were six small-market signees versus five large-market signees. In other words, large-market teams did not make use of the free agent market for pitchers much more than did small-market teams. Again, because the *BE* sample covers only a third of all free agent transactions, it could be providing a slightly distorted picture. For the recent period described in Table 2.7, the full free agent sample indicates that small-market teams signed 109 pitchers, while large-market teams signed 145. This suggests that large-market teams now are slightly more likely to sign free agent pitchers. However, given all the data presented here, it is unlikely that free agency has been that great a boon to large-market teams in satisfying their pitching needs. And, as described in Chapter Four, pitching, not hitting, is the necessary ingredient in creating a league champion.

The figures in Tables 2.6 and 2.7 only summarize free agent performance in the year of the pitcher's signing. That information may, therefore, yield an incomplete impression of these transactions. Although Table 2.5 indicated that large-market free agents didn't stay with their new teams any longer than did small-market free agents, and Tables 2.6 and 2.7 indicate that their immediate impact was no greater than for small-market free agents, large-market signees may be bringing a different sort of star power. That is, as big-name players, they may be better able to fill the stands. The additional resources they provide may enable these players to provide benefits to their teams in excess of their on-field performance.

The free agents best able to boost attendance are likely to be those with the longest, most glorious careers. If the large-market teams are better able to afford such stars, it might be reflected in the career statistics of their free agent signees. However, Table 2.8 indicates that the career statistics of the large-market free agent pitchers were no better than those for small-market signees. Prior to 1981, small-market pitchers, on average, held career advantages in ERA (3.80 vs. 3.90), innings pitched (2,243.8 vs. 1,358.1) and record (131–124 vs. 73–77). They were at a disadvantage in terms of average career saves (7.3 vs. 51.0), again largely due to reliever Bill Campbell, who was signed by the large-market Red Sox. The three large-market signees were Campbell, Jim Barr (Angels), and John D'Acquisto (Angels). The small-market signees were Doyle Alexander (Rangers), Jim Bibby (Pirates), and John Curtis (Padres). If anything, the star power factor would appear to tip toward the small-market signees. From 1981 to 1990, results were mixed. Small-market pitchers had a better ERA, 3.90 vs. 4.20; but they trailed in innings pitched, 1,403.5 vs. 1,636.7; record, 80–79 vs. 101–96; and saves, 30.8 vs. 46.1. After 1990, small-market pitchers held a slight advantage: 3.80 vs. 4.10 ERA; 2,066.6 vs. 1,361.6 innings pitched; 129–105 vs. 80–77 record; and 11.8 vs. 3.4 saves.

The small-market advantage after 1990 is no doubt the result of a small sample. Table 2.9, which provides data from the full sample of free agents from 1998 to 2003, indicates that, as in the 1980s, pitchers signed by small-market teams had slightly worse average career statistics than those signed by large-market teams: 4.33 versus 4.18 ERA; 1,091.2 versus 1,259.6 innings pitched; 63–62 versus 76–69 record. The small-market pitchers did however hold a slight edge in career saves, 34.1 versus 32.5. Viewed in its totality, the evidence indicates that large-market free agent pitchers did not and do not, on average, have much better career statistics than small-market free agent pitchers.

Table 2.8 — Career Performance of Free Agent Pitchers, by Market Size

	No.	Avg.	Min.	Max.
Prior to 1981				
Small-market				
ERA	3	3.8	3.8	4.0
Innings Pitched	3	2,243.8	1,641.0	3,367.7
Saves	3	7.3	3	11
Wins	3	131.3	89	194
Losses	3	124.0	97	174
Large-market				
ERA	3	3.9	3.5	4.6
Innings Pitched	3	1,358.1	779.7	2,065.3
Saves	3	51.0	12	126
Wins	3	72.7	34	101
Losses	3	77.0	51	112
1981–1990				
Small-market				
ERA	12	3.9	3.2	4.2
Innings Pitched	12	1,403.5	626.3	2,188.3
Saves	12	30.8	0	96
Wins	12	79.5	35	134
Losses	12	79.4	33	134
Large-market				
ERA	12	4.2	2.8	6.2
Innings Pitched	12	1,636.7	33.0	3,017.0
Saves	12	46.1	0	126
Wins	12	101.4	31	177
Losses	12	95.8	26	182
Post–1990				
Small-market				
ERA	6	3.8	3.3	4.1
Innings Pitched	6	2,066.6	1,205.3	2,898.7
Saves	6	11.8	0	32
Wins	6	128.5	67	194
Losses	6	105.3	62	134
Large-market				
ERA	5	4.1	3.7	4.6
Innings Pitched	5	1,361.6	540.3	2,725.0
Saves	5	3.4	0	11
Wins	5	80.2	31	151
Losses	5	77.0	34	164

Note: All cities with MSA population below the MLB median are considered small-markets; those above the median are large-markets.

Table 2.9 — Career Performance of Free Agent Pitchers Signed 1998–2003 by Market Size

	Average	Median	Min.	Max.
Small-market (109 Free Agents)				
ERA	4.33	4.33	3.10	7.37
Innings Pitched	1,091.2	883.3	105.0	3,197.3
Saves	34.1	5	0	304
Wins	63.2	47	2	230
Losses	61.6	52	3	186
Large-market (145 Free Agents)				
ERA	4.18	4.16	2.74	5.50
Innings Pitched	1,259.6	982.7	11.7	4,278.7
Saves	32.5	5	0	424
Wins	75.7	60	0	310
Losses	68.5	56	0	186

Notes: All cities with MSA population (adjusted for the number of teams in the market) below the MLB median are considered small-markets; those above the median are large-markets. Only those pitchers that appeared in a major league game in the year of their acquisition (for the team that they signed with) are included in the calculations.

In short, in terms of pitching, there is no strong evidence that free agency has been a tool that differentially benefits large-market teams. However, it is interesting to note that in the last six years large-market teams signed more free agent pitchers than did small-market teams. Surprisingly, the reverse is true with respect to position players (see Table 2.11). This could indicate that, as in the early years of the amateur draft, large-market teams at first misguidedly focused on position players in signing free agents. For example, even more recently, when White Sox owner Jerry Reinsdorf asked Frank Thomas what free agent he would most like to hit next to in the lineup, Thomas named Albert Belle, who was later acquired (and then left after the White Sox stumbled through consecutive sub-.500 seasons). He should have asked Thomas what pitcher was toughest to face. He could have named Roger Clemens, or Pedro Martinez, or Randy Johnson, or Curt Schilling. All were available (reportedly or actually) at one time or another since 1998. Based on the data from 1976 to 1992, it is plausible that large-market teams didn't use the free agent pitching markets as effectively as they might have. The evidence from the past six years is consistent with them shifting their efforts in that direction.

In any event, as with the pitchers, any performance advantage enjoyed by large-market free agent position players over small-market signees is small, although the *BE* data suggest that the gap might be widening. Prior to 1981, there was little or no perceptible advantage for the large-market free agent in the year of his signing (Table 2.10). Small-market position players averaged

308.2 AB, 6.2 HR, 35.2 RBI, a .217 BA, and a .285 OBP. Large-market signees averaged 304.9 AB, 5.8 HR, 34.1 RBI, a .240 BA, and a .317 OBP. By the 1980s, however, the average large-market free agent held a sizable edge over his small-market counterpart on all five measures of offensive production. After 1991, the sole small-market signee, Chili Davis (Twins, 1991), did have better production than the typical large-market free agent, but perhaps the most alarming statistic was that there was but *one* position player signed by a small-market team.

The full sample results from 1998 to 2003, which appear in Table 2.11, indicate that the post–1990 results in Table 2.10 are a bit misleading. Position players signed by large-market teams in the last six years were a little better than their small-market counterparts, but not much better. The large-market signees averaged 284 AB; 10 HR; 39 RBI; a .251 batting average; and a .324 OBP. The small-market signees had the same average RBI, and higher OBP (.335) and batting average (.262). They lagged the large-market signees, but only slightly, on the other two measures of offensive production (278 AB; 9 HR). Moreover, the gap on those two measures is eliminated when looking at median performance: 249 AB, 6 HR for large-market position players versus 257 AB, 6 HR for the small-market players. Based on these numbers, it is hard to argue that large-market teams derive a sizable advantage from signing free agent position players. Perhaps as importantly, the small-market teams signed two *more* position players than the large-market teams during the last four years (164 versus 162). Again, teams from smaller cities have participated in these markets a lot more than some of their owners would like us to believe.

While the statistics in the year of signing are remarkably similar for free agent position players in small- and large-markets since 1981, the large-market signees did have better career statistics in the 1980s (Table 2.12). Results are, again, similar for both groups prior to 1981—the typical small-market signee averaged 4,770 AB, 94 HR, 523 RBI, a .262 BA, and a .343 OBP; his large-market counterpart averaged 3,915 AB, 114 HR, 522 RBI, a .275 BA, and a .348 OBP. In the 1980s, career statistics for the large-market signees were clearly better than for small-market signees, especially with respect to home runs (149 vs. 44) and RBI (687 vs. 323). Also in the 1980s, large-market teams signed 23 position players, small-market teams only 17. In the '90s, the career averages tip in favor of the small-market teams, but not by that much, and the disparity is again due to Chili Davis being the only small-market signee.

The full sample results from 1998 to 2003 in Table 2.13 indicate that, as with the yearly statistics, the career statistics of the free agent position players signed by small-market teams are comparable to those for players signed by large-market teams. The typical small-market signee had 3,964 career AB, 117 HR, 528 RBI, a .335 OBP, and a .266 batting average. The typical large-market signee had the same OBP, slightly more career at bats (4,108), home runs (131) and RBI (561), and a slightly higher batting average (.268). Unlike for the

Table 2.10 — Performance of Free Agent Position Players in Year of Signing, by Market Size

	No.	Avg.	Min.	Max.
Prior to 1981				
Small-market				
At Bats	6	308.2	0	580
Home Runs	6	6.2	0	17
RBI	6	35.2	0	82
Avg.	6	.217	.000	.281
On Base Pct.	6	.285	.000	.378
Large-market				
At Bats	8	304.9	80	650
Home Runs	8	5.8	0	25
RBI	8	34.1	4	75
Avg.	8	.240	.181	.296
On Base Pct.	8	.317	.253	.364
1981–1990				
Small-market				
At Bats	17	174.5	0	405
Home Runs	17	2.1	0	11
RBI	17	17.9	0	45
Avg.	17	.212	.000	.300
On Base Pct.	17	.271	.000	.378
Large-market				
At Bats	23	345.1	34	621
Home Runs	23	11.0	0	49
RBI	23	45.3	3	137
Avg.	23	.256	.118	.350
On Base Pct.	23	.326	.118	.402
Post–1990				
Small-market				
At Bats	1	534.0	534	534
Home Runs	1	29.0	29	29
RBI	1	93.0	93	93
Avg.	1	.277	.277	.277
On Base Pct.	1	.387	.387	.387
Large-market				
At Bats	8	381.8	104	573
Home Runs	8	13.9	0	46
RBI	8	61.0	15	123
Avg.	8	.269	.243	.336
On Base Pct.	8	.356	.318	.463

Note: All cities with MSA population below the MLB median are considered small-markets; those above the median are large-markets.

Table 2.11—Performance of Free Agent Position Players Signed 1998–2001 in Year of Signing, by Market Size

	Average	Median	Min.	Max.
Small-market (164 Free Agents)				
At Bats	278.2	257	1	632
Home Runs	8.8	6	0	46
RBI	39.0	33	0	145
Avg.	.262	.262	.000	.441
On Base Pct.	.335	.336	.000	.582
Large-market (162 Free Agents)				
At Bats	284.2	249	2	673
Home Runs	9.7	6	0	52
RBI	39.0	30	0	148
Avg.	.251	.258	.000	.500
On Base Pct.	.324	.326	.000	.500

Notes: All cities with MSA population (adjusted for the number of teams in the market) below the MLB median are considered small-markets; those above the median are large-markets. Only those players that appeared in a major league game in the year of their acquisition (for the team that they signed with) are included in the calculations.

1980s, when large-market signees held a distinct advantage over small-market signees, there is much less difference in the career statistics of the two groups since 1998. This could suggest that the crop of free agents signed by large-market teams in the 1980s was especially good, or that the *BE* sample for the 1980s is incomplete and thus misleading, or that small-market teams are now doing a better job with their position player signings. Whatever the explanation, the current data suggest that the typical position player signed by a small-market team produces about as much the typical large-market signee in the year that he arrives, and he also has relatively comparable career statistics.

Recall also that there are at least a couple of key indications that the combination of free agents signed by small-market teams and the young non-free agents that populate the infields and outfields of teams like the Twins and A's provides a reasonable substitute for the collection of more expensive veteran free agents signed by large-market teams. First, the share of teams with winning percentages below .400 continues near its lowest levels since World War II (see Chapter 1), and, second, there is little or no correlation between winning percentage and city size.

So the evolution of free agency described here has not coincided with any obvious decline in competitive balance. The question is why hasn't it? A large part of the answer is that free agents aren't worth what teams end up paying for them. There will be more on the free agent salary mechanism in the next subsection. For a given budget, a team can afford more young players than it can free agents. Because injuries occur and individual performance varies from

Table 2.12 — Career Performance of Free Agent Position Players by Market Size

	No.	Avg.	Min.	Max.
Prior to 1981				
Small-market				
At Bats	6	4,769.5	1,997	8,684
Home Runs	6	93.7	15	242
RBI	6	522.8	193	1,039
Avg.	6	.262	.252	.282
On Base Pct.	6	.343	.311	.389
Large-market				
At Bats	8	3,914.6	1,294	8,198
Home Runs	8	114.3	16	351
RBI	8	522.0	151	1,276
Avg.	8	.275	.229	.311
On Base Pct.	8	.348	.329	.381
1981–1990				
Small-market				
At Bats	17	3,334.6	865	7,245
Home Runs	17	43.9	2	105
RBI	17	322.5	80	826
Avg.	17	.254	.221	.281
On Base Pct.	17	.321	.270	.350
Large-market				
At Bats	23	5,552.8	1,061	9,927
Home Runs	23	149.0	19	438
RBI	23	687.2	131	1,591
Avg.	23	.262	.220	.290
On Base Pct.	23	.335	.302	.383
Post–1990				
Small-market				
At Bats	1	8,673.0	8,673	8,673
Home Runs	1	350.0	350	350
RBI	1	1,372.0	1,372	1,372
Avg.	1	.274	.274	.274
On Base Pct.	1	.360	.360	.360
Large-market				
At Bats	8	6,380.4	1,189	9,927
Home Runs	8	262.0	10	658
RBI	8	1,022.9	240	1,742
Avg.	8	.282	.245	.328
On Base Pct.	8	.367	.307	.433

Note: All cities with MSA population below the MLB median are considered small-markets; those above the median are large-markets.

Table 2.13 — Career Performance of Free Agent Position Players Signed 1998–2003 by Market Size

	Average	Median	Min.	Max.
Small-market (164 Free Agents)				
At Bats	3,963.9	3,507	69	9,288
Home Runs	117.4	77	3	658
RBI	528.2	422	15	1,742
Avg.	.266	.265	.208	.338
On Base Pct.	.335	.333	.277	.454
Large-market (162 Free Agents)				
At Bats	4,107.8	3,759	269	10,961
Home Runs	130.8	91	7	528
RBI	561.1	435	40	1,687
Avg.	.268	.269	.208	.319
On Base Pct.	.335	.334	.266	.428

Notes: All cities with MSA population (adjusted for the number of teams in the market) below the MLB median are considered small-markets; those above the median are large-markets. Only those players that appeared in a major league game in the year of their acquisition (for the team that they signed with) are included in the calculations.

year to year, a broad portfolio of young players can conceivably outperform a smaller number of free agents. Relying on a small group of high-priced free agents can be like putting too many eggs in one basket.

So why not do both? That is, if you have the resources, why not outspend other teams on both dimensions — free agents and player development? This is clearly what teams like the Braves and the Yankees have done since the early 1990s. For every Fred McGriff the Braves signed, their minor league system produced a Chipper Jones or a Ryan Klesko. One reason the Braves' success hasn't been duplicated by other teams is, simply, because it's hard to consistently select the best free agents and draft and groom the best young talent. Just ask the generally disappointing Dodgers, Cubs, and Angels of the 1990s, all large-market teams that had considerable resources.

Another important reason why teams find it difficult to hold on to a large stable of free agents and young players is that most players simply want to play. Although there remain impediments to the free movement of players, there is enough flexibility that players will gravitate toward situations where their skills are best put to use. Moreover, teams that are loaded with talent never get to find out how good some of their young players are. It takes time for young players to develop and each team has only so many innings and at-bats at the major league level in a given year, and minor league experience is not a perfect substitute. Take Paul Byrd, for example, an all-star pitcher for the Phillies in 1999, who had kicked around the Braves system for years with little or no opportunity to crack that formidable rotation. So, there exists a natural constraint on the stockpiling of talent, and this too partially accounts for the competitive balance since the '80s.

FREE AGENT SALARIES

Even if free agent salaries were reasonable, it seems likely that competition would continue to be relatively balanced for the reasons described in subsequent chapters, such as the introduction of the amateur draft and the variability of pitching performance. However, one of the enjoyable aspects of major league baseball is that teams tend to get less than they pay for when signing free agents. This affects large-market teams most, as they sign the most expensive free agents, and thus contributes to competitive balance. A considerable academic literature has sprung up to document and explain the mispricing in this market, which is briefly summarized here. As demonstrated above, and as this literature predicts, the link between team salaries and winning percentage is not as strong as some would have you believe.

DO YOU GET WHAT YOU PAY FOR?

This subsection describes econometric results that help resolve one of baseball's key riddles. Namely, since the inception of free agency, team payrolls have escalated and the payroll disparities between large-market and small-market teams have grown ever wider (in absolute terms). At the same time, however, winning percentages have, if anything, narrowed, and there is no obvious statistical relationship between city size and winning percentage.[5]

To figure out whether a player is worth his salary, an economist named Gerald Scully devised a three-step procedure. In step one, a standard regression equation is used to figure out how much winning boosts team revenues. The equation is of the form:

$$TR_j = a_0 + a_1 X_j + a_2 WPCT_j$$

where TR_j is the jth team's total revenues, WPCT is that team's winning percentage, and X represents other factors affecting the team's revenues (market population, local economic conditions, etc.). The researcher collects these data for each team over a period of years (say five). Then he uses a computer statistical package to select those a's that best explain the variation across teams, and across time, in total revenues (TR). Of the estimated coefficients, the most important is a_2, which indicates how much winning is worth in terms of team revenue.[6]

Armed with an estimate of what winning is worth, the next step is to describe how teams win. In economic parlance, the goal is to describe how teams use inputs (hits, HR, defense, stolen bases, etc.) to produce output, that is, wins. Again, a standard regression equation is used, but this time of the form:

$$WPCT_j = B_0 + B_1 PERF_j$$

where $PERF_j$ represents the jth team's performance measures. These could include anything that contributes to winning. In practice, economists have opted for simple, broad summary statistics. Scully (1974, 1989) chose to focus on slugging percentage for position players and strikeout-to-walk ratios for pitchers. Zimbalist (1992) pointed out that these are not especially reliable predictors of winning percentage and opted for OPS (on-base plus slugging percentage) for position players and ERA for pitchers. Krautmann (1999) argues that, for statistical purposes, total bases is a better measure than slugging percentage or OPS, and he also incorporated ERA as a measure of pitching performance. There are advantages and disadvantages to each measure of performance, and economists could go on debating their merits for days. The main point is, a lot of different performance measures have been used, and the qualitative results that are derived are similar.

After running the second regression, the researcher has an estimate of how performance (say, OPS) affects winning, which is summarized in the coefficient B_1. And, from regression one, the effect of winning on team revenues is summarized by a_2. To determine how much a given change in performance affected team revenues, the researcher simply multiplies that change by B_1 and then by a_2:

$$\text{Change in TR} = (\text{Change in PERF}) * B_1 * a_2$$

This simple calculation underlies the estimates of how much a player is worth to a team. The intuition is that, after figuring out how big a change in team performance is derived from including, say, Robby Alomar on your team, instead of Joe Blow, the regression coefficients indicate how much additional revenue that would imply.

And measuring Robby Alomar's (or any other player's) relative contribution to team performance is the third, and final, step in the Scully procedure. It can be done in at least a couple of ways, and the method does appear to affect results. Scully took a straightforward, so-called proportional approach. He simply calculated the share of total team performance attributable to a given player by multiplying that player's slugging percentage by his share of the team's at-bats, which he then called the player's marginal product. For example, if a player slugged .500 and had 10 percent of his team's at-bats, his marginal product would be $(.5)(.1) = .05$. That marginal product would then be multiplied by a_1 and B_1, as just described, to derive the player's marginal revenue product (MRP), or his dollar value to the team.

Scully's method produced some erratic estimates of MRPs, and so Zimbalist proposed some refinements. A key critique of Scully's approach was that it didn't really take into account the value of Robby Alomar's performance *relative* to the guy he would replace, namely Joe Blow. So, Zimbalist proposed an approach which is based on a comparison of a team's performance with, versus without, the player on its roster, and his estimates appear to be a bit more reasonable.

The young stars tended to have MRPs far in excess of their 1989 salaries. For example, looking at the first four players with three or fewer years of major league experience in Zimbalist's Table 4.6 (Roberto Alomar, Barry Bonds, Bobby Bonilla, and Ellis Burks), their MRPs were *about four times* their salaries. By contrast, the older stars tended to have salaries much higher than their estimated MRPs. For example, George Brett, Andre Dawson, and Carlton Fisk, the first players listed with 13 or more years of major league experience, had salaries substantially higher than their MRPs, about twice as high for Brett and Dawson. One can debate the fine points of the Zimbalist-Scully methodology, but those are big differences, so big in fact, that no amount of methodological tweaking will undermine the main conclusion—older players typically get more money than they're worth, while younger players, especially the budding stars, get a lot less than they're worth. This is due, no doubt, to the reserve system which prevents a player from becoming a free agent until he has played six years in the major leagues.

This is an important equalizer for small-market teams. In 1989, Alomar, Bonds, and Bonilla gave their teams about the same production as Brett, Dawson, and Fisk, but at about one-fourth the cost. So this isn't necessarily a situation where a large-market team spends a lot more money to get better performance than teams that go with younger players. In many cases, a team could get equal or better performance from a young player that costs much less. This makes one wonder why teams, especially those from large-markets that have more money to spend, consistently overpay their veterans. It is easy to understand how a team would make the occasional mistake, but the econometric results demonstrate that, on average, teams continue to make the same types of mistakes.

There are at least a couple of potential explanations, one having to do with the way people make decisions under uncertainty, and the other having to do with the relationship between a team and its fans. The first is that bidders in auctions—and the wooing of veteran free agents is just that, an auction—are susceptible to something called the winner's curse. In his highly readable *Against the Gods: The Remarkable Story of Risk*, Peter L. Bernstein notes that the highest bidder in an auction often suffers from the "Winner's Curse—overpaying out of a determination to win."

There's a large literature in economics on auctions that looks at this issue from a much more mathematical perspective, but Bernstein's definition captures at least some of the intuition. Let's say two-time American League MVP Juan Gonzalez comes on the free agent market (as occurred in 2001), and, to simplify things, let's assume that he'll have the same expected productivity wherever he goes. This is simply assuming that, among the teams that are interested in him, he wouldn't be an obviously better fit at any one of them. If those assumptions hold, and they're probably not too terrible an approximation of reality, major league general managers are competing in what is known as a common value auction. Juan Gonzalez's future productivity is at auction, and general managers, using all the information at their disposal, have to make an educated guess about how much that productivity will be worth in dollar terms.

The idea is that there is some underlying "true" value to Gonzalez's productivity, and that each general manager uses his information, at least some of which is private to him, to make his assessment. Now who is going to win that auction? If he has enough money, the general manager with the rosiest assessment, and, provided the other general managers weren't all seeing the situation incorrectly, he is likely to be wrong. Moreover, once Bernstein's "determination to win" notion kicks in—after all, GMs are a competitive lot, and this auction proceeds in stages, and pressure to win intensifies as each detail is thoroughly digested by the press and fans—the probability of overpayment becomes even greater. Viewed in that context, the Scully-Zimbalist econometric results make more sense.

There are a couple of potential problems with this story. First, in dollar terms the value of Gonzalez's productivity is likely to be higher in a large-market than in a small one. Note, however, that the story doesn't really require that Gonzalez's value be uniform across teams. To end up with a winning bidder that overpays requires only reasonable similarity across large-market teams regarding his value and a handful of them participating in the auction. In the vast majority of cases, those conditions appear to apply. The beauty is that, despite all the complaining about not being able to compete effectively for free agents, the small-market teams indirectly benefit from the bidding among their large-market competitors. Large-market teams expend resources competing with each other, which leaves the winner of the free agent auction with fewer resources to pursue other opportunities.

A second, but minor, potential problem with this story is that this isn't really a pure common value auction. Gonzalez and his specific talents are likely to be a better fit with some teams than others. In that sense, teams might really each have a private, rather than a common, value for him. Bidders in most auctions have both private and common components to their overall valuations for an item. The relevant question is which component is more important. It seems likely that all the talk about where a player fits into a lineup, or a pitching rotation, and the support he gets around him, is interesting but overemphasized. Moreover, the teams sort themselves. That is, only the ones that think Gonzalez will be a good fit will participate in the auction. In an auction among those teams, the common value component is likely to overwhelm any private value components to valuations.

A third, less academic, explanation of the Scully-Zimbalist results is that large-market teams sometimes don't have much choice but to overpay for a given player. Look at the Orioles. Do you think they had any choice but to keep

Cal Ripken? They probably would have been able to get similar productivity over the 1990s for far less money, but their fans would have killed them if they had let him go. Now it could be that Cal is loved more by Baltimore fans than he would be by fans in another town. In that sense, he may really have been worth more to the Orioles than another team. But this seems unlikely — players like Ripken are pretty universally loved.

It's also true that some players might be willing to take less money than they could get on the free agent market to stay with a team. While this could occur, it's much more the exception rather than the rule. Overpaying your most popular veterans and signing them to longer contracts than is warranted by their expected productivity is almost certainly the more frequent outcome. The key point is that whether it's Winner's Curse, or overpaying out of loyalty, or some other factor, the evidence strongly indicates that free agent veterans are overpaid, so much so that it helps ensure competitive balance. The detailed evidence about team payrolls and their effects on team performance in Chapter 2 further substantiates that statement.

TRADES

In terms of player movement between teams and its effects on competitive balance, the workings of the free agent market and the reserve system for younger players are currently most important. In the past, however, some teams maintained their dominance, and perhaps they did it through player trades (at least in part).[7] The introduction of the amateur draft and the advent of free agency have changed the incentives of general managers and thus the market for trades. This section analyzes a sample of trades to determine if and how trades changed.

The basic hypothesis is that if teams in smaller cities are at a sufficient financial disadvantage, then we might expect that when their young stars mature and are eligible for greater compensation, they might have to trade them to wealthier large-market teams in return for unproven prospects. If those prospects do not, on average, perform as well as the established players that the small-market teams have to trade, this could be a source of competitive advantage for large-market teams.

If these conjectures are correct, we would expect to see evidence in support of them in data from trades. That is, we would expect that small-market teams would receive less-proven players at earlier stages of their careers in return for more-proven players at more advanced stages of their careers. In other words, we would expect to see small-market teams trading the relatively known for the relatively unknown. So, one indication that financial pressures dictate the structure of trades would be that the players received by small-market teams would be younger than those received by large-market teams. In addition, although the small-market players might play for more years than those received by large-market teams in the same trade, their initial performance would be worse, or at least more variable.

THE PITCHERS

Let us look first at evidence from trades involving pitchers. The advent of free agency is what made these financial pressures more pronounced. By contrast, under the reserve clause, when players could not move freely between teams, and salary structures for teams were similar, trades were less apt to reflect small-market financial pressures. So we should expect to see a difference in the characteristics of trades after the mid–1970s.

Assessing how well teams do in trades is not easy. The main problem, from a statistical viewpoint, is that trades come in all shapes and sizes. Teams often trade two players for one, or three for two. Even when a trade is symmetric in terms of the number of players changing hands, those players often play different positions, which makes comparing their subsequent performance difficult. How do you compare the performance of a middle reliever with that of a utility infielder or a designated hitter?

This difficulty is addressed by looking at the subset of trades in which one player was exchanged for another, and both players played the same position. As noted, there are 1,500 transactions in the *BE* database, one-third of the total transactions from 1945 to 1992. However, symmetric trades involving players of the same position comprise only a small fraction of the total.

Table 2.14 provides performance data for players involved in pitcher-for-pitcher trades. The data come from the year of the trade, and thus Table 2.14 indicates the immediate value of these trades to the respective teams. The data are averaged across eras, and trades are broken up into three categories: (1) "large to large," meaning pitchers were exchanged between two large-market teams, (2) "small to small" for trades between small-market teams, and (3) "small to large" for trades between a small- and a large-market team. For the small to large trades, the average performance of the pitchers that went to the small-market teams is presented in rows labeled "(S)," and the performance for those that went to large-markets in rows labeled "(L)." Again, a large-market team is defined as having a population above the median for major league cities.

To test the hypotheses described above, the key trades are the small to large ones. For simplicity, they are referred to as mixed trades hereafter. Before discussing the results from mixed trades, however, there is one simple indication that small-market teams *aren't* typically pressured into veterans-for-prospects trades with large-market teams. If trades occurred at random between large- and small-market teams, we would expect one-quarter of the sample to be comprised of small-to-small trades, one-quarter to be large-to-large trades, and one-half to be mixed trades.

Table 2.14 — Pitcher for Pitcher Trades Performance in Year of Trade

Market Type(s)	N	ERA	IP	W	L	SV	Year Left	Left with Team
1945–1962 (Mickey Mantle Era)								
Large to Large	6	4.49	139.6	7	9	2	2.7	1.5
Small to Small	10	4.59	62.9	4	3	2	4.2	1.5
Small to Large	16							
(S)	8	5.49	80.7	3	5	1	3.3	1.6
(L)	8	1.96	61.8	4	3	1	2.6	0.9
1963–1977 (Henry Aaron Era)								
Large to Large	4	5.29	110.6	5	4	2	2.3	0.8
Small to Small	18	3.52	71.7	4	5	3	2.5	1.1
Small to Large	26							
(S)	13	4.40	92.8	4	5	3	3.3	1.0
(L)	13	3.81	105.6	7	5	5	4.5	2.8
1978–1992 (Marvin Miller Era)								
Large to Large	16	4.75	61.8	3	4	1	4.0	1.4
Small to Small	14	4.53	54.7	2	4	0	3.6	0.6
Small to Large	34							
(S)	17	3.11	46.6	2	3	0	4.4	2.1
(L)	17	2.87	56.7	3	3	0	3.1	1.2

Notes: N is the number of players involved in the trades. If N=6, the number of trades in that category is three. Trades are broken up into three categories: (1) "large to large," meaning pitchers were exchanged between two large-market teams, (2) "small to small" for trades between small-market teams, and (3) "small to large" for trades between a small- and a large-market team. For the small to large trades, the average performance of the pitchers that went to the small-market teams is presented in rows labeled "(S)," and the performance for those that went to large-markets in rows labeled "(L)." A large-market team is defined as having a population above the median for major league cities.

If small-market teams felt the pressures mentioned above, mixed trades would likely be more frequent than others, and thus would comprise more than half of the sample.

Mixed trades comprised 8 of the 16 trades during the Mantle Era (1945–1962); 13 of 24 (or 54%) of the trades in the Aaron Era (1963–1977); and 17 of 32 (53%) of the trades in the Miller Era (1977–1992). So, although mixed trades are slightly more likely than they were, escalation in player salaries hasn't made them that much more likely. It's safe to say that, at least through the early 1990s, mixed trades were about as frequent as you would expect if small-market teams faced no financial pressures that made veterans-for-prospects trades with large-market teams more likely. Perhaps more importantly, although we lack trade data from the most recent years, the sheer number of free agent signings from 1998 to 2003 indicates that trades are now a much less important method of player movement.

Although mixed trades weren't more frequent than other trades, maybe they did exhibit some of the characteristics of veterans-for-prospects trades mentioned above. One expectation might be that in mixed trades the small-market team would, on average, receive players at earlier points in their major league careers. Table 2.14 provides some support for that proposition. Since 1978, the small-market team in mixed trades received pitchers with just over four years left in their careers, two of which were spent with that small-market team. The pitchers received by the large-market teams in those transactions averaged a little more than three years left in their careers, and a little more than one of those years was spent with that team.

Prior to 1978, before the steep escalation in player salaries, the record was less consistent. In the mixed trades from 1945 to 1962, small-market teams received pitchers that had more years ahead of them than did the pitchers received by large-market teams in those same trades. But, from 1963 to 1977, the figures were reversed. In mixed trades, large-market teams received pitchers with 4.5 years left in their careers, 2.8 of which were spent with those teams. Small-market teams received pitchers that had, on average, 3.3 years left in their careers, only one of which was spent with those teams.

Based on the career duration figures for pitchers in mixed trades, there is some support for the idea that, in the most recent era, small-market teams might have felt financial pressures that resulted in veterans-for-prospects trades with large-market teams. That is, since 1978, there is some evidence — not overwhelming evidence, just some evidence — that small-markets have tended to receive slightly less-seasoned pitchers in trades with large-market teams.

Did those younger pitchers received by the small-market teams in mixed trades perform worse than the pitchers received by the large-market teams? Not really. Table 2.14 presents data on ERA, innings pitched, wins, losses, and saves for large- and small-market pitchers that were part of mixed trades. Again, the data come from the year of the trade. From 1978 to 1992, the large-market pitchers and the small-market pitchers were nearly identical in terms of their average wins, losses, and saves. The pitchers received by large-market teams had a slight advantage in ERA (2.87 versus 3.11 for small-market pitchers) and average innings pitched (56.7 versus 46.6). Based on this evidence, the large-market teams got the better of the mixed trades in the year of the trade during the Marvin Miller Era, but the advantage was not a big one.

Note also that the data suggest that small-market teams were most likely to be making veterans-for-prospects trades in the Mantle Era, well before the steep escalation in player salaries. Prior to 1962, the small-market pitchers had 3.3 years left in their careers, and in the year of the trade, their ERAs averaged 5.49 in 80.7 innings pitched; the large-market players had 2.6 years left, and average ERAs of 1.96 in 61.8 innings pitched. So, it looks like the young pitchers were more apt go to the small-market teams in mixed trades, places where they received more opportunities to pitch, but where they tended to struggle.

This would appear to lend some support to the idea that small-market teams were pressured into veterans-for-prospects trades. Because the veterans-for-prospects interpretation of what the small-market teams received in mixed trades works at least as well in the '50s as the '80s, and because it doesn't work so well in the '70s or the '60s, it is difficult to conclude that salary escalation has forced small-market teams into these trades.

What about the careers of the small-market pitchers? Did they approach those of the pitchers for which they were traded? Table 2.15 makes it clear that, since 1978, the pitchers received by the small-markets had careers comparable to those received by the large-markets. They had slightly longer careers, pitched more total innings, had slightly lower ERAs, and had very similar won-loss records. Based on the evidence, it would be impossible to conclude that free agency and the resulting escalating salaries pressured small-markets into accepting pitchers that had worse careers than the pitchers they gave up, at least through 1992. Indeed, the only period in which the large-market teams received pitchers with substantially better career numbers was from 1963 to 1977, prior to free agency, and prior to the period when teams started using their first-round picks in the amateur draft to acquire pitching.

THE HITTERS

How about mixed trades for position players? Reliable comparisons on that score are even harder to come by, since one-for-one trades of players that play the same position are rare. The most data are available for trades where one outfielder was exchanged for another. There are some differences between the pitcher mixed trades and those involving outfielders. The conjecture offered here was that if financial pressures were really squeezing the small-market teams, veterans-for-prospects trades would have become increasingly prevalent. Mixed trades comprised four of the eight outfielder-for-outfielder trades from 1945 to 1962 (see Table 2.16). They made up eight of the 18 outfielder-for-outfielder trades (44%) from 1963 to 1977, and eight of 14 (57%) from 1978 to 1992. So, the figure hovered near 50% from 1945 to 1992. It did grow a bit in the Miller Era, but probably not so much that it should cause concern.

The trades since 1978 also provide some evidence that the small-market team received the younger player. Small-market outfielders in mixed trades had about five years left in their careers; large-market outfielders averaged a little over two. That disparity, however, cannot be attributed to free agency and escalating salaries. In both the Mantle and the Aaron eras, the small-market outfielders in mixed trades had five to six years left in their careers; the large-market outfielders had three to four years left. Based on those figures, it would appear that the pressures that force small-market teams into veterans-for-prospects trades, if they exist, have been with us since the end of World War II.

Moreover, the performance data in Table 2.16 do not indicate that the

Table 2.15 — Pitcher for Pitcher Trades Career Performance

Market Type(s)	N	ERA	IP	W	L	SV	Career
1945–1962 (Mickey Mantle Era)							
Large to Large	6	4.23	893	49	53	8	7.3
Small to Small	10	4.22	737	41	46	18	9.0
Small to Large	16						
(S)	8	4.42	471	25	25	5	7.6
(L)	8	3.89	455	21	22	9	8.6
1963–1977 (Henry Aaron Era)							
Large to Large	4	3.87	1449	79	76	11	11.0
Small to Small	18	3.91	806	43	49	22	9.2
Small to Large	26						
(S)	13	3.79	1087	62	60	31	10.6
(L)	13	3.70	1394	83	75	38	11.3
1978–1992 (Marvin Miller Era)							
Large to Large	16	4.02	1067	60	61	28	10.1
Small to Small	14	4.69	768	36	48	17	9.9
Small to Large	34						
(S)	17	4.29	671	36	36	16	8.6
(L)	17	4.49	612	33	33	17	7.9

Notes: N is the number of players involved in the trades. If N=6, the number of trades in that category is three. Trades are broken up into three categories: (1) "large to large," meaning pitchers were exchanged between two large-market teams, (2) "small to small" for trades between small-market teams, and (3) "small to large" for trades between a small- and a large-market team. For the small to large trades, the average performance of the pitchers that went to the small-market teams is presented in rows labeled "(S)," and the performance for those that went to large-markets in rows labeled "(L)." A large-market team is defined as having a population above the median for major league cities.

small-market teams received relatively ineffective inexperienced players. Since 1978, the small-market outfielders in mixed trades averaged more at bats, home runs, and RBI than their large-market counterparts in the year of the trade, and they had higher batting averages. In the Miller Era, the small-market outfielders averaged 213 AB, .226 BA, 6 HR, and 26 RBI. The players received in exchange for them by the large-market teams averaged 211 AB, .213 BA, 4 HR, and 24 RBI.

The career statistics (Table 2.17) also indicate that the small-market teams weren't forced to accept inferior players in mixed trades as salaries escalated due to free agency. Since 1978, the small-market outfielders averaged 2,437 career AB, .263 BA, 81 HR, and 346 RBI; the large-market outfielders averaged 2,440 AB, .252 BA, 73 HR, and 342 RBI. The disparity, small as it is, tips in favor of the small-market players. The disparity in the Aaron Era in favor of the small-market outfielders is even more pronounced. If all the data since 1963

Table 2.16 — Outfielder for Outfielder Trades Performance in Year of Trade

Market Type(s)	N	AB	AVG	HR	RBI	Year Left	Left with Team
1945–1962 (Mickey Mantle Era)							
Large to Large	2	136	.292	4	20	9.5	1.5
Small to Small	6	310	.234	5	32	3.0	0.5
Small to Large	8						
(S)	4	304	.315	10	43	6.0	2.5
(L)	4	386	.257	20	60	4.5	2.5
1963–1977 (Henry Aaron Era)							
Large to Large	12	235	.216	8	32	3.6	1.2
Small to Small	8	304	.210	8	36	3.4	1.3
Small to Large	16						
(S)	8	271	.232	4	28	5.1	1.3
(L)	8	136	.136	2	10	2.9	1.1
1978–1992 (Marvin Miller Era)							
Large to Large	8	196	.233	2	17	2.6	0.6
Small to Small	4	244	.140	9	37	2.8	2.0
Small to Large	16						
(S)	8	213	.226	6	26	5.0	1.1
(L)	8	211	.213	4	24	2.1	0.9

Notes: N is the number of players involved in the trades. If N=6, the number of trades in that category is three. Trades are broken up into three categories: (1) "large to large," meaning outfielders were exchanged between two large-market teams, (2) "small to small" for trades between small-market teams, and (3) "small to large" for trades between a small- and a large-market team. For the small to large trades, the average performance of the outfielders that went to the small-market teams is presented in rows labeled "(S)," and the performance for those that went to large-markets in rows labeled "(L)." A large-market team is defined as having a population above the median for major league cities.

are pooled, the small-market teams have done at least as well in outfielder-for-outfielder trades with large-market teams. They tend to get the slightly younger player, and that player ends up playing pretty well.

Before closing the discussion of the trade data, a serious limitation of the analysis needs to be mentioned. Because it is extremely difficult to measure quantitatively which team benefited more from a given trade, the focus on one-for-one trades is defensible. Two-for-two trades of players at the same position could also have been incorporated, but those are so rare that the sample would not have grown much. But defensible or not, the focus on one-for-one trades might be responsible for a bias against concluding that small-market teams have been increasingly forced into veterans-for-prospects trades in which they tend to get the short end of the deal. This is because the typical veteran-for-prospect trade might not be one-for-one. The typical one could be one vet-

Table 2.17 — Outfielder for Outfielder Trades Career Performance

Market Type(s)	N	AB	AVG	HR	RBI	Career Length
1945–1962 (Mickey Mantle Era)						
Large to Large	2	1844	.255	45	236	11.5
Small to Small	6	3454	.265	68	414	11.0
Small to Large	8					
(S)	4	5124	.271	115	610	14.8
(L)	4	5279	.274	261	898	13.5
1963–1977 (Henry Aaron Era)						
Large to Large	12	2661	.262	97	371	9.3
Small to Small	8	4356	.251	103	506	13.0
Small to Large	16					
(S)	8	2614	.257	54	282	10.9
(L)	8	1345	.218	25	131	8.4
1978–1992 (Marvin Miller Era)						
Large to Large	8	2469	.263	44	272	9.8
Small to Small	4	2267	.271	90	375	7.5
Small to Large	16					
(S)	8	2437	.263	81	346	10.1
(L)	8	2440	.252	73	342	8.6

Notes: N is the number of players involved in the trades. If N=6, the number of trades in that category is three. Trades are broken up into three categories (1) "large to large," meaning outfielders were exchanged between two large-market teams, (2) "small to small" for trades between small-market teams, and (3) "small to large" for trades between a small- and a large-market team. For the small to large trades, the average performance of the outfielders that went to the small-market teams is presented in rows labeled "(S)," and the performance for those that went to large-markets in rows labeled "(L)." A large-market team is defined as having a population above the median for major league cities.

eran from a small-market team in exchange for two or three prospects from a large-market team. And those three prospects tend to play different positions. So, without resorting to a much more elaborate econometric methodology, which is beyond the scope of the current research effort, there is no way to draw inferences from a number of asymmetric trades that are potentially important to analyze. It is possible that, with a more complete sample of trades, the disadvantages of small-market teams stemming from financial pressures might become more evident.

But based on all of the data presented here, it would be difficult to argue that, at least through the early 1990s, financial pressures increasingly forced small-market teams to give up high-quality established players in exchange for low-quality prospects. Sometimes the small-market team might have had to trade for the cheaper, younger player, but that player often ended up playing pretty well. The large-market team often ends up paying many times as much for roughly the same productivity.

The best player at a position might get paid 10 times more than the seventh or eighth best, but his performance isn't 10 times better. This is why winning percentages are narrowing, and why small-market teams can often compete with large-market teams. It's perverse, but escalating salaries, which force large-market teams to pay too much for the productivity they receive, are in some sense an equalizing force in baseball. Small-market teams lose veterans in trades and through free agency, and, barring dramatic revenue sharing, that's going to continue or get worse. Rather than focus on those departures, which is what the media likes to do, fans should be a little more clear-eyed about their implications. As long as the small-market teams can get reasonable, cheaper substitutes for departing veterans, and the major league compensation structure assures that they can, shrewd small-market teams can and will overcome their disadvantages and compete for the playoffs. Every time it happens, Bud Selig or Bob Costas or some other commentator will call it an aberration and wonder aloud how it can possibly occur. Do yourself a favor. Total up the aberrations over the next 10 or 20 years.

3

Player Development: The Evolution of the Draft

Each June the major league baseball draft passes with little fanfare. It goes sufficiently unnoticed that you might conclude that it produces little in the way of major league talent. Even casual football fans probably were acquainted with University of Mississippi quarterback Eli Manning's desire to play for the New York Giants rather than the San Diego Chargers, who held the first pick, and the 2004 draft day uncertainty it produced. Manning was taken by the Chargers but ended up with Giants via a draft day trade. Similarly, most basketball fans were well aware that the Cleveland Cavaliers would use the first pick in 2003 to select LeBron James, perhaps as fine a high school player as ever entered the NBA draft. In contrast, in June 2004 how many baseball fans knew that Jered Weaver, a pitcher from Long Beach State University, and brother of Dodgers pitcher Jeff, was likely to be his sport's first draft pick?

Why the basketball and football drafts generate so much attention relative to baseball is subject to debate. Clearly, baseball doesn't promote its draft the way the other sports do. Basketball determines the team order for the first nine picks via televised "lottery" at halftime of an important playoff game. Football and basketball both have extensive live draft coverage on ESPN; by contrast, baseball is typically covered in the "transactions" section of the paper, although the internet has made it possible to follow the proceedings live. Football and basketball have their drafts well after their college champions have been crowned on national television, and after all the accolades have been awarded. College baseball waits all year for its World Series to be televised by ESPN, only to hold its draft before its completion, and thus before the viewing audience becomes acquainted with the top collegiate players.

Maybe it's the number of high school players taken in baseball's draft that makes it impossible for fans to know baseball's finest amateurs. Then again, basketball hasn't suffered a loss of interest because of high school draftees Kevin Garnett or Kobe Bryant.[1] Whatever the reason, baseball's draft slinks past quietly year after year, so quietly that it's easy to forget that its first round has produced the likes of Will Clark, Roger Clemens, Frank Thomas, Dave Winfield,

Paul Molitor, Robin Yount, and Dale Murphy, to name but a handful. In fact, since the draft's inception in 1965, teams have become increasingly adept at selecting talented future major leaguers. The first round, in particular, has changed dramatically. Originally the province of position players fresh out of high school, today's first round is populated largely by college pitchers. This chapter traces the evolution of the first round from 1965 to 2003, and documents that the draft has become an increasingly effective means of ensuring competitive balance.[2] Of course, Commissioner Bud Selig might disagree, arguing that the draft is hardly sufficient to protect small-market clubs from their large-market rivals, and thus some revenue sharing is a necessity. However, the evidence indicates that unlike Selig's Brewers, some teams from small-markets have been able to use the draft to build competitive clubs.

THE WAY IT WAS

The draft did not spring forth from thin air. In the early 1960s, the majority of owners became dissatisfied with the existing system of player development. In *The Baseball Draft: The First 25 Years*, Baseball America offered three related reasons for the owners' growing dissatisfaction in 1964. The first was the Yankees dynasty, a team that had won 14 of the previous 16 American League titles. The second was the escalating bonuses being paid to young prospects, which had reached a new high with the $205,000 paid by the Los Angeles Angels to University of Wisconsin outfielder Rick Reichardt. That bonus was more than the annual salaries of the game's top stars. The third was the decline of the minor leagues. Once a fertile ground for nurturing young talent, the number of minor league affiliates had declined from 460 in 1949 to only 121.[3]

Those issues were related because dominant teams like the Yankees and Dodgers were wealthy enough to outspend the rest of the league on top prospects ("bonus babies"). To the extent that they concentrated on the "right" prospects, these teams could use their financial muscle to sustain their dynasties. Other teams tried to compete for prospects with their wealthier competitors, leaving fewer resources for the rest of their operations, including the minor leagues.

To attribute the decline of the minor leagues to spending on prospects is, however, an oversimplification. The expansion of television increasingly brought baseball into the homes of Americans living outside major league cities, and probably had a dampening effect on minor league attendance. Indeed, it has been the minors' ability to differentiate itself from the majors, not only in terms of price, but also in terms of general wackiness and local flair, that appears to be at the core of its recent resurgence. Moreover, it is highly unlikely that concern for the viability of the minors led major league owners to adopt a draft.[4] Rather, the data indicate that the cause of the draft was what was considered outrageous spending on prospects and, to a lesser extent, the sustained dominance of a few clubs.

As demonstrated in the Introduction, there was a lack of competitive balance in the majors between 1946 and 1964. Winning teams tended to be wealthier teams and, provided they made the right decisions about player personnel, wealthier teams had the resources to sustain their winning traditions. With regard to prospects, this could be achieved in at least a couple of ways. If there was great uncertainty about the quality of individual prospects, a wealthy team could exercise its dominance on the quantity dimension by signing as many players as possible for roughly the same price. If, on the other hand, it were relatively easy to predict which prospects would eventually become good major league ballplayers, dominant teams could offer them more money, thus outstripping their weaker rivals on the price dimension. No doubt the Dodgers and Yankees employed both the price and quantity strategies simultaneously to maintain their dynasties. However, as the period progressed, larger signing bonuses for top prospects suggest increased emphasis on price competition. In addition, by 1960 the gap between franchises in the number of affiliated minor league teams had closed dramatically, indicating decreased reliance on the quantity strategy of player development (Table 3.1). For example, from 1945 to 1949, the Yankees averaged 17.6 minor league affiliates per year, three more than the Indians, their nearest rival. By contrast, from 1960 to 1964 all American League teams averaged between five and seven affiliations. The Yankees' 6.6 affiliations per year were still near the top, but the days when they had five or six more minor league clubs than most of their rivals were gone.

Table 3.1— Average Number of Minor League Affiliates by Team

AL	1945–49	1950–54	1955–59	1960–64
Yankees	17.6 (2)*	11.8 (4)	9.8 (4)	6.6 (5)
Indians	14.4 (1)	10.8 (1)	8.4 (0)	5.4 (0)
Browns/Orioles	13.4 (0)	11.4 (0)	8.2 (0)	6.8 (0)
Red Sox	11.0 (1)	6.8 (0)	5.6 (0)	5.6 (0)
White Sox	10.6 (0)	7.2 (0)	5.6 (1)	5.6 (0)
Tigers	10.0 (1)	7.8 (0)	8.8 (0)	6.6 (0)
A's	9.4 (0)	9.2 (0)	6.4 (0)	6.4 (0)
Senators/Twins	7.0 (0)	7.8 (0)	7.2 (0)	6.6 (0)
NL				
Dodgers	21.4 (2)	17.6 (2)	13.4 (3)	9.4 (1)
Cardinals	17.2 (1)	18.0 (0)	14.0 (0)	6.6 (1)
Giants	16.8 (0)	12.6 (2)	10.2 (0)	7.8 (1)
Cubs	16.6 (1)	11.4 (0)	8.0 (0)	5.4 (0)
Pirates	12.6 (0)	12.0 (0)	11.2 (0)	6.8 (1)
Braves	11.2 (1)	9.8 (0)	12.6 (2)	8.0 (0)
Phillies	10.8 (0)	10.4 (1)	8.2 (0)	7.4 (0)
Reds	7.2 (0)	6.6 (0)	9.6 (0)	5.4 (1)

*Number of league championships in parentheses. Source: Total Baseball, 1993, p. 514.

It's not clear from Table 3.1 that the Yankees or Dodgers necessarily suffered from increased reliance on the price strategy — the Yankees enjoyed their most dominant quinquennium from 1960 to 1964 winning all five American League titles; the Dodgers did their best from 1955 to 1959 winning three league titles. Of course, neither had suffered greatly in the days of the quantity strategy either (the Yankees won six of 10 titles from 1945 to 1954, the Dodgers four), and, to the extent that competing with rivals on price was growing more costly over time, it seems unlikely that either dynasty was the impetus behind the change in strategy. Rather, this competition was probably imposed upon them by zealous upstarts; they probably would have welcomed a return to the days of the vast minor league system.

Timing effects, however, make Table 3.1 a little difficult to interpret. For example, should the Yankees' success from 1960 to 1964 be attributed to a successful transition to pricing strategies, or to the quantity advantage they held throughout the '50s? A good case could be made that player development decisions operate at a lag, and thus the Yankees' success in the early '60s was largely the product of their decisions in the late '50s. Viewed from the lagged perspective, big spending on prospects in the early '60s contributed to greater competitive balance in the late '60s. From 1965 to 1969, the Tigers, Orioles, Twins and Red Sox each won at least one AL title; the Cardinals, Dodgers, and Mets won NL titles. In that five-year period, eight different teams appeared in the World Series; from 1950 to 1954 there had been only five different teams, from 1955 to 1959 four, and from 1960 to 1964 six.

It may not be so surprising that the dynasties found it more difficult to maintain their advantage in the era of the bonus baby. Although some baseball people (general managers, scouts, etc.) might tell you differently, predicting which 18-year-olds are going to become major league stars is not at all easy. The list of bonus babies mentioned in Baseball America's discussion of the origins of the draft includes more busts than stars. For every Al Kaline or Frank Howard, there were two Rick Reichardts, Von McDaniels, Bob "Hawk" Taylors, or Stew McDonalds. And the bonuses paid to these highly uncertain prospects had grown from a 1942 high of $52,000 to pitcher Dick Wakefield to $100,000 for pitcher Paul Pettit in 1950, to $130,000 for pitcher Danny Murphy in 1960, to Reichardt's $205,000 in 1964.

While the signing of bonus babies may have afforded the game's best teams a somewhat more tenuous grasp on their dynasties than they enjoyed during the era of vast minor league systems, they much preferred it to a draft of amateur players. Former Dodgers general manager Buzzie Bavasi gave several reasons for his opposition to the draft:

> No. 1, I don't think [the draft] will equalize the talent because clubs that were making personnel mistakes under the old system will make them under this one. No. 2, it won't save the money some expect because you still have to pay a boy what he's worth. No. 3, it's a form of socialism because the boy can sell his talents in

only one place — unlike football which has the NFL, AFL and Canada. No. 4, it penalizes the industrious.[5]

It was reason four — the draft penalizes the industrious — rather than concerns about socialism that probably colored Buzzie Bavasi's perception of the draft. However, the Dodgers Cardinals, and Yankees persuaded other owners that courts would find the restraint of trade imposed by the draft illegal (although basketball and football already had amateur drafts). In August 1964 the owners split 10–10 on a vote to impose the draft. In late October, however, the general managers convened and voted 14–4 in favor of the draft (interestingly, the Dodgers were not present). Finally, at the Winter Meetings the draft was approved in a 14–6 vote of the owners.[6]

Baseball America concludes that the draft has, for the most part, accomplished its twin goals — keeping payments to untested amateurs reasonable and restoring competitive balance. American League president Lee MacPhail went further, saying, "It's been an unqualified success. Certainly, it's evened competition. It's given teams that have a difficult time competing for free-agent talent a fair share, or even more than a fair share. Close races in all divisions today goes [sic] back to the free-agent draft. If you didn't have it today, it would be a disaster."[7] That assessment may overstate the benefits of the draft, at least initially. After all, eight teams appeared in the World Series from 1965 to 1969; by contrast, from 1970 to 1974, years when many of the first drafted players were entering the majors, the Orioles, A's, and Reds dominated their divisions, and only six different teams appeared in the series. While the competitive balance that MacPhail attributes to the draft grew over time, the first drafts were hit-or-miss affairs described in the next sections.

THE DRAFT: RULES CHANGES

The draft evolved in fits and starts. Predictably, the first draft was rigged in favor of teams like the Dodgers. In 1965, a team with a greater number of Class A minor league affiliates was given a proportionately greater number of selections beginning in the eighth round. By 1966, however, that injustice was eliminated. Next, a 1967 rule change shifted the regular draft's focus to high school players. Initially, college players were eligible for the draft if they had attained sophomore standing. The new rule prohibited the signing of college players until they were 21 years old. Moreover, players drafted out of high school that had chosen to attend college could enter the league only through the secondary phase of the draft. This meant that there were really two drafts. The most talented high school players came in the early rounds of the regular draft, most of the best collegiate players in the early rounds of the secondary draft. Interestingly, with their reliance on high school talent, the first rounds of these early regular drafts produced far less major league talent than subsequent first rounds.

In 1972, previously drafted players became eligible for the regular phase of the draft if more than 13 months had passed since they were last selected. Although college players still had to be 21, this rule made far more college players eligible for the regular draft than had been in the past, and the quality of first round picks began to improve. For the statistical comparisons below, the drafts are broken up into eras. The first, the high school era, runs from 1965 to 1971. The intermediate era begins in 1972 with the change in secondary phase rules. In 1976, the 21-year-old rule was modified so that college players became eligible for selection following their junior year regardless of their age. This may have made a few more college players eligible a bit earlier, but probably did little to alter the high school-college balance in the first round. As a result, the draft's intermediate era extends to 1981, well after the 1976 rule changes.

It was in 1981 that college players really began to dominate the first round of the regular draft. There was a rule change in 1981, but it wasn't one that could easily account for the shift over to college talent. The new Basic Agreement between players and management provided for greater compensation for teams that lost free agents. Compensation for those players ranked in the top 20% at their positions (Type A players) became a draft pick and a major league player from the compensation pool. For players ranked from 20% to 30% at their position (Type B), compensation became a draft pick in the supplemental draft between the first and second rounds. The compensation system has evolved over the years. Currently, a Type A player is ranked among the top 30% of major leaguers at his position according to a rating system established by Elias Sports Bureau. A Type B player is ranked in the top half (but below the top 30%) at his position. A team that loses a Type A player receives the first-round pick of the team that signed him and a supplemental pick after the first round. In 2004, those picks all occurred in the third round or earlier. A team that loses a Type B player receives only the signing team's top pick.[8]

It is possible that teams that needed to replace an established free agent using a draft pick were more inclined to choose an older college player who could make the major league team more quickly. Whatever the reason, the period from 1981 to 1989 will be referred to as the college era of the draft. There have been a few more rule changes since 1981 (some of which are discussed below), but none that have affected the nature of the first round as dramatically as the ones described above.[9] Finally, the recent era covers the drafts from 1990 to 2003.

THE EVOLUTION OF THE DRAFT:
THE SHIFT TO COLLEGE PLAYERS

Table 3.2 summarizes the high school-college breakdown for the first round of the regular draft from 1965 to 2003. In no year during the high school era (1965–1971) did the percentage of first-round draftees selected from high schools ever fall below 75%. In 1971, *all* 24 players selected in the first round were high schoolers. The shift to collegiate players began in 1972, albeit slowly. From 1965 to 1971 a little over 13% of the players selected were from four-year colleges or universities; in no year was the percentage over 25; in four of the seven years the percentage was 12.5 or less. In the intermediate era (1972–1980), about twice as many (25.8%) of the players selected in each year were from the college ranks. In no year was the percentage of college players less than 12.5; in three of nine years over a third of the selections were collegiates.[10]

The dramatic shift to collegiate players began in 1981, when, for the first time in the history of the draft, the majority of players selected in the first round had played for an American college or university. This trend persisted throughout the draft's college era (1981–89). In only two of those years were college players in the minority in the first round; in no year did the percentage of collegiates fall below 40. The high water mark came in 1984 when 18 of 26 first-round picks (69%) were former college players. That 1984 class eventually produced 19 major leaguers, tied with the classes of '79, '80, '81, and '85 for the best ever prior to 1990. The 1990 draft produced 22 major leaguers, while the '91, '92, '93, and '94 drafts each produced 21.

The trend toward college players reached a plateau in the 1990s where it has more or less held steady. From 1990 to 2003, 49% of the players selected in the first round have come straight out of high school. In some years, like 1996, the high schoolers held an edge (63% versus 37% for college players); in others, like 1992, the college players held an edge (71% versus 25%). For the most part, however, it's been about a 50–50 split between the collegiates and the high schoolers since 1990, which is a far cry from the drafts of the late 1960s and 1970s.

Why the shift to college players? The simple answer is that they were surer bets to contribute to the major league team than high school draftees. Through a painful process of trial and error, scouts and management types eventually realized that the expected payoff was slightly higher (and the variance in performance somewhat lower) for college players than for high schoolers. As Table 3.3 indicates, the percentage of first-round draft picks that eventually made it to the major leagues has increased somewhat over time. In the high school draft era, 61% of draftees made the big leagues. For the intermediate era the figure was 62%; for the college era it jumped to 71%. From 1990 to 2003, only 53% of first-round draft picks had made it to the majors through the 2003 season. However, that's not really a fair comparison since many of the players from recent drafts haven't had sufficient time to mature. Looking only at the drafts from 1990 to 1998, 72% of the first-rounders have made it to the big leagues, so the generally increasing trend continued throughout the '90s.

The switch from high school to college draftees also coincided with a slight decrease in the number of first-round busts—players who never advanced beyond Class AA ball (Table 3.3). For the drafts from 1965 to 1989, Baseball

Table 3.2 — High School-College Breakdown First Round of Regular Draft, 1965–2003

Year	Picks	HS	JC	Coll.	Univ.	% HS	% Coll.
1965	20	15	0	0	5	75%	25%
1966	20	16	0	0	4	80	20
1967	20	19	0	0	1	95	5
1968	20	16	0	1	3	80	20
1969	24	21	0	0	3	88	13
1970	24	21	0	0	3	88	13
1971	24	24	0	0	0	100	0
1972	24	19	0	1	4	79	21
1973	24	17	0	0	7	71	29
1974	24	18	0	0	6	75	25
1975	24	16	0	2	6	67	33
1976	24	21	0	0	3	88	13
1977	26	21	0	0	5	81	19
1978	26	20	1	0	5	77	19
1979	26	16	0	0	10	62	38
1980	26	17	0	1	8	65	35
1981	26	9	0	1	16	35	65
1982	26	15	0	2	9	58	42
1983	26	11	0	4	11	42	58
1984	26	8	0	2	16	31	69
1985	26	9	0	1	16	35	65
1986	26	15	0	0	11	58	42
1987	26	11	1	0	14	42	54
1988	26	8	2	0	16	31	66
1989	26	12	0	0	14	46	54
1990	26	16	1	1	8	62	35
1991	26	11	1	1	13	42	54
1992	28	7	1	1	19	25	71
1993	28	12	0	2	14	43	57
1994	28	16	0	0	12	57	43
1995	28	15	0	0	13	54	46
1996	30	19	0	0	11	63	37
1997	31	16	1	0	14	52	45
1998	30	14	0	0	16	47	53
1999	30	15	0	0	15	50	50
2000	30	18	2	0	10	60	33
2001	30	12	0	0	18	40	60
2002	30	16	1	0	13	53	43
2003	30	12	1	0	17	40	57

Notes: HS — *drafted out of high school;* JC — *drafted out of junior college;* Coll. — *drafted out of a four-year college;* Univ. — *drafted out of a university;* %HS — *percentage of picks drafted out of a high school;* %Coll — *percentage of picks drafted out of four-year colleges or universities.*

Sources: *The Baseball Draft: The First 25 Years* (1990) and the *Baseball America Draft Almanac* (2003).

University of North Carolina shortstop B.J. Surhoff was the first pick in the 1985 amateur draft, which had one of the strongest first rounds ever. Eighteen of 26 first-round picks were collegiate players, and 19 of the first-rounders made it to the major leagues, tied for the most of any draft prior to 1990. The 1985 first round also produced collegiate players Barry Bonds, Will Clark, Barry Larkin, and Rafael Palmeiro.

America also provided information on the top level achieved by those that didn't make it to the majors. The same information was not available for the 1990s drafts in the *Baseball America Draft Almanac* (2003). In both the high school and intermediate eras, about a quarter of first-round draft picks never advanced to Triple-A baseball. For the college era of the draft, 19% of the

Table 3.3 — Highest Level of Attainment for First-Round Draft Choices (Percentage, by Era)

Era		Reached MLB	Never advanced beyond AA	Drafted out of high school	Drafted out of colleges and universities
1.	(1965–1971)	61%	24%	87%	13%
2.	(1972–1980)	62%	24%	74%	26%
3.	(1981–1989)	71%	19%	42%	57%
4.	(1990–2003)	53%	.	49%	51%
4a.	(1990–1998)	72%	.	49%	51%

Note: For simplicity, players drafted out of junior colleges are also included in % drafted out of colleges and universities.

players picked had not advanced beyond the low minor leagues by 1992.[11] The percentage changes in Table 3.3 make it clear that as teams increasingly spent their first-round draft choices on college players, the chances of a successful pick improved.

Why might the college players be safer picks? One obvious reason is that they're older. Being better developed physically and more polished, college players make it easier on scouts—there is less guesswork about whether an 18-year-old will gain five to seven miles per hour on his fastball when he fills out, or whether he'll be able to hit a major league breaking ball. Most college pitchers are sufficiently developed that projecting their throwing velocity is easy, and most position players have probably faced a number of pitchers with decent breaking stuff by the time they leave the university. Many high school stars have faced only the relatively thin talent pool in their local area or in their state by the time they're drafted. By contrast, a college star at Arizona, LSU, or UCLA has faced former high school stars from across the nation. Apparently, the increased quality of the competition at the college level reduces the probability that a college star will be a professional disappointment.

If college players are safer picks, why hasn't the first round always been dominated by them? As noted above, because previously drafted players could be selected only in the secondary phase of the draft, many of the best college players were not taken in the early years of the regular draft. However, after the 1972 rule change that permitted players to reenter the regular draft 13 months after their initial selection, the heavy reliance on high school players is more difficult to understand. It could simply be that baseball people were slow to realize that college players were better bets than high school stars. It is also likely that the quality of play at the college level has been improving largely due to changes in economic conditions. Just after World War II, U.S. dominance in manufacturing (and other nonservice industries) meant that a young man didn't need a college education to provide a comfortable life for his family. Knowing that if he failed, a young prospect could return to the local factory, foundry, or mill, there was little risk associated with pursuing a baseball career. By the 1980s, the U.S. economy had shifted from manufacturing to services, and a college degree became an increasingly important ingredient for financial success. Given the choice between a scholarship education at a school like Stanford or heading directly from high school to the low minor leagues, parents and players alike had a more complicated decision to make than their early post–war counterparts. Those prospects that chose to head directly to the minors and didn't eventually make the major leagues were in a less advantageous position than those that took the college scholarship and graduated. The early entrants could return to college, but they would be much older than their classmates, and the university certainly wouldn't pick up the tab. Although it's only a theory, it appears that as a college degree has grown in importance, the quality of the college game and its drafted players has improved — at least with regard to the first-round picks.

An alternative hypothesis could be that, although college players were more likely to make the majors, the biggest stars came from the high school ranks. Thus teams that chose college players suffered less risk but could expect smaller rewards from their best selections. The data, however, indicate that first-round college draftees were not only more likely to make the majors, but also to do it more quickly, and that the quality of their major league careers was on a par with those drafted out of high school. Table 3.4 demonstrates that, on average, those college players that made it to the majors did it at least a year before high school players taken in the same draft.

Table 3.4 — Average Time (in Years) to the Major Leagues First-Round Draft Choices, 1965–2003[12]

	Era 1 (65–71)	Era 2 (72–80)	Era 3 (81–89)	Era 4 (90–03)	Era 4a (90–98)
High School					
Pitchers	3.15 (2.1)*	3.55 (2.6)	3.75 (1.5)	3.86 (1.6)	4.00 (1.6)
Position Players	3.26 (1.5)	3.78 (1.8)	4.19 (1.7)	3.82 (1.6)	3.84 (1.6)
College					
Pitchers	—	2.10 (2.1)	2.20 (1.6)	2.43 (1.6)	2.66 (1.7)
Position Players	1.91 (1.3)	1.42 (1.2)	2.50 (1.6)	2.56 (1.3)	2.71 (1.3)

Note: *The standard deviations in parentheses are measures of the typical dispersion about the mean value. Roughly two-thirds of the observed values for an era fall within the interval one standard deviation above and one standard deviation below its mean.

There's not a lot of difference in the time required by pitchers and position players to make the majors. For players drafted out of high school, the average is a little over three and a half years, although that number has increased over time. High school pitchers drafted from 1965 to 1971 attained the majors in just over three years; those drafted from 1981 to 1989 averaged a 3.8-year apprenticeship in the minor leagues. From 1990 to 2003, the average was 3.9 years. For college players, pitchers and position players alike, the average was about two years for those drafted before 1981 and about two and a half years for those taken subsequently.

Some might take the increase in the time to reach the majors as an indication that the prospects coming out today are less polished players than past draftees. However, modern ballplayers are probably in better physical condition than their predecessors, and thus have longer careers, which leaves fewer spots for young ballplayers. In addition, the designated hitter rule provides American League roster spots for 15 or so players that might otherwise be retired. At the minor league level, the talent pool might have actually grown deeper as franchises mine places like the Dominican Republic, Mexico, and Venezuela ever more effectively, even as they begin to dip their toes into Japan, South Korea, and Australia, to say nothing of the players defecting from the powerful Cuban national team.[13]

There are, of course, other factors that suggest that the present crop of American prospects may indeed be somewhat weaker than past classes. Expansion has brought six additional franchises since 1976. These additional roster spots should make it easier to escape the minors. We also hear a lot about how fewer American kids are playing baseball, which implies less talented draftees and, perhaps, longer average apprenticeships at the minor league level.[14] In short, there are a couple of factors that should make it more difficult for first-round draftees to make the majors and a couple that should make it easier. The net effect of these factors is difficult to measure given the data in Table 3.4. However, one shouldn't use the increase in the average time to the majors for first-round picks as irrefutable evidence that the quality of American players is waning. It is conceivable that the United States is producing its best talent ever, and that the competition for major league roster spots is simply more difficult than in the past.[15]

The main point of Table 3.4 is that it takes less time for first-round picks out of college to make the majors than it does for high schoolers. College players require a little over two years, high school players almost four. So, not only are college players more likely to make the majors, they're likely to do it in a little over half the time it takes high school picks. For a struggling franchise in a small-market, a top college prospect seems the best choice — they obtain a player that will likely contribute at the major league level relatively quickly, and they don't have to pay him too much (at least until he renegotiates his contract).[16] Yet, teams like Commissioner Selig's Milwaukee Brewers have rolled the dice on a couple of notable high schoolers, only to get burned. In 1986, they used the sixth pick overall to draft Gary Sheffield out of Hillsborough High School in Tampa; his immaturity eventually compelled him to blow plays on purpose in an effort to get traded. He's mellowed somewhat, and put up great numbers for the Padres, Marlins, Dodgers, Braves, and Yankees but the Brewers had to deal a problem player a cut-rate price. Actually, the Sheffield deal could have been a lot worse for the Brewers. For Sheffield and minor league pitcher Geoff Kellogg they received Ricky Bones, Jose Valentin, and Matt Mieske. All three contributed at the major league level, though, with the possible exception of Valentin, none became a star.[17] And none of those players puts fans in the seats like Sheffield. In 1996, for example, Sheffield hit .314, with 42 home runs, and 120 RBI. More impressive were his .624 slugging percentage (second in the NL) and his league-leading .465 on base percentage.

The Brewers took another chance on a high school prospect in the 1988 draft, and got far less than they did for Sheffield. With the 24th pick in the first round, the Brewers selected Alex Fernandez out of Pace High School in Miami. Rather than sign with the Brewers, Fernandez chose to attend the University of Miami. After a stellar freshman season, he enrolled in Miami-Dade Community College so that he could become eligible for the draft before the end of his junior year. He eventually ended up with the White Sox and emerged as the ace of the staff before joining the Marlins as a free agent in 1997. His 1996 record was 16–10 with a 3.45 ERA and 200 strikeouts (third in the AL).

It's probably unfair to pick on the Brewers; in the past 10 to 15 years most teams probably took chances on high school players that didn't pan out. Yet, large-market teams that can afford to play the free agent game are in a better position to take those chances than teams like the Brewers. Many of those wealthier teams, however, have gone with proven college stars. During the late '80s, the White Sox, for example, drafted Robin Ventura out of Oklahoma State, Frank Thomas out of Auburn, Jack McDowell out of Stanford, and Fernandez, after he left Miami-Dade. A first-round draft choice has become a precious commodity for any team, but especially for a Pittsburgh, Milwaukee, or a Montreal. Rather than focus so much on revenue sharing, so that they too can play the free agent game, why not draft more effectively?[18] As demonstrated in Chapter Three, moreover, given the salaries paid to veteran players, signing free agents can be as risky as relying on college draftees.

The argument could be made that small-market teams can't afford to rely on dependable college players. Rather, knowing they can't obtain top veteran talent through the free agent market, they must hit a home run with their first-round choice, and thus they tend to take the chance on the high school "phenom." Ken Griffey Jr., for example, was an excellent choice for the Seattle Mariners in 1987. On average, however, the data indicate that, among those first-round picks that make it to the majors, there are as many superstars among the college players as among the high schoolers.

The next tables group first-round draft choices by the quality of their careers. Those that didn't play a game in the majors comprise the first group. Table 3.5 displays quality of career results for all position players taken in the first round. Prior to 1981, a little over 40% of the position players drafted became career minor leaguers. In the '80s that figure was only 27%. Since 1990, 47% of the first-round choices had not advanced beyond the minor leagues by the end of the 2003 season. Again, however, many players drafted in later years have not had a reasonable chance to attain major league status, and thus the 1990–98 results are more representative of the quality of the later drafts. And indeed, of those players drafted from 1990 to 1998, only 27% have not reached the majors, which is identical to the 1980s figure. Clearly, among position players, the percentage of picks that were major disappointments has diminished since the inception of the draft.

Table 3.5 — Quality of Career, First-Round Draft Choices (1965–2003) Broken Down by Era (Position Players)

	Era 1 (65–71)	Era 2 (72–80)	Era 3 (81–89)	Era 4 (90–03)	Era 4a (90–98)
Minors	41 (41%)	59 (41%)	34 (27%)	91 (47%)	35 (27%)
Brief Stint (1–150 games)	11 (11%)	25 (17%)	21 (16%)	27 (14%)	19 (15%)
Marginal Player (151–450 games)	11 (11%)	10 (7%)	16 (13%)	26 (13%)	25 (19%)
Established Player (451–1,200 games)	19 (19%)	24 (17%)	25 (20%)	45 (23%)	45 (35%)
Veteran Player (1,200+ games)	17 (17%)	27 (19%)	32 (25%)	6 (3%)	6 (5%)

In Table 3.5, first-round choices that made it to the majors are separated into four categories. Those position players that appeared in fewer than 150 games (roughly one full season as a regular player) are in the brief stint category. It contains obscure players like Drungo Hazewood, Rick Seilheimer, and Jerry Tabb. Brief stint players were only slightly less disappointing picks than the career minor leaguers. The next category is for marginal players, who played in 151–450 games, roughly one to three years as a major league regular. Players drafted from 1972 to 1980 that fall into this category include Danny Goodwin, Buddy Biancalana, Steve Nicosia, and Brad Komminsk — players that you remember as hanging around for a few years, some of them as a regular, but not any all-star appearances. Marginal players weren't picks totally wasted. Some were disappointing, but the franchise did receive a player that contributed at the major league level.

Established position players, those that played 451–1,200 games (roughly three to eight years as a regular), are lumped into the next category. For the most part, franchises had to be pleased with these selections. The 1972–80 drafts, for example, produced Dave Roberts, Roy Howell, Dave Chalk, Jamie Quirk, John Stearns, Gary Roenicke, Steve Swisher, Scot Thompson, Clint Hurdle, Dale Berra, Leon Durham, Wally Backman, Nick Esasky, Darnell Coles, Cecil Espy, Glenn Wilson, Kelly Gruber, and Dion James. Solid ballplayers with an occasional all-star appearance, but no serious candidates for the Hall of Fame. Still, the general manager who selected these guys did his job well—he converted his first-round pick into a solid major league contributor.

The final category is reserved for the grizzled veterans, position players that appeared in over 1,200 games. Not all of those in the category were Hall of Famers, but most were stars in one way or another. Apparently, you can't stick around the majors for over eight years without some real ability. Veterans selected from 1972 to 1980 included Rick Manning, Chet Lemon, Robin Yount, Dave Winfield, Lee Mazzilli, Bill Almon, Lonnie Smith, Dale Murphy, Garry Templeton, Lance Parrish, Paul Monitor, Tim Wallach, Darryl Strawberry, and Harold Baines. There are another 10 or so in the category, but you get the picture. This is where the stars are. The Bill Almons are the exception, not the rule. The GMs that selected these players earned their salaries.

More recently the first round has produced position players of greater quality. If career minor league and brief stint players are grouped together as disappoints, it becomes clear that the first round has increasingly become a source for major league talent. From 1965 to 1971, 47% of the position players drafted in the first round became marginal, established, or veteran players. From 1972 to 1980 that figure dipped to 42%, but the percentage that became established or veteran players held constant at about 35%. The marginal and above figure for first-round picks from 1981 to 1989 was 57% as of 2003. For the most recent era (1990–2003), that figure was 39%, almost tied with the 1972–80 era. Again, however, many players taken in later drafts hadn't had sufficient time to break into the top categories by 2003, so Table 3.5 overstates the actual percentage of draft disappointments in the past 14 years. Restricting our attention to the drafts from 1990 to 1998, 58% of the position players taken in the first round had become at least marginal major leaguers by 2003, which is the highest share for any era and quite an increase over the 45% success rate prior to 1980.

The results for pitchers drafted in the first round are similar, if somewhat less pronounced (Table 3.6). The percentage that spent their careers in the minors decreased from 36% for the high school era to 33% for the intermediate and 31% for the 1980s. That figure dipped further, to 29%, for the drafts from 1990 to 1998. Moreover, a higher percentage of pitchers achieved at least marginal status (36–100 starts, or 51–150 appearances as a reliever) in the 1980s drafts than for the two prior eras. From 1981 to 1989, 56% of first-round pitchers reached the majors for more than a brief stint. For 1965–71 that figure was 45%; from 1972 to 1980 it was 53%. To this point, however, only 44% of the first-round picks from the 1990–98 drafts have been in the majors for more than a brief stint. Again, the last draft era will probably catch up to the 1980s when the figures are recalculated to account for seasons after 2003, especially because, as Table 3.4 indicated, it often takes pitchers more time than position players to reach the majors.

Table 3.6 — Quality of Career, First-Round Draft Choices (1965–2003) Broken Down by Era (Pitchers)

	Era 1 (65–71)	Era 2 (72–80)	Era 3 (81–89)	Era 4 (90–03)	Era 4a (90–98)
Minors	19 (36%)	26 (33%)	33 (31%)	100 (48%)	36 (29%)
Brief Stint (1–50 games, 1–35 starts)	10 (19%)	11 (14%)	14 (13%)	47 (22%)	34 (27%)
Marginal Pitcher (51–150 games, 36–100 starts)	5 (9%)	15 (19%)	17 (16%)	24 (11%)	17 (14%)
Established Pitcher (151–450 games, 101–300 starts)	15 (28%)	19 (22%)	24 (23%)	35 (17%)	34 (27%)
Veteran Pitcher (450+ games or 300+ starts)	4 (8%)	8 (13%)	18 (17%)	4 (2%)	4 (3%)

With respect to established pitchers (101–300 starts or 151 appearances) and veterans (more than 300 starts or 450 appearances), the 1990s should lag the other eras substantially because the best pitchers from those drafts are still playing. Indeed, only 30% of the pitchers taken from 1990 to 1998 had achieved at least established status by 2003. For the high school era that figure was 36%; for the intermediate era it was 34%. In the 1980s, 40% of the first-rounders achieved at least established status, and 17% achieved veteran status. That 17% figure is twice the figure for the 1965 to 1971 drafts, and also larger than the 13% figure for 1972 to 1980. Only four pitchers drafted in the 1990s had achieved veteran status as of 2003, and all of them did so recently. During the 2001 season, 1990 draftee Mike Mussina started his 300th game, and in 2003 relievers Jay Powell, Paul Shuey, and Billy Wagner all reached the 450 appearance level. No doubt others will soon follow them into the veteran category. It's pretty much a certainty that the 1990s will eventually outperform the two early eras by a substantial margin in the production of established and veteran pitchers.

Table 3.6 also hints at an important shift from position players to pitchers in the first round. The high school era produced only 24 pitchers that pitched in the majors for something longer than a brief stint; the intermediate era 42. The 1980s produced 59 such pitchers. In part, this merely reflects the fact that, due to expansion, there were more first round picks over time. However, the 1990–98 drafts have already produced more major league pitching talent (89 pitchers, including 55 that have been in the majors for more than a brief stint) than did the earliest eras despite the fact that, as of 2003, many of those draftees had not had sufficient time to fully establish themselves.

THE SHIFT TO PITCHERS

The shift to pitchers coincided with both the shift to college players and the increased probability of success for first-round draft picks. In the high school and intermediate eras, 35% of first-round draft choices were pitchers. In the college era, the number increased to 45%; in the 1990s the figure crept near 50% (Table 3.7). The increased reliance on pitchers and the improvement in the quality of individual first-round draft choices have combined to produce more major league starters over the years. In the high school era, the first round produced 4.6 major league starters per year. The intermediate era averaged 5.3 per draft; the college era averaged over seven; and the abbreviated recent era (1990–98) over eight. For all the drafts since the 1990s that figure is 6.4, but again, not enough time has elapsed to determine how many starters recent drafts will produce. Of course, as the majors expanded, there were more first-round picks per year, and thus one would expect the number of starters per draft to increase. A more instructive measure is the number of starters per pick. From 1965 to 1971 the first round produced .21 starters per pick. In other words, there was about one major league starter produced for every five first-round picks in the high school era. From 1972 to 1980 that figure held at .21 starters per pick. By the college era, the figure was up to 0.28 — about three picks to produce one major league starter; and from 1990 to 1998 the figure increased slightly to 0.29. The number of major league pitching starts per pick, however, does not tilt in favor of the recent era. The high school and intermediate eras averaged about 25 starts per pick; the 1980s 37.7. The drafts from 1990 to 1998 have produced 22.2 starts per pick, while, for all drafts since 1990 the figure is 15.3 starts per pick. Again, this is largely because many of the pitchers that were drafted since 1990 are still active, and many of those haven't had enough time to become established. The starts per pick figure for the 1990s will no doubt increase and likely eclipse the previous eras. At the least, the 1990s will surpass the pre–1980 drafts by a substantial margin.

The results in Table 3.7 indicate that the first round has increasingly become a source of major league starters. Given the importance of pitching, which will be described in greater detail in Chapters 5 and 6, this is an impor-

Table 3.7 — Position Player/Pitcher Breakdown First-Round Draft Picks (1965–2003)

	Era 1 (65–71)	Era 2 (72–80)	Era 3 (80–89)	Era 4 (90–03)	Era 4a (90–98)
Pitchers	99	79	106	210	125
Position Players	53	145	128	195	130
Percent Pitchers	34.9%	35.3%	45.3%	51.9%	49.0%
Major League Starters Per Draft	4.57	5.33	7.22	6.43	8.11
Major League Starters Per Pick	0.21	0.21	0.28	0.22	0.29
Major League Starts Per Pick	24.0	26.3	37.7	15.3	22.2

tant result. Although difficult to demonstrate definitively, the competitive balance enjoyed at the major league level in recent years is due in no small part to the relatively egalitarian way that young talent — and increasingly young pitching talent — is allocated among major league teams through the draft. The statistics in Table 3.7 are not sufficient, however, to demonstrate that the quality of the individual pitchers selected in the first round has improved over time, although the data on the length of careers in Table 3.6 suggests that it has. It could, however, be that the starters per pick measure has increased *only* because the number of picks devoted to pitchers has increased. Table 3.8 presents results that better assess whether first-round picks devoted to pitchers in the 1980s and 1990s were more successful than those in the 1960s and 1970s.

The shift to pitchers predated the shift to college draftees in the '80s, but only by a few years. With the exception of the drafts of 1966 (in which nine of the 20 selections were pitchers) and 1971 (11 of 24 selections were pitchers), prior to 1976 about two-thirds of the first-round selections in each draft were position players. In 1976, half of the selections were pitchers; in 1977 over 40% were pitchers. In 1978 there was a return to reliance on position players, but otherwise from 1975 to 1988 at least nine pitchers were selected in the first round of each draft — in nine of those 14 years at least 11 pitchers were taken. In four 1980s drafts ('83, '84, '87, '88) at least half of the first-round selections were pitchers. The 1989 draft, however, marked a temporary switch back to a pre–1975-style first round dominated by position players. In the drafts since 1989, there were at least 11 pitchers taken in every year, and pitchers made up more than half of the first-round picks in 1993, 1996, and all four drafts from 1999 to 2002.

The yearly figures in Table 3.8 somewhat obscure the fact that, in terms of both games and starts per pitcher selected, the drafts got better over time as shown in Figure 4. The 1965 to 1971 drafts averaged 121 appearances per pitcher selected; the 1972 to 1980 drafts 134 appearances per pitcher; and the 1981 to

Table 3.8 — Major League Pitchers Drafted in the First Round by Year, 1965–2003

Year	Pitchers	Position Players	Starters	Starts	Games Per Pitcher	Starts Per Pitcher
1965	7	13	5	377	77.3	53.9
1966	9	11	6	835	180.2	92.8
1967	6	14	3	433	133.2	72.2
1968	3	17	2	153	121.7	51.0
1969	8	16	6	645	159.8	80.6
1970	9	15	3	181	51.6	20.1
1971	11	13	7	1,019	120.0	92.6
1972	8	16	6	999	158.8	124.9
1973	7	17	4	171	47.7	24.4
1974	8	16	7	525	124.6	65.6
1975	9	15	4	129	36.7	14.3
1976	12	12	7	1,104	149.1	92.0
1977	11	15	5	1,217	122.9	110.6
1978	5	21	4	773	210.8	154.6
1979	10	16	5	484	185.7	48.4
1980	9	17	6	496	174.2	55.1
1981	11	15	7	995	134.7	90.5
1982	12	14	5	587	182.3	48.9
1983	13	13	7	1,161	182.1	89.3
1984	13	13	8	967	141.1	74.4
1985	11	15	7	764	97.7	69.5
1986	9	17	7	994	282.4	110.4
1987	15	11	11	1,278	171.9	85.2
1988	14	12	7	1,536	168.9	109.7
1989	8	18	6	543	98.0	67.9
1990	12	14	9	1,044	140.5	87.0
1991	11	15	8	957	101.2	87.0
1992	13	15	7	408	122.4	31.4
1993	19	9	10	901	155.5	47.4
1994	11	17	6	539	90.7	49.0
1995	13	15	8	592	54.7	45.5
1996	17	13	10	522	79.6	30.7
1997	15	16	7	194	38.3	12.9
1998	14	16	8	502	51.4	35.9
1999	20	10	8	408	27.8	20.4
2000	17	13	5	35	3.4	2.1
2001	20	10	4	102	5.6	5.1
2002	17	13	0	0	0	0
2003	11	19	0	0	2.6	0

1989 drafts 162. Similarly, the 65–71 drafts averaged 69 starts per pitcher selected, while the 72–80 drafts averaged 75, and the 1981–89 drafts 83. It's still too early to tell how the recent drafts will pan out, but it is highly likely that they'll look a lot more like the 1981–89 drafts than the pre-'80s drafts.

It seems likely that few pitchers are drafted with the intention that they

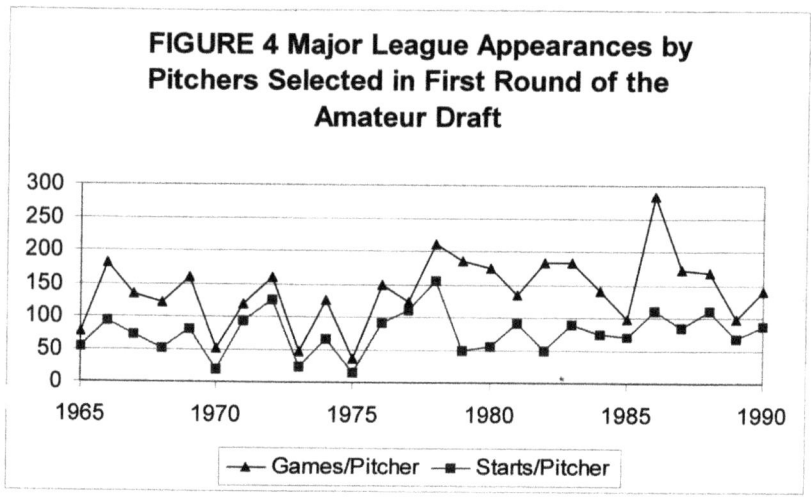

will become relievers. If a kid eventually does become an effective reliever, that's great, but the general manager that spends his first-round pick on a pitcher probably wants a major league starter. Not surprisingly, increased reliance on pitchers in the first round has yielded more major league starters in the post–1975 drafts. No draft before 1976 produced more than seven major league starters. Of the drafts from 1981 to 1989, only two produced less than seven starters. From 1990 to 1999, every draft produced at least six starters and the average was eight.

Only two of the pre-1976 drafts produced seven starters, and none of those selections were exactly Cy Young. The 1974 draft produced luminaries like Tommy Boggs (94 starts), Tom Brennan (20 starts), Butch Edge (9 starts), Larry Monroe (2 starts), Rod Scurry (7 starts), and Cliff Speck (1 start). The seventh starter, Rick Sutcliffe, was drafted by the Dodgers with the 21st pick. No doubt, he had a very good career—six seasons with 16 or more victories and the National League Cy Young Award in 1984. Not good enough to make up for the rest of the disappointing class of 1974, but quite good nonetheless. The 1971 class also produced seven starters—Jay Franklin (1 start), Roy Branch (2 starts), Roy Thomas (13 starts), Frank Tanana (584 starts), Frank Riccelli (5 starts), Rick Rhoden (380 starts), and Randy Stein (2 starts). Rhoden certainly had a solid career, and Tanana was always interesting, especially after he transformed himself from a young fireballer to a junkballer that survived on guile, but the 1971 class was also disappointing in some respects—and remember that '71 and '74 were two of the better early drafts for pitching.

Contrast the '71 and '74 classes with the pitchers selected in the first round of the 1985 draft (Table 3.9), one of the worst drafts for pitching of the '80s, and one that, like the '71 and '74 drafts, produced seven major league starters. In 1985, 11 pitchers were selected—seven from colleges, four directly out of high school. In the 1971 draft, all 11 pitchers picked were high schoolers. Again, that may have been because many of the best college pitchers had been drafted out of high school, and previously drafted players weren't eligible for the regular draft. For example, *Baseball America* notes that, had they been eligible, major leaguers Pete Broberg and Burt Hooten, who were drafted out of high school in 1968, would have gone 1–2 in the 1971 regular draft as they did in the secondary phase.[19] By 1974, however, previously drafted players were no longer relegated to the secondary phase of the draft, and yet only one college pitcher (Tom Brennan of Lewis University in Romeoville, IL) was selected in the first round. Seven of the eight pitchers selected were from the high school ranks. The data indicate that the heavy reliance on high school pitching talent in the first 15 years of the draft did not, however, serve teams well. As noted, 1971 and 1974, two of the most successful early drafts for pitching, each produced seven pitchers that started at least one game in the majors. On average, the first round produced about five starters from 1965 to 1976. And yet, in some respects neither the '71 nor '74 drafts compares favorably with the '85 draft, a weak draft for the '80s.

The hit-or-miss nature of the drafts dominated by high school prospects created a lot of variance in first-round draft performance among teams, and produced drafts of lower median quality than those of the '80s. Before the late '70s, therefore, the first round was not a very effective way for struggling clubs to redress pitching deficiencies, and first-round choices did little to alleviate competitive imbalance. The best early drafts produced only one or two pitchers that were regular major league starters for over four years. The '71 and '74 drafts produced Tanana, Sutcliffe, and Rhoden, who undoubtedly helped the teams that selected them (the Angels for Tanana, Dodgers for Sutcliffe and Rhoden), but the teams that selected the other 16 pitchers received very little in return. The 1985 draft, by contrast, produced a number of pitchers that were regular starters for at least four years. A healthy starter probably gets about 25–30 starts in a year. If a bona fide major league starter is defined as having 100 starts (four years times 25 starts per year), the 1985 draft produced three such pitchers—Joe Magrane, Willie Fraser, and Bobby Witt. In addition, Tommy Greene just misses the bona fide starter category with 97 career starts. While none of these pitchers had as good a career as Sutcliffe or Tanana, the 1985 draft produced three of four bona fide starters and provided pitching to four teams (Witt to the Rangers, Greene to the Braves, Fraser to the Angels, and Magrane to the Cardinals). Collegiates Witt, Magrane, and Fraser all paid dividends for the teams that drafted them. Greene, the high school draftee, took longer to develop and never really produced for the Braves. He was traded along with an aging Dale Murphy to the Phillies for Jeff Parrett, Jim Vatcher, and Victor Rosario in 1990. The Braves didn't get much for their pick, but Greene did eventually become an effective starter (when healthy) for a struggling Phillies club, which is also a contribution to competitive balance.

Table 3.9 — Comparison of Pitchers Selected in the First Round of 1971, '74, and '85 Drafts

Name	School	MLB Record	Games	Saves	ERA
1971 Draft					
Jay Franklin	HS (VA)	0–1	3	0	6.00
Roy Branch	HS (MO)	0–1	2	0	8.18
Roy Thomas	HS (CA)	20–11	182	7	3.83
Roger Quiroga	HS (TX)	—	—	—	—
David Sloan	HS (CA)	—	—	—	—
Frank Tanana	HS (MI)	233–219	606	1	3.63
Jeff Wehmeier	HS (IN)	—	—	—	—
Sugar Bear Daniels	HS (MI)	—	—	—	—
Frank Ricelli	HS (NY)	3–3	17	0	4.39
Rick Rhoden	HS (FL)	151–125	413	1	3.60
Randy Stein	HS (CA)	5–6	65	1	5.75
1974 Draft					
Tommy Boggs	HS (TX)	20–44	114	0	4.23
Tom Brennan	Lewis U.	9–10	64	2	4.40
Butch Edge	HS (CA)	3–4	9	0	5.19
Larry Monroe	HS (IL)	0–1	8	0	4.09
Rod Scurry	HS (NV)	19–32	332	39	3.24
Cliff Speck	HS (OR)	2–1	13	0	4.13
Rick Sutcliffe	HS (MO)	171–139	457	6	4.08
Steve Reed	HS (IN)	—	—	—	—
1985 Draft					
Bobby Witt	U. Okla.	142–157	430	0	4.83
Mike Campbell	U. Hawaii	12–19	51	0	5.86
Mike Poehl	U. Texas	—	—	—	—
Jeff Bumgarner	HS (WA)	—	—	—	—
Tommy Greene	HS (NC)	38–25	119	0	4.14
Willie Fraser	Concordia	38–40	239	7	4.47
Joe Magrane	U. Ariz.	57–67	190	0	3.81
Mike Cook	South Car.	1–6	41	0	5.55
Dan Gabriele	HS (MI)	—	—	—	—
Dave Masters	U. Calif.	—	—	—	—
Randy Nosek	HS (MO)	1–3	5	0	10.22

It's not very surprising that, among the four best pitchers in the first round of the '85 draft, it was the high school draftee, Greene, that provided the least benefit to the team that picked him. In general, high school pitchers taken in the first round of the '80s drafts remained riskier choices than pitchers selected out of college. Five of the seven college pitchers (71.4%) selected in the '85 draft played in the majors, each remaining there for at least four years, although not necessarily with the team that drafted him. Among the four high school draftees, only Greene made it to the majors for more than a handful of games. Of the 11 high school pitchers selected in the first round in 1971, seven (63.6%)

made the majors, but only four (36.3%) remained in the big leagues for four or more years. In the 1974 draft, perhaps the best of those dominated by high schoolers, six of the seven pitchers selected (85.7%) made the majors, but only three (42.9%) appeared in more than sixty-five games. In short, the '71, '74, and '85 draft data suggest that the influx of college pitchers has both improved the median quality and reduced the variance in performance of first-round choices.

A skeptic might argue that the '71 and '75 drafts were superior to the '85 draft because Tanana, Sutcliffe, and Rhoden were so much better than Fraser, Witt, Magrane, and Greene. However, Witt has posted career numbers pretty similar to Sutcliffe's and Rhoden's. His winning percentage is lower, but that is due, in part, to the mediocre Ranger teams of the late '80s and early '90s (560–573 from 1986 to 1992, Witt's first seven seasons).

One could also belabor the point that the '71 and '74 drafts were among the best of the first 15 drafts while 1985 was a weak draft for the late '80s. For example, the first round of the 1986 draft produced three high-quality college pitchers in Greg Swindell, Kevin Brown, and reliever Roberto Hernandez, and a couple of high schoolers that made it to the majors in Kent Mercker and Scott Scudder. The 1987 draft had college stars Jack McDowell, Kevin Appier, Jack Armstrong, and Mike Harkey, in addition to high schooler Willie Banks. Collegiate first-round choices in the 1988 draft included Andy Benes, Alex Fernandez, Charles Nagy, Gregg Olson, and Jim Abbott. That first round also produced high schooler Steve Avery. The 1989 draft may have been the weakest in the late '80s, but it still produced college stars Ben McDonald (who emerged as the ace of the Brewers staff before injuries derailed his career), Cal Eldred (who also started for the Brewers and started for the division champion White Sox in 2000), Greg Gohr (who started for the Tigers),[20] and Kyle Abbott (who by 1992 had started for both the Angels and Phillies), along with high schoolers Roger Salkeld (Reds) and Jeff Juden (a former reliever for the Expos that previously started for the Phillies). The pattern for pitchers selected in the first round in the late '80s has remained the same—four or five college pitchers who became solid major league starters (or in the case of Roberto Hernandez and, for a time, Greg Olson, dominant relievers), and one or two of the high school pitchers who also made it to the majors. Not all of them became stars, but most lasted for more than a few years, and some like McDowell, Appier, Fernandez, Nagy, Benes, and Brown have careers on par with those of Rhoden, Sutcliffe, and Tanana. In short, in the '80s, the shift to college pitchers made the first round an effective means of distributing major league pitching talent across numerous teams, and, therefore, helped ensure competitive balance. That trend, moreover, continues to this day.

Two further indications that the quality of the pitchers selected in the first round has improved are the starts per pitcher and games per pitcher measures in Table 3.8. As noted above, part of the reason that the '80s drafts have produced more major league pitchers is simply because more pitchers were selected in the later drafts. Ideally, if all the pitchers selected by 2003 had completed their careers, the starts and games per pitcher selected statistics would be an accurate measure of draft quality. Unfortunately, because so many of the players selected in the later drafts are still active, the starts and games per pitcher measures understate the quality of the 1990s' selections. Ten or 15 years from now, it will be possible to update these figures and demonstrate that, on a per-pick basis, the first-round selections in the '90s were far superior to those of the '60s and '70s. In the meantime, however, the per-pick measures do provide important indications that first-round draft choices increasingly have become an effective means of acquiring major league pitching talent. For example, by the end of the 2003 season, every first round from 1980 to 1989 had produced at least 98 major league appearances and 48 starts per pitcher selected. By contrast, three of the early drafts (1970, 1973, and 1975) produced fewer than 55 appearances per pitcher selected and, perhaps more damning, fewer than 25 major league starts per pitcher. These three drafts were pretty awful for pitchers. In the 1975 draft, the worst by the numbers (36.7 appearances and 14.3 starts per pitcher), only four of the nine pitchers selected made the majors. One of the four, Jim Gideon, appeared in only one major league game. Of the other three—Chris Knapp, Bo McLaughlin, and Dave Ford—none appeared in more than 156 games and none started more than 99 games. Of the 16 pitching selections in the 1970 and 1973 drafts, only nine achieved the major leagues.[21] Only two of those pitchers—John D'Acquisto and Steve Dunning—remained in the major leagues for more than five years. None of them had more major league starts than D'Acquisto's 92.

This is not to suggest that all of the drafts before the late '70s produced little pitching talent. Some were quite good, but the variance in quality from year to year is striking when compared with the consistency of the '80s drafts. The best early first rounds in terms of games and starts per pitcher selected were the '66 and '72 drafts, which, although dominated by high schoolers, displayed a depth similar to that of the later drafts. The '66 draft yielded four bona fide major league pitchers—Ken Brett (83–85, 3.93 ERA, 349 games), Wayne Twitchell (48–65, 3.98 ERA, 282 games), John Curtis (89–97, 3.96 ERA, 438 games), and Gary Nolan (110–70, 3.08 ERA, 250 games)—and two marginal major leaguers, Al Santorini (17–38, 4.28 ERA, 127 games) and Bob Reynolds (14–16, 3.15 ERA, 140 games). The '72 draft produced high-quality starters Larry Christenson (83–71, 3.79 ERA, 243 games), Dick Ruthven (123–127, 4.14 ERA, 355 games), and Scott McGregor (138–108, 3.99 ERA, 356 games), along with major leaguers Preston Hanna (17–25, 4.62 ERA, 156 games), Rob Dressler (11–23, 4.18 ERA, 82 games), and Dan Larson (10–25, 4.39 ERA, 78 games). These were two good drafts for pitchers, but once the players drafted in the '90s have completed their careers, many of the later drafts will perform as well as them in terms of games and starts per pitcher.

A look at the 1998 draft makes it clear how important these young arms have become to all franchises, but especially to the so-called small-market franchises (Table 3.10). Fourteen of the 30 players selected in the first round were pitchers. Of the 14, only three were coming out of high school. The three teams who took the high school pitchers were Cleveland and Colorado, two teams often described as large-market, and Milwaukee, a team that never seems to do what one would predict. The teams that took college pitchers included Oakland, Kansas City (who took two), Minnesota, Detroit, Pittsburgh, Seattle, and San Francisco.

One should be cautious about reading too much into one draft, but look at that list. All of the usual suspects are there except perhaps Milwaukee, Montreal, and Cincinnati. As noted in previous chapters, the population statistics for major metropolitan areas indicate that Oakland, San Francisco, and Detroit should not be considered small-market teams. With the possible exception of San Francisco, the common thread among all of the teams that took college pitchers is not their market size but that they were in a rebuilding process. Based on the trends presented here, it seems that teams that need to retool look more and more toward pitchers in the first round, and because many of them can't afford to make a mistake, they are increasingly apt to select college players. To the extent that these teams hold onto these pitchers for a few years, it seems likely that the strategy will be somewhat successful.

The first-round data indicate that the draft has indeed become a more effective vehicle for distributing talent across the league, and thus helps to ensure competitive balance. But will it continue to play this role?

THE FUTURE OF THE DRAFT

The draft, at least the first round, has undoubtedly become an effective means of distributing American talent among the major league teams. But what of foreign talent? For the most part, this increasingly important source of major league talent has been distributed in the same manner that American talent was distributed prior to 1965 — every team for itself. In theory, in much the way that the dominant teams of the '50s and '60s were able to sign a disproportionate share of the top prospects to preserve their dynasties, the teams that have sufficient resources to scout the entire world — especially Latin America — and to pay high signing bonuses, have an advantage over their less wealthy competitors. Lacking data on the amount that teams spend on foreign scouting and signings, it is not possible to examine this systematically, but it is probable that a team like the Dodgers (with a starting rotation that has included Ramon Martinez, Hideo Nomo, Pedro Astacio, Chan Ho Park, and Ismael Valdes) has benefited substantially from foreign players' exemption from the draft. On the other hand, the small-market Montreal Expos were able to focus scarce resources on select parts of Latin America and the Caribbean to produce a

Table 3.10 — The 1998 Draft

	Name	Team	Position	School
1	Pat Burrell	Phillies	1b	University of Miami
2	Mark Mulder	A's	p	Michigan State University
3	Cory Patterson	Cubs	of	Harrison HS (GA)
4	Jeff Austin	Royals	p	Stanford University
5	J.D. Drew	Cardinals	of	Florida State University
6	Ryan Mills	Twins	p	Arizona State University
7	Austin Kearns	Reds	of	Lafayette HS (CA)
8	Felip Lopez	Blue Jays	ss	Lake Branley HS (FL)
9	Sean Burroughs	Padres	3b	Wilson HS (CA)
10	Carlos Pena	Rangers	1b	Northeastern University
11	Josh McKinley	Expos	ss	Malvern Prep HS (PA)
12	Jeffrey Everett	Red Sox	ss	University of South Carolina
13	J.M. Gold	Brewers	p	Toms River North HS (NJ)
14	Jeff Weaver	Tigers	p	Fresno State University
15	Clint Johnston	Pirates	p	Vanderbilt University
16	Robert Kip Wells	White Sox	p	Baylor University
17	Brad Lidge	Astros	p	University of Notre Dame
18	Seth Etherton	Angels	p	University of Southern California
19	Anthony Torcata	Giants	3b	Woodland HS (CA)
20	Carsten Sabathia	Indians	p	Vallejo HS (CA)
21	Jason Tyner	Mets	of	Texas A&M University
22	Matthew Thornton	Mariners	p	Grand Valley State University
23	Bubba Crosby	Dodgers	of	Rice University
24	Andy Brown	Yankees	of	Richmond HS (IN)
25	Nate Bump	Giants	p	Penn State University
26	Rick Elder	Orioles	of	Sprayberry HS (GA)
27	Chip Ambres	Marlins	of	West Brook HS (TX)
28	Matt Roney	Rockies	p	Edmond North HS (OK)
29	Arturo McDowell	Giants	of	Forest Hill HS (MS)
30	Matt Burch	Royals	p	Virginia Commonwealth University

steady stream of major league players that have enabled them to remain somewhat competitive.

Interestingly, however, not all foreign-born players are exempt from the draft. In 1985, the owners amended the draft rules to include foreign players attending school in the United States (the so-called "Juan Nieves Rule"). Although the rule would appear to presage draft eligibility for all foreign players, the owners have taken no formal action, even though a Blue Ribbon panel examining competitive balance recently endorsed expanding the draft in this way. Some of this could be attributable to the players union and the need to bargain collectively over draft changes. It is, however, strange that a distinction was made between foreign players that attend a U.S. university for a couple of years and those that do not. Clearly, if the owners really want to preserve competitive balance, all foreign-born players, even those who are just graduating from high school, should be eligible for the draft. This would not, of course, put all teams on even footing with respect to foreign talent — those that have well-developed foreign scouting operations would continue to enjoy an advantage. However, for those young foreign prospects that are well known to all teams, the draft would ensure that the prospect could negotiate with only the team that drafted him, thus eliminating the sort of bidding competition that priced poorer clubs out of the market for American talent in the early '60s and foreign talent in the '90s.

While it remains uncertain why the owners and players association haven't made all foreign players eligible for the draft, the rash of defections from the Cuban national team may put some additional pressure on them. Orlando "El Duque" Hernandez went to the Yankees, Livan Hernandez to the Marlins, and Rolando Arrojo defected just prior to the 1996 Olympics. It seemed like the entire Cuban pitching staff was being auctioned to the highest bidder, one at a time, with the latest being the Yankees' (now White Sox') Jose Contreras. Joe Cubas, who staged many of the early defections and then acted as the agent for many of these players, would, no doubt, argue against the draft eligibility for his players, preferring instead to play teams against one another. He would also likely argue that these players deserve whatever the market will bear. Similar arguments were, of course, made prior to the first draft — recall that Dodger general manager Buzzie Bavasi referred to the draft as a form of socialism. The Cubans and all other foreign-bornplayers should, however, be included in the draft. It is true that some of them are a bit older than typical American prospects, and thus Cubas might argue that they should be treated more like free agents than like prospects. The draft could deprive the Cubans of some income early in their careers, but, rather than ensure that none of them ends up with Pittsburgh, or Milwaukee, or Minnesota, which is what will happen if agents for these players have their way, the older players should merely be granted free agency somewhat more quickly than the younger ones. In this way, the Twins might receive a few good years out of an established Cuban star like hard-hitting third baseman Omar Linares (if he had defected). As the foreign talent pool becomes a more important source for prospects, ownrs that are concerned about competi-tive balance will have to change the draft rules. When will this occur? It's tough to say, because some clubs are clearly benefiting from the present arrangement. In much the way that it took time to muster the votes for an amateur draft in the early '60s, it could take time to form a winning coalition on eliminating the foreign draft exemption. But it has to happen some time ... doesn't it?

Summary

The data indicate that over time the draft has become a more effective means of distributing American talent to insure competitive balance. This cuts against some conventional wisdom. As late as 1989, no less an authority than Toronto general manager Pat Gillick put it this way:

> In football or basketball, they're drafting guys after they've spent three or four years in what is the equivalent of our farm system. The caliber of play in college baseball is not equivalent to that of basketball and football. It's not a very exacting science. No matter how much testing you try to do, you never really know how a young guy's going to react to a pro situation until he plays in one.[22]

Gillick's assessment absolves general managers of a lot of poor draft choices, and that's probably why the conventional wisdom is perpetuated by baseball people. To be fair, since 1989 college baseball has become much more popular, and Gillick may, therefore, have revised his opinions, but the data indicate that, long before 1989, the draft had become an increasingly effective conduit for major league talent. To summarize the results:

(1) *The draft has come to be dominated by college players.* Before 1980, about three-quarters of the players selected in the first round came out of the high school ranks. In one year, *all* of the first-round selections were high schoolers. After 1980, over half of the first-round selections were collegiate players. In part, this can be explained by draft rules that relegated many college players (those that had been drafted out of high school) to the secondary phase of the draft. But that rule was eliminated in 1972, and so the shift to college players marks a real shift in the preferences of teams. Despite Gillick's criticisms of the college game, major league teams have increasingly indicated a preference for its players. This result, moreover, is not confined to the first round of the draft. Baseball America notes that in every year since 1977 more college players than high school were selected overall: "By 1981, the swing to college talent had become so pronounced that the ratio of players entering the professional ranks from college programs was nearly five to one."[23]

(2) *First-round college draftees have been, on average, less risky selections than high school players. More generally, players selected in more recent drafts have been less risky selections, regardless of whether they were selected out of high school or college.* Before 1980, about 60% of the first-round selections made it to the majors. One-quarter of the selections never advanced beyond double-A baseball. After 1980, about 70% of first-rounders made the majors; less than 20% did not advance beyond double-A. Although the figures here are only through 2003, the quality of the careers of those that have made the majors is better for those selected in later drafts. For example, 58% of the position players selected in first rounds from 1981 to 1989 played in at least 150 major league games. Only 43% of the position players selected from 1972 to 1980 played in as many games. The careers of many of those selected in the 1990s were still in progress in 2003, but the percentage of first-round draftees from 1990 to 1998 that had become at least marginal major leaguers was already about 60. In addition, the increased reliance on collegiate players has meant that, for the most part, only those high school players that "can't miss" are now drafted in the first round. The result

is that a first-round pick means more now than it ever has, especially in terms of competitive balance. Start holding your team accountable for rotten selections.

(3) *The shift to collegiate draftees coincided with a shift to pitchers.* Another striking trend in first-round selections is the shift to pitchers. Although pitchers are not always a majority of first-round picks, they now comprise about half of first-round selections, whereas in the '60s and '70s that figure was about 35 percent, and they never were a majority in any year. These recent pitching selections appear to be better than those of past drafts. Many of the recent drafts have already produced more bona fide major league starters than did the early drafts, even the best ones. Given the importance of starting pitching, these results can only imply good things for struggling teams.

There is some evidence that weak teams are now having trouble signing their first-round picks due to escalating salary demands. This is worrying and will be discussed more in the concluding chapter. However, the data in this chapter suggest that the draft has become an increasingly effective way to distribute amateur talent across teams, especially pitching. This is one important reason why the gloom-and-doom prognostications for baseball, in particular for its weaker franchises, are overdone. Moreover, under the 2002 labor agreement, teams that are unable to sign their first-round draft pick receive a pick at the same position in the next draft.[24] The next two chapters describe in detail how pitching performance varies widely from year to year. This variability, along with the more equitable method for distributing pitching talent through the draft, have been the key drivers of increased competitive balance over time.

4
Pitching Quality on Championship Teams

This chapter seeks to establish two simple propositions: (1) good pitching is necessary (but not sufficient) to win a championship, and (2) good hitting is neither necessary nor sufficient on championship teams. Branch Rickey used to say that pitching was 75% of the game. There's now an army of SABRmetricians (SABR is the Society for American Baseball Research) that has used various statistical tests to demonstrate that pitching performance really explains about 50% of the variance in winning percentage. Those analysts are correct, but they miss a key point. The data establish convincingly that a team must have good pitching to win a title. The best pitching team doesn't always prevail, but a lousy pitching team almost never does. Excluding 1981, the first strike year, a year when things were highly atypical (first-half champions, second-half champions, etc.), there were 144 champions from 1945 to 1992 (two per year from 1945 to 1968, four thereafter). Of those, only eight finished in the bottom half of their division (or league, before 1969) in ERA (Table 4.1). The post–1992 data are presented at the end of the chapter, but let's start with these.

Table 4.1— Championship Teams 1945–1992 Finished Bottom Half of League or Division in ERA*

1962 San Francisco Giants (6th)	1975 Boston Red Sox (4th)
1964 St. Louis Cardinals (6th)	1982 Atlanta Braves (6th)
1967 Boston Red Sox (8th)	1984 Chicago Cubs (6th)
1971 San Francisco Giants (4th)	1987 Minnesota Twins (6th)

*League ranking in parentheses for pre–1969 teams; division ranking in parentheses thereafter.

Four of the eight ('62 and '71 Giants, '64 Cards, and '75 Red Sox) finished just one place shy of the top half, so they weren't awful pitching teams. The other four teams played their home games in ballparks where a lot of runs are (or were) scored — Fenway, Wrigley, Fulton County Stadium (the launching pad), and the Metrodome. High ERAs for these teams do not necessarily indicate that they were below-average pitching teams. The ERA data are purged of home park bias via a simple statistic. Using runs allowed per game both at home and on the road, park-adjusted runs allowed are computed as follows:[1]

Park-adjusted Runs Allowed =   (1/N) × Average Runs Allowed in Home Games +
(N-1/N) × Average Runs Allowed in Away Games

where N is the number of teams in the league.[2] In 1962 there were 10 teams in each league. So each team's runs allowed at home contribute 10% to the park-adjusted figure; the away figure contributes 90%. In this way, runs allowed in each ballpark contribute an equal amount (10%) to the park-adjusted figure. It's a crude measure that has its limitations (to be explained shortly), but it helps demonstrate that most of these high-ERA champions were above-average pitching teams (Table 4.2).

Table 4.2 — High-ERA Champions 1945–1992 Park-Adjusted Runs Allowed Per Game*

1962 San Francisco Giants (4th)	1975 Boston Red Sox (3rd)
1964 St. Louis Cardinals (2nd)	1982 Atlanta Braves (1st)
1967 Boston Red Sox (2nd)	1984 Chicago Cubs (2nd)
1971 San Francisco Giants (4th)	1987 Minnesota Twins (7th)

*League ranking in parentheses for pre–1969 teams; division ranking in parentheses thereafter.

Ah yes, that's a bit better. Bob Gibson's 1964 Cardinals team, which played in the relatively small Sportsman's Park, becomes the second best pitching team in the National League. Gibson went 19–12 with a 3.01 ERA; Curt Simmons went 18–9 (3.43 ERA); Ray Sadecki went 20–11 (3.68 ERA). They comprised a good (if not great) starting rotation, good enough to take care of the Yankees in the World Series. Similarly, the 1962 Giants (who extended the Yankees to seven games), had a good staff (Juan Marichal 18–11, Jack Sanford 24–7, Billy Pierce 16–6, and Billy O'Dell 19–14); they ranked fourth out of 10 in park-adjusted runs allowed. The 1982 Braves become the top-ranked pitching team in the NL West despite what appeared to be a rather weak rotation (besides Phil Niekro they started Rick Mahler, Rick Camp, and Bob Walk). The 1984 Cubs (Rick Sutcliffe 16–1) and the 1967 Red Sox (Jim Lonborg 22–9) ranked second in park-adjusted ERA. The 1975 Red Sox (Bill Lee 17–9, Luis Tiant 18–14, Rick Wise 19–12) ranked third.

Two of the eight remain a problem. The 1971 Giants are worse on the park-adjusted measure than on ERA. Why? They were an ordinary road team — .630 home winning percentage, .481 away. Since the park-adjusted measure weights away performance much more heavily than does the straight ERA measure, the Giants look worse than they actually were. Their team ERA was a respectable 3.33. Within their division, they ranked behind Houston (3.13), San Diego (3.23) and the Dodgers (3.23). Theirs was the better pitching division: they ranked sixth of the 12 NL teams in ERA. The average NL ERA was

The 1987 Minnesota Twins — The world champions were the only league champion from 1945 to 1992 that was below their league median in ERA and park-adjusted runs allowed per game. On the park-adjusted measure they ranked last in their division. They also gave up more runs than they scored, one of only four playoff participants to do so since 1945.

3.47, well above the Giants' mark. They started Gaylord Perry (16–12) and Juan Marichal (18–11). They were a decent pitching team.

The same cannot be said of the 1987 Twins. They are, however, a fluke, the proverbial exception that proves the rule. With the exception of the 1973 Mets (.509 winning percentage), they were the weakest champ ever (85–77, .525 winning percentage). The Twins qualified for the playoffs by winning a division in which only one other team (the Kansas City Royals) played better than .500 ball. Once in, how did the Twins win it all? First, the short series playoff format maximized the few strengths on the Twins' suspect pitching staff— starters Frank Viola and Bert Blyleven, and closer Jeff Reardon.[3] Second, they had home field advantage throughout the playoffs (something no other sport would tolerate). Noted sportswriter Tom Boswell put it well:

> Let's make one thing clear: The noise conditions here are not equal for both teams. The reason that this jet-landing level of noise does not bother the Twins is that the crowd explodes only when it will rattle the visitors. These nice midwesterners have Dome booming down to a science. When their boys need quiet time to think, you can hear the air conditioners hum. When the bad guys need some peace, the world's largest high school gym feels as if it's about to rip itself apart.... Thanks to the *Elias Analyst*, we already know that, year in and year out, the Twins have the biggest home field edge in baseball; they play about 16 percent better at home than on the road.[4]

During the season, they had a .691 home winning percentage and a *.358* road winning percentage. The .333 home-road differential was by far the largest for any of the 144 champions (the next highest was .259 for the 1961 Yankees) — the average differential was .074. In park-adjusted runs allowed per game (which, again, weights road performance more heavily), they ranked last in the

AL. They also gave up more runs than they scored, one of only four playoff participants to do so since 1945 (the others being the 1984 Royals, the 1994 Rangers, and the 1997 Giants). In the World Series they won the four games in their peculiar little stadium, and lost the three in the Cardinals' Busch Stadium.[5]

The 1987 Twins were just plain odd. They are the only one of the "high-ERA" champions with truly weak pitching.[6] However, it can not be concluded that they were the only weak pitching team ever to win a championship, at least not yet. It remains to be seen whether all of the 136 champions whose pitchers ranked in the top half of their league (or division) in ERA truly pitched well. Some teams might have had low ERAs primarily due to their relatively spacious home ballparks. Table 4.3 lists all champions that ranked in the lower half of their division (or league, before 1969) in park-adjusted runs per game.

Table 4.3 — Championship Teams 1945–1992 Finished Lower Half of League or Division in Park-Adjusted Runs Allowed Per Game*

1951 New York Yankees (5th)	1977 Phil. Phillies (4th)
1960 New York Yankees (6th)	1979 Cal. Angels (6th)
1962 New York Yankees (6th)	1982 Milwaukee Brewers (7th)
1970 Pittsburgh Pirates (4th)	1987 Minnesota Twins (7th)
1971 San Fran. Giants (6th)	1989 San Fran. Giants (5th)
1974 Pittsburgh Pirates (4th)	

*League ranking in parentheses for pre–1969 teams; division ranking in parentheses thereafter.

The '71 Giants and the '87 Twins have already been discussed. The rest of the list is a bit surprising. Five of the nine had winning percentages over .586 (95–67 in a 162-game season); three of the teams from the Yankees dynasty appear. Most appear not because they were weak pitching teams, but rather because of the way the park-adjusted runs allowed statistic is constructed. For example, the 1960 Yankees led the league in ERA; the '62 Yanks, '70 Pirates, '77 Phillies, and '89 Giants finished second in their respective leagues or divisions in ERA (Table 4.4).

Table 4.4 — Championship Teams 1945–1992 ERA Rank of Teams in Lower Half of League or Division in Park-Adjusted Runs Allowed Per Game*

1951 New York Yankees (3rd)	1977 Phil. Phillies (2nd)
1960 New York Yankees (1st)	1979 California Angels (4th)
1962 New York Yankees (2nd)	1982 Milwaukee Brewers (3rd)
1970 Pittsburgh Pirates (2nd)	1987 Minnesota Twins (6th)
1971 San Fran. Giants (4th)	1989 San Fran. Giants (2nd)
1974 Pittsburgh Pirates (3rd)	

*League ranking in parentheses for pre–1969 teams; division ranking in parentheses thereafter.

In constructing the park-adjusted statistic the implicit assumption is that any disparity in home versus away runs allowed is due to a team's home ballpark. By reweighting the runs allowed data, the ERA figures are, hopefully, purged of home ballpark bias. However, some champions had home ballparks that favored neither hitters nor pitchers, yet, for whatever reason, they pitched much better at home than on the road. All of the 11 teams in Table 4.3 gave up at least half a run more in road games than in home games; six gave up at least an additional run in their road games (Table 4.5). These differentials are quite large. For comparison, in the Mantle Era, *all* teams gave up, on average, .136 more runs on the road than at home; in the Aaron Era that figure was .129; in the Miller Era it was .164 runs per game.

Many of the teams in Table 4.5 were very good pitching teams, but, because the park-adjusted runs allowed statistic weights away performance heavily, they appear to be weak. This uneven pitching performance is ultimately reflected in winning percentages. And these teams often had home-away winning percentage differentials two to four times the size of the average for championship teams. In the Mantle Era (1945–62) champs won 7.7% more of their home games, in the Aaron Era (1963–76) 6.1% more, and in the Marvin Miller Era (1977–92) 8.1% more. Nine of the 11 teams in Table 4.5 had home-away differentials of at least 12%. Uneven pitching performance clearly contributed to their high park-adjusted runs allowed figures. With the exceptions of the '71 Giants and the '87 Twins, the combination of their low team ERAs and their large home-away pitching performance differentials leads to the conclusion that the teams in Table 4.3 were good pitching teams that were especially dominant at home.

The 1982 Milwaukee Brewers are peculiar enough to warrant a few additional words. They put up a lot of runs both at home and on the road. Five players had at least 97 RBI — Cecil Cooper 121, Robin Yount 114, Gorman Thomas 112, Ben Oglivie 102, and Ted Simmons 97. Yount, Cooper, Thomas, and Oglivie each hit at least 29 home runs. The team's pitching, however, was much better at home than on the road (although County Stadium wasn't a particularly large ballpark). At home, the Brew Crew scored 5.75 per game and gave up only 3.89. On the road, they scored 5.71 but gave up 4.97. Oddly, despite giving up the additional run on the road, their home and road winning percentages were nearly identical — 48–34 at home (.585), 47–33 away (.588). Given their runs produced and allowed, it is very surprising that their home winning percentage wasn't better and their road percentage wasn't worse.

In any event, the high-scoring Brewers were not a bad pitching team. They were tied for third in the AL East in ERA; sixth out of 14 in the American League. Five of the pitchers on this balanced staff posted double-digits in victories (Mike Caldwell 17–13, 3.91 ERA, Pete Vukovich 18–6, 3.34 ERA, Moose Haas 11–8, 4.47 ERA, Bob McClure 12–7, 4.22 ERA, Jim Slaton 10–6, 3.29 ERA). Rollie Fingers was very good as their closer (5–6, 29 saves, 2.60 ERA). Why the

Table 4.5 — Champions 1945–1992 Finished Bottom Half of League or Division in Park-Adjusted Runs Allowed Per Game; Home and Away Runs Allowed Per Game, Winning Percentage Differentials

Team	Runs Allowed Per Game (Home)	Runs Allowed Per Game (Away)	Winning Percentage Differential (Home-Away)
'51 Yankees	3.30	4.77	16.5%
'60 Yankees	3.54	4.59	16.9%
'62 Yankees	3.82	4.56	6.4%
'70 Pirates	3.84	4.36	12.2%
'71 Giants	3.70	4.24	14.8%
'74 Pirates	3.74	4.37	19.8%
'77 Phillies	3.69	4.55	23.4%
'79 Angels	4.18	5.29	12.3%
'82 Brewers	3.89	4.97	-0.2%
'87 Twins	4.29	5.65	33.3%
'89 Giants	3.14	4.25	17.3%

MLB AVERAGES: Run Differential, Home — Away
Mantle Era (1945–62)   0.14
Aaron Era (1963–76)   0.13
Miller Era (1977–92)   0.16

'71 Giants were above average in pitching has already been explained. This leaves only the '87 Twins unexplained — the exception that proves the rule. Proposition 1 has been well established: all championship teams (at least through 1992) had better than average pitching.

How about the second proposition, namely, that above-average hitting is not found on all championship teams? Thirteen championship teams finished in the bottom half of their division or league in runs scored per game (Table 4.6) — five more than finished in the bottom half in ERA. A number of the likely suspects are on this list: the Go-Go White Sox of 1959, The Koufax-Drysdale Dodger teams of the '60s, and the Seaver-Koosman-Matlack Mets teams of the late '60s and early '70s. Others, however, might have made the list primarily because of their relatively spacious home parks ('80 and '86 Astros, '84 and '85 Royals).[7] Some are more surprising: the 1990 Red Sox appear, a team that played half of its games in tiny Fenway; the 1974 Orioles and the 1991 Blue Jays, two teams not typically thought of as weak in hitting, are also listed.[8]

To correct for home park bias, park-adjusted runs scored per game is computed in the same way as was the park-adjusted runs allowed measure (Table 4.7). In a number of cases, the park-adjusted figures produced more sensible results: by that measure the 1963 Dodgers ranked second, the 1966 Dodgers snuck into the top half of the league (fifth), and the 1980 and '86 Astros and

Table 4.6 — Champions 1945–1992 Finished Bottom Half of League or Division in Runs Scored Per Game*

1959 Chicago White Sox (6th)
1963 Los Angeles Dodgers (6th)
1965 Los Angeles Dodgers (8th)
1966 Los Angeles Dodgers (8th)
1969 New York Mets (4th)
1973 New York Mets (6th)
1974 Baltimore Orioles (4th)

1980 Houston Astros (4th)
1984 K.C. Royals (5th)
1985 K.C. Royals (6th)
1986 Houston Astros (4th)
1990 Boston Red Sox (5th)
1991 Toronto Blue Jays (5th)

*League ranking in parentheses for pre-1969 teams; division ranking in parentheses thereafter.

the 1984 Royals moved into third in their respective divisions. For other teams, however, the park-adjusted figures echo the runs scored results. The '65 Dodgers, '69 and '73 Mets, '85 Royals, '90 Red Sox, and '91 Blue Jays are weak hitting teams by either measure.

Table 4.7 — Low Scoring Champions 1945–1992: Park-Adjusted Runs Scored Per Game*

1959 Chicago White Sox (3rd)
1963 Los Angeles Dodgers (2nd)
1965 Los Angeles Dodgers (6th)
1966 Los Angeles Dodgers (5th)
1969 New York Mets (4th)
1973 New York Mets (4th)
1974 Baltimore Orioles (1st)

1980 Houston Astros (3rd)
1984 K.C. Royals (3rd)
1985 K.C. Royals (5th)
1986 Houston Astros (3rd)
1990 Boston Red Sox (6th)
1991 Toronto Blue Jays (5th)

*League ranking in parentheses for pre-1969 teams; division ranking in parentheses thereafter.

Two teams—the 1959 White Sox and the 1974 Orioles—didn't play in especially large ballparks, but their park-adjusted runs scored figures ranked them near the top of their league or division (White Sox third, Orioles first). These two appear to be strong offensive teams, but only because of the way the park-adjusted statistics are constructed. Most championship teams, even weak-hitting teams that played in neutral or pitcher-friendly home parks ('80, '86 Astros, and '84, '85 Royals) scored at least as much in home games as in road games. Because the park-adjusted figures weight road performance so heavily, a team that does not suffer the typical drop-off in run production on the road could appear strong relative to the rest of the league, despite being relatively mediocre offensively. The '59 White Sox and the '74 Orioles not only suffered no road drop-off in runs scored they actually scored significantly more runs in their road games. The White Sox averaged 4.06 runs in their home games, 4.62 in their road games. The Orioles scored 3.46 at home, 4.66 away—a whopping 1.2-run differential. In terms of home versus road offensive production, these two teams were clearly different from the other low scoring champs in Table

4.8. Despite their impressive park-adjusted rankings, they were relatively weak offensive teams.

Table 4.8 — Low Scoring Champions 1945–1992 Home-Away Differentials: Winning Percentage, Runs Per Game

Team	Runs Scored Per Game (Home)	Runs Scored Per Game (Away)	Winning Percentage Differential (Home-Away)
'59 White Sox	4.06	4.62	0.0%
'63 Dodgers	3.65	4.24	8.6%
'65 Dodgers	3.30	4.19	3.7%
'66 Dodgers	3.53	3.95	13.6%
'69 Mets	3.80	4.00	3.4%
'73 Mets	3.87	3.67	4.3%
'74 Orioles	3.46	4.66	1.2%
'80 Astros	4.06	3.75	21.6%
'84 Royals	4.24	4.06	4.9%
'85 Royals	4.35	4.12	9.7%
'86 Astros	4.03	4.03	9.9%
'90 Red Sox	4.86	3.76	17.3%
'91 Blue Jays	4.43	4.01	1.2%

So far that is eight champions that were below-average offensive teams. Note that these weak hitting teams were not all marginal champions like the weak pitching '87 Twins (.525 winning percentage). Three were .600 ball clubs (or very close)—'59 White Sox .610, '65 Dodgers .599, and '69 Mets .617. Three others—the '85 Royals, '91 Blue Jays, and '74 Orioles—had winning percentages of .562 (91–71 in a 162 game season). The '90 Red Sox, also a stronger champion than the '87 Twins, posted a .543 winning percentage. Excluding the '73 Mets (.509 winning percentage), these teams were not fluke champions. They were good (in some cases very good) teams that all had below-average offensive production.

Identifying weak offensive champions is not yet complete, however. It may be that some champions appear to be high-scoring teams primarily because of their small home ballparks. Table 4.9 lists all champions that ranked in the bottom half of their league (or division) in park-adjusted runs scored per game. Six are weak offensive teams that have already been discussed ('65 Dodgers, '69–'73 Mets, '85 Royals, '90 Red Sox, '91 Blue Jays); six are new ('54 Giants, '70 Reds, '72 Tigers, '83 Dodgers, '89 A's, and the '91 Twins).

A couple of these new teams did play their home games in hitters' ballparks (Tigers, Twins), and thus the park-adjustment probably does reveal something about their true offensive prowess. The 1983 Dodgers, however, are more difficult to explain. By down-weighting their runs scored in home games, the

Members of the 1955 Chicago White Sox — (left to right) Ed McGhee, Bob Neiman, Minnie Minoso, Jim Rivera, and Johnny Groth — look quizzically at a bat, a reflection, perhaps, of their struggles at the plate. While the 1959 version of that team was the prototypical low-scoring champion, the Sox were also very competitive earlier in the decade. The 1957 edition finished 90–64; the 1955 team was a game better at 91–63. The 1955 team was fourth out of eight in the AL in on base percentage (.340) and fifth in slugging percentage (.388).

park-adjusted figure should benefit a team that played half its games in the relatively spacious Chavez Ravine. Instead, they ranked third in the NL West in runs per game but fourth in park-adjusted runs per game. Although they ranked near the division median on both measures of offensive production, they were eighth out of 12 in the National League in runs scored. The team had one star offensive performer (Pedro Guerrero: .298 batting average, 32 home runs, 102 RBI); no other Dodger hit over .284, had more than 17 home runs, or 73 RBI. A strong case can be made for including them among the weak offensive champions, but the argument that above-average hitting is not a necessary ingredient on a championship team can be made without including the '83 Dodgers.

Three of the teams in Table 4.9 appear to be low scoring because of the way the park-adjusted figure was constructed — the '54 Giants, '70 Reds and

Table 4.9 — Champions 1945–1992 Finished Lower Half of League or Division in Park-Adjusted Runs Scored Per Game*

1954 New York Giants (5th)
1965 Los Angeles Dodgers (6th)
1969 New York Mets (4th)
1970 Cincinnati Reds (4th)
1973 New York Mets (4th)
1972 Detroit Tigers (5th)
1983 Los Angeles Dodgers (4th)
1985 K.C. Royals (5th)
1989 Oakland A's (5th)
1990 Boston Red Sox (6th)
1991 Toronto Blue Jays (5th)
1991 Minnesota Twins (5th)

*League ranking in parentheses for pre–1969 teams; division ranking in parentheses thereafter.

'89 A's. Though none played in a ballpark that especially favored hitters, each scored more runs in, and won a much higher percentage of, their home games (Table 4.10) than other low-scoring champions. Among the 12 teams in Table 4.9, only the '90 Red Sox had a higher home-away winning percentage differential than the Giants, Reds or A's.[9] Each of the three scored at least .34 more runs per game at home (roughly three times the typical differential) and had winning percentage differentials of at least 11.1 (roughly twice the historic average). In short, it would be wrong to conclude that these three were weak offensive teams on the basis of park-adjusted runs per game. By contrast, the '72 Tigers and '91 Twins had typical home-away winning percentage differentials, and thus their runs scored differentials primarily reflect the size of their home ballparks.

Table 4.10 — Low Scoring Champions 1945–92: Park-Adjusted Runs Per Game Home-Away Differentials: Winning Percentage, Runs Per Game (Teams Not Already Listed in Table 4.8)

Team	Runs Scored Per Game (Home)	Runs Scored Per Game (Away)	Winning Percentage Differential (Home-Away)
'54 Giants	5.09	4.42	13.3%
'70 Reds	5.13	4.43	14.4%
'72 Tigers	4.00	3.15	2.6%
'83 Dodgers	3.95	4.12	7.6%
'89 A's	4.56	4.22	11.1%
'91 Twins	4.98	4.59	8.6%

The '72 Tigers and the '91 Twins can therefore safely be added to the original eight low-scoring champions ('59 White Sox, '65 Dodgers, '69 Mets, '73 Mets, '74 Orioles, '85 Royals, '90 Red Sox, '91 Blue Jays). Neither of these additions were particularly weak champions—the Tigers posted a .551 winning percentage, the Twins .586. Notice that there were weak offensive champions in each era; this phenomenon was not, therefore, caused by weak champions under the division format. Ten weak offensive champions, one weak pitching champion—and that one was the '87 Twins, perhaps the biggest fluke among all champions; both propositions are substantiated. That is, from 1945–1992, better-than-average pitching was a necessary ingredient on a championship team; above-average offensive production was not.

THE RECENT EVIDENCE

This is all wonderful, but the data extend only through 1992. You might fairly ask, "What's happened in recent years? Didn't all those strong Cleveland Indians teams of the 1990s have lousy pitching?" or something to that effect. Table 4.11 shows all the teams that made the playoffs that were either above-average (actually above the league median) in runs allowed (i.e., weak pitching teams), or below-average in runs scored (i.e., weak hitting teams).[10] Again, any team that is above (below) the median on *both* the park-adjusted and the unadjusted measures is termed a below-average or weak pitching (hitting) team.

In the park-adjusted figures for all years except 1993, N is the number of teams in the league, not the division, and thus all below (above) median calculations in Table 4.11 are made relative to the full league. This is because of the new playoff format. Under the old division format (1969–1993), one team made it to the playoffs out of each division, and thus it made sense to compare performance only relative to division opponents. Under the new format, the wild-card team can come from any division. Because teams in different divisions are in more direct competition for a playoff spot, it made sense to do the runs scored and allowed calculations relative to all teams in the league.

At first glance, the listing in Table 4.11 suggests that good pitching is no more necessary than good hitting. Nine playoff teams were below the league median in runs scored; nine were above the league median in runs allowed. Eleven were below the median in park-adjusted runs scored; 11 were above the median in park-adjusted runs allowed. Six teams—the 1996 Yankees, 1997 Marlins, 1999 Red Sox, 2001 Braves, and the A's in both 2002 and 2003—were below the median on both measures of runs scored; and five teams—the 1997 Mariners, 1997 Giants, 1998 Cubs, 2001 Indians, and 2003 Red Sox—were above the median on both measures of runs allowed. Based solely on those lists one could reasonably conclude that among recent playoff teams, weak hitting is just as rare as weak pitching. This would undercut the argument presented here about the necessity of solid pitching, but, necessary or not, pitching is still very important. And since pitching performance is still highly variable, it would remain a key source of competitive balance in baseball.

However, if you look at the list in Table 4.11 a little more closely, you could still conclude that, even recently, good pitching is necessary on a championship team, and good hitting is not. Of the five teams that are weak on both measures of runs allowed ('97 Mariners, '97 Giants, '98 Cubs, '01 Indians, and '03 Red Sox), only the Red Sox got past the first round of the playoffs, eventually losing to the Yankees in a heartbreaking American League Championship Series. Four of the six teams that are weak on both measures of runs scored reached the league championship series, and two of them won the World Series (the '96 Yankees and the '97 Marlins). So, like the rest of the data since World War II, the recent data also indicate that it is possible to win a league championship and even a World Series with below-average offensive production. This is not so for teams with below-average pitching, or at least no such team had done it as of 2003 (except for the 1987 Twins).

In addition, the weak scoring playoff participants were simply better teams than those that were weak on runs allowed. The average winning percentage for the teams that were below average on both measures of offensive production was .581, equivalent to a 94–68 record. Teams that were weak on both measures of run prevention had a .562 winning percentage (91–71). So, based on their playoff performances and their yearly winning percentages, it is clear that the weak hitting playoff participants were a more capable bunch than the weak pitching teams. This further underscores that MLB's most coveted prizes are still more likely to be won by a below-average offensive team than a below-average pitching team.

As with the pre–1993 data, the lists in Table 4.11 are just a starting point for identifying weak hitting and pitching playoff participants. A number of teams that appear on the list are not truly weak, but are victims of the way the statistics are constructed or their own uneven play at home versus on the road. Consider the three teams that were below average in runs scored per game, but not in park-adjusted runs per game (Table 4.11, Panel A). The 1996 Dodgers were victims of their large ballpark, and thus the park-adjusted figures reveal them to have been the fifth best run producing team in the National League, well above average. Conversely, the 2003 Cubs were below average in runs scored because they did not score much in their relatively small home ballpark. They scored 378 runs on the road, but only 346 in Wrigley Field. And unlike most other teams, their home record was not better than their road record (44–37 both at home and away). This is similar to the situation for the 1959 White Sox and 1974 Orioles, except that the Cubs played in a more hitter-friendly park, which should have meant well-above-average scoring on their part. Using park-adjusted runs scored, which weights their relatively stronger road performance more heavily, they rank sixth in the NL, but they were actually a below-average offensive team, as indicated by their ranking in runs scored per game (ninth).

The 2002 Twins are similar in that they did not score much more in their relatively small home ballpark (396 runs) than on the road (372 runs). Thus,

Table 4.11—Playoff Participants 1993–2003
(Includes only full seasons)

BATTING

PANEL A. Teams with Below-Median Runs Scored Per Game
(League Rank in Parentheses)

1996 New York Yankees (9th)
1996 Los Angeles Dodgers (12th)
1997 Florida Marlins (8th)
1999 Boston Red Sox (9th)
2001 Atlanta Braves (13th)
2002 Oakland A's (8th)
2002 Minnesota Twins (9th)
2003 Oakland A's (9th)
2003 Chicago Cubs (9th)

PANEL B. Teams with Below-Median Park-Adjusted Runs Scored Per Game

1996 Texas Rangers (8th)
1996 New York Yankees (9th)
1996 Atlanta Braves (10th)
1997 Florida Marlins (8th)
1998 Cleveland Indians (9th)
1999 Boston Red Sox (11th)
2001 St. Louis Cardinals (9th)
2001 Atlanta Braves (10th)
2002 Oakland A's (8th)
2003 Oakland A's (9th)
2003 San Francisco Giants (9th)

PITCHING/DEFENSE

PANEL C. Teams with Above-Median Runs Allowed Per Game
(League Rank in Parentheses after 1993, Division Rank in 1993)

1997 Seattle Mariners (10th)
1997 San Francisco Giants (11th)
1998 Texas Rangers (14th)
1998 Chicago Cubs (11th)
1999 Cleveland Indians (8th)
2001 Cleveland Indians (9th)
2001 Houston Astros (10th)
2003 Boston Red Sox (9th)
2003 Atlanta Braves (9th)

PANEL D. Teams with Above-Median Park-Adjusted Runs Allowed Per Game

1993 Philadelphia Phillies (5th)
1996 Baltimore Orioles (12th)
1997 Seattle Mariners (9th)
1997 Cleveland Indians (10th)
1997 San Francisco Giants (11th)
1998 Chicago Cubs (11th)
2000 Oakland A's (9th)
2000 San Francisco Giants (11th)
2001 Cleveland Indians (10th)
2003 Boston Red Sox (9th)
2003 Florida Marlins (10th)

Source: Home-Road runs and runs allowed data: www.baseballreference.com

they too perform better on the park-adjusted runs statistic (seventh in the AL), although unlike the 2003 Cubs their winning percentage at home was still much higher than on the road (.667 versus .500). The high differential is attributable to better pitching at home (336 runs allowed) than on the road (376 runs allowed). Had they scored just a bit more in their games in the Metrodome, they wouldn't appear on this list. They didn't, which makes it difficult to classify them. Because they don't quite have the same profile as the '59 White Sox, '74 Orioles, and '03 Cubs—that is, balanced home-road winning percentages and more scoring in road than in homes games despite a home ballpark that does not favor pitchers—they are left off the list of truly weak offensive teams.

4—Pitching Quality on Championship Teams 119

Another reason to exclude them is that they were very near the league median on both measures of offensive production.

Turning to teams that were above average in runs allowed but not in park-adjusted runs allowed (Table 4.11, Panel C), the 1998 Texas Rangers and 2001 Houston Astros both appear to be weak pitching teams because of their small ballparks. The Astros further compounded the problem by playing worse in their small home ballpark (44–37) than on the road (49–32). The park adjustment helps both teams with the Rangers ranking seventh and the Astros ranking third. The 1999 Indians were another team that played better on the road (50–31) than at home (47–34). They therefore did much better in terms of park-adjusted runs allowed, ranking third in the AL. Because their home ballpark also favored hitters slightly, the adjusted figures are a fairer indication of their ability to prevent runs.[11] Even on the unadjusted measure, they rank just below the league median (eighth), having given up just .006 more runs per game than the seventh-place Texas Rangers. Looking at all the information, the 1999 Indians were not a weak pitching team. Finally, the 2003 Braves were not victims of the way the statistics were constructed, but were very near the league median in both runs allowed (ninth) and park-adjusted runs allowed (seventh). They, too, should not be considered a below-average pitching team for the same reason that the 2002 Twins were not obviously a weak offensive team.

While only one of the teams that appeared on the runs scored or runs allowed lists, but not on the adjusted measures, was truly weak at scoring or preventing runs, those weak on both measures and those weak on only the park-adjusted measures are more likely candidates. To begin exploring that possibility, Table 4.12 presents data on average runs scored at home and on the road, and the home-road winning percentage differential for all teams that were below the league median on park-adjusted runs scored.

Some teams are low scoring on the park-adjusted measure because they played much better in their home games than in their road games. If their home ballpark was one that favored pitchers, it would be unfair to classify them as weak offensive teams. For example, the 2003 Oakland A's played in a home ballpark that favored pitchers more than any other listed in Table 4.12. However, they scored 386 runs in their road games and 382 in their home games. Those 382 runs scored in a tough hitting environment were an impressive achievement, as evidenced by their winning 22.3% more of their home games than their road games (the largest differential on the list). Again, the typical home-road winning percentage differential is 5%–10%. Because their home ballpark masked their true offensive achievements, they rate below the league median in runs scored per game. Yet, because their offensive performance was so much poorer in road games, they also rank below the median on park-adjusted runs per game. But they weren't really a weak offensive team. The statistics just punish them for combining a pitcher-friendly ballpark with highly uneven home-road performance.

Table 4.12 — Low Scoring Playoff Teams 1993–2003 (in Park-Adjusted Runs Scored Per Game) Home-Away Differentials: Winning Percentage, Runs Per Game

Team	Runs Scored Per Game (Home)	Runs Scored Per Game (Away)	Winning Percentage Differential (Home-Away)
'96 Texas Rangers (101)	6.27	5.12	12.3%
'96 New York Yankees* (101)	5.60	5.16	8.8%
'96 Atlanta Braves (104)	5.36	4.19	19.7%
'97 Florida Marlins* (96)	4.42	4.72	14.8%
'98 Cleveland Indians (103)	5.67	4.83	3.7%
'99 Boston Red Sox* (104)	5.59	4.73	4.9%
'01 St. Louis Cardinals (99)	5.40	4.64	17.1%
'01 Atlanta Braves* (101)	4.37	4.63	9.9%
'02 Oakland A's* (104)	5.27	4.60	6.2%
'03 Oakland A's* (94)	4.72	4.77	22.3%
'03 San Francisco Giants (100)	4.91	4.46	16.6%

indicates below league median on both runs scored per game and park-adjusted runs scored per game. Park adjustment factors are in parentheses. Figures over 100 indicate that the ballpark favored hitters.

By contrast, teams that had much higher home winning percentages and played in parks that favored hitters are more likely to have been weak offensive teams. For example, the 1996 Atlanta Braves played in a home ballpark that favored hitters as much as any in Table 4.12. More damning, their high home-road winning percentage differential was driven by their pitching, not their hitting. They scored 434 runs at home, 339 on the road, a reasonable difference given their hitter-friendly ballpark (then referred to as the launching pad). However, they actually gave up *fewer* runs at home (300) than on the road (348), which is remarkable. Because their home ballpark inflated their scoring, and because it is clear that it was not superior offensive performance in home games that drove their high differential in winning percentage, their park-adjusted runs scored are especially meaningful. They were, therefore, a weak offensive team.

The 1996 Rangers are similar to the 1996 Braves. Their home ballpark typically favors hitters, although the park-adjustment factor for 1996 shows only a slight edge for hitters. In subsequent years, the adjustment factor hovered near 104, spiking to 110 in 2002–2003. A word about the park factors is probably in order here. You will note that in some cases the same park can have a wildly different adjustment factor from one year to the next. This is likely because the team's own offensive and defensive production is used in calculating the factor.[12] Thus, a ballpark can conceivably be rated as favoring hitters just because its team's pitchers performed poorly in their home games. Despite this potential circularity, the adjustment factor for a park typically fluctuates little enough to reliably classify it as either a hitters' or pitchers' park. And the Ballpark at Arlington is safe to classify as a hitters' park.

Playing in a home park that favored hitters, the '96 Rangers scored 508 runs. On the road they scored 420, a reasonable differential. However, like the Braves, it was their pitching that was responsible for them winning 12.3% more of their home games than their road games. They gave up 392 runs on the road, and only 407 in their hitter-friendly home ballpark. Admittedly, the Braves' home pitching performance was more impressive than the Rangers,' and thus it was clearer that pitching was driving their winning percentage differential. In the Rangers' case, it does however seem safe to conclude that uneven pitching is primarily responsible for their relatively high home winning percentage. To be consistent, the 1996 Rangers are also classified as a weak offensive team on the basis of their ranking on park-adjusted runs scored.

In other cases, a higher winning percentage at home was driven by uneven hitting performance rather than ballpark effects. For whatever reason, some teams just played much better offensively in their home parks, and should not be classified as weak offensive teams. For example, the 2001 Cardinals played in a park that didn't particularly favor pitchers or hitters. They scored 19% more runs in their home than their road games (443 home, 371 road), and they gave up 18% fewer runs at home (308 home, 378 road). Since both strong hitting and pitching were responsible for their high home winning percentage, their unadjusted runs scored per game (which weights home scoring more heavily than the adjusted measure) is a valid measure of their offensive performance. On that basis, they were not a weak offensive team. Similarly, in their home games the 2003 Giants scored 11.3% more and gave up 11.8% fewer runs in a park that favored neither pitchers nor hitters. They too were a team that simply played better (both offensively and defensively) at home, but they were not the weak offensive team that their adjusted runs scored per game suggests.

Of the remaining five teams that ranked below the median on both measures of offensive production (starred entries in Table 4.12), four had typical home-road winning percentage differentials (1996 Yankees, 1999 Red Sox, 2001 Braves, and 2002 A's). It seems safe to conclude that all four were below-average offensive teams. The last remaining team ranked below the league median on both scoring measures was the 1997 Marlins, who won 15% more of their home than their road games. That split is not, however, indicative of truly superior offensive performance in their home ballpark. The Marlins scored 382 runs on the road and gave up 345. At home they scored 358 and gave up 324. One would expect that their winning percentage at home and away would have been similar, and yet they were 52–29 at home versus 40–41 away. Their winning percentage differential is simply a fluke. While their home ballpark was an offensive disadvantage, the park-adjusted statistic is a valid indication that they were also a weak offensive team.

Of the teams in Table 4.12, that leaves only the 1998 Cleveland Indians to discuss, another team that is difficult to classify. The played in a home ballpark that favored hitters, which casts some suspicion on their runs scored per game ranking (sixth in the AL). On the park-adjusted measure they ranked ninth. They won 4% more of their home games than their road games, scoring 68 more runs and letting up 59 more than they did on the road — none of which was out of the ordinary. This is another team that was very near the league median in offensive production. To be consistent, they too are not included among the truly weak offensive teams.

That makes eight below-average offensive teams that participated in the playoffs from 1993 to 2003: 1996 Braves, Rangers, and Yankees, 1997 Marlins, 1999 Red Sox, 2001 Braves, 2002 A's, and the 2003 Cubs. That seems a large number considering that there were only 10 weak offensive playoff participants from 1945 to 1992. To better assess how large that number is, and to test whether above-average pitching remains more indispensable than above-average offensive production for a playoff team, Table 4.13 presents data on average runs allowed at home and on the road and the home-road winning percentage differential for all teams that were above the league median in park-adjusted runs allowed. As was the case with runs scored, some teams appear to be weak pitching teams because of a combination of the way the adjusted runs allowed statistic is constructed, their ballpark, or their uneven home-road performance.

For example, both the 1998 Cubs and the 2003 Red Sox played in home ballparks that favored hitters and had much higher winning percentages at home than on the road. Their small ballparks make it hard to detect that they pitched well at home. The Cubs, for example, allowed only four more runs in their home than their road games, and because of the one-game playoff against the Giants at Wrigley Field to determine the wild-card entrant to the playoffs, they played one more home than road game. Thus, they actually allowed fewer runs per game at home than on the road. Similarly, the 2003 Red Sox allowed fewer runs at Fenway Park than on the road (395 versus 414). In both cases, relatively strong pitching in their home games was substantially responsible for their large home versus road winning percentage differential, and neither was therefore a weak pitching team.

In two other cases, teams played much better at home than on the road, and their pitcher-friendly home ballparks help reflect their superior home pitching performance. The 2003 Florida Marlins allowed 293 runs in their homes games, 399 away. They ranked second in the NL in fewest runs allowed per game at home, and they won over 18% more of their home than road games. The 2000 Giants gave up 306 runs at home, 441 on the road, and they won 16% more home than road games. They also ranked first in the NL with the fewest runs allowed per game at home. Both teams simply played and pitched much better in their home games, and although their pitchers were aided by a friendly home ballpark, neither was a weak pitching team.

4—Pitching Quality on Championship Teams

In four other cases, teams played at least as well on the road as at home, which is uncommon and could have had an impact on their runs allowed rankings. For example, the 1997 and 2001 Cleveland Indians played in offense-friendly Jacobs Field, and let up over five runs per home game. They won only 2% more of their home than road games in 1997, and won 2% *less* home than road games in 2003. The combination of a hitter-friendly home ballpark and relatively weak home performance should make the park-adjusted runs allowed statistics more meaningful for those Indians teams. And yet they also ranked below the league median in park-adjusted runs allowed (10th in both years). These were simply below-average pitching teams.

Like the 2001 Indians, the 1996 Orioles had a slightly higher road winning percentage, although they differ in that they played in a park that favored pitchers slightly. Despite winning a higher share on the road, they let up 5.7 runs per road game, the highest runs allowed per game figure listed in Table 4.13. In park-adjusted runs per game they ranked 12th in the AL. Their strange home-road winning percentage differential is more attributable to offense than defense. At home they scored 438 runs and let up 441, and yet were lucky enough to win 53% of their games (43–38). On the road, they scored much more (511 runs), while letting up only a bit more than at home (462 runs). One would have expected their road winning percentage to have been roughly what it was (45–36, .556 winning percentage). Although the home winning percentage is higher than would be expected, it is not attributable to uneven home-road pitching performance, and thus the adjusted figures are probably an accurate reflection that this was a weak pitching team. In addition, in a park that favored pitchers slightly, they ranked only seventh in the AL in unadjusted runs per game, just above the median. It seems safe to conclude that this was a below-average pitching team.

The final team to play at least as well on the road as at home was the 1997 Mariners. Playing in a park that favored neither hitters nor pitchers much, they ranked below the league median on both measures of runs allowed. They let up over five runs per game both at home and on the road, one of only three teams in Table 4.13 to do so. They could easily be classified as a weak pitching team, and yet a closer look at their statistics makes the assessment more complicated. Their main three starting pitchers posted the following numbers: Randy Johnson, 20–4, 2.28 ERA; Jamie Moyer, 17–5, 3.86 ERA; and Jeff Fassero, 16–9, 3.61 ERA. And yet their team ERA was a pretty wretched 4.79, 11th in the AL. Although they did have some trouble finding a fourth starter, the real problem was their bullpen. Consider Norm Charlton's 1997 statistics: 71 games, 69 innings pitched, 3–8 record, 7.27 ERA, 14 saves. He was their closer for much of the year and he had a 7.27 ERA! The calculations here mix the Mariners' strong starting pitching with their atrocious relief. Since most of the arguments presented to this point and in the next chapter about competitive balance and pitching concern starters (namely that they display highly variable perform-

Table 4.13 — Playoff Teams 1993–2003 That Allowed More Runs Than Average (in Park-Adjusted Runs Allowed Per Game) Home-Away Differentials: Winning Percentage, Runs Allowed Per Game

Team	Runs Allowed Per Game (Home)	Runs Allowed Per Game (Away)	Winning Percentage Differential (Home-Away)
'93 Philadelphia Phillies (99)**	4.58	4.56	8.6%
'96 Baltimore Orioles (98)	5.38	5.70	-2.5%
'97 Seattle Mariners* (99)	5.21	5.07	0.0%
'97 Cleveland Indians (103)	5.02	5.10	1.8%
'97 San Francisco Giants* (92)	4.78	5.01	7.4%
'98 Chicago Cubs* (103)	4.85	4.86	14.1%
'00 Oakland A's (96)	4.67	5.44	3.0%
'00 San Francisco Giants (98)	3.78	5.44	16.0%
'01 Cleveland Indians* (101)	5.20	4.94	-2.3%
'03 Boston Red Sox* (104)	4.88	5.11	13.5%
'03 Florida Marlins (94)	3.62	4.93	18.5%

*indicates above league median on both runs allowed per game and park-adjusted runs allowed per game. **Park adjustment factors are in parentheses. Figures over 100 indicate that the ballpark favored hitters.

ance from year to year, and by design pitch only every fourth or fifth day), it can be said that the Mariners weren't a weak pitching team. In any event, the conclusions of this analysis are not greatly affected by their inclusion or exclusion among the weak pitching playoff participants.

Finally, there are three remaining teams in Table 4.13 that had typical home-road differentials in winning percentage. Only one is easily classified as a weak pitching team, the 1997 Giants. Despite playing in a home ballpark that favored pitchers, they ranked well below the league median (11th) in runs allowed per game. They also ranked 11th in park-adjusted runs allowed per game. Looking at their splits, it is a wonder that they made the playoffs. On the road they scored 407 runs, gave up 406, and were a little lucky to end up with 42–39 record (.519). At home, in a ballpark that favored pitchers more than any other listed in Table 4.13, they let up 387 runs, almost as many as on the road. They also scored *fewer* runs than they let up at home (377), but remarkably ended up with a 48–33 record (.593). They were just incredibly lucky, and they were not a good pitching team.

The final two cases are close calls, but neither was a bad pitching team. The 2000 Oakland A's played in a pitcher's park, and thus one might be skeptical of their runs allowed per game figures. In unadjusted runs they ranked fourth in the AL, and they had the third lowest team ERA. By contrast, they were ninth in park-adjusted runs allowed. However, it is unfair to conclude that the park-adjusted figure is the more valid one without first considering their splits. On the road, they scored 481 runs and let up 435, and their .550 winning percentage (44–36) was a little better than expected. At home, they scored almost the same number of runs (466) as on the road, but they let up far fewer (378). Their home record (47–34, .580 winning percentage) was probably a little worse than expected given their runs scored and allowed. So, although their home winning percentage did not reflect it, they played and pitched much better at home than on the road. Thus, their unadjusted runs allowed per game and their ERA were valid indications that this was not a weak pitching team.

Finally, the 1993 Philadelphia Phillies had a typical home-road winning percentage differential, played in a park that favored neither hitters nor pitchers, and let up almost the same runs per game at home and away. They ranked fourth (the median) in a seven-team division in runs allowed per game, giving up just .006 more than the third-ranked Cubs. They ranked just below the median (fifth) in park-adjusted runs allowed per game, giving up only .007 runs per game more than the fourth-ranked Mets. They were also the sixth-ranked team of 14 in the NL in ERA. Looking at all of the information, they were the median pitching team in the NL, or maybe a bit better. Therefore, like the other teams ranked at the league (or division) median, the 1993 Phillies should not be classified as a weak pitching team.

That makes four truly weak pitching teams that appeared in the playoffs from 1993 to 2003: 1997 and 2001 Indians, 1997 Giants, and 1996 Orioles. That is half as many as the number of weak-hitting playoff participants that appeared during the same period. In that sense, above-average pitching can still be viewed as more indispensable than above-average hitting on a playoff-caliber ball club. Still, from 1969 to 1992 only one team won a division title that had below-average pitching. It is clear that a more expansive playoff format is permitting some weak pitching teams to enter the playoffs.

It is highly likely that none of the four weak pitching teams would have made the playoffs under the old playoff format. There is some speculation involved here, because it is difficult to know for sure how MLB would have organized the divisions after expansion, but it seems highly likely that the 1997 Indians would have lost the AL East to the Orioles (98–64), the 2001 Indians would have lost to the Yankees (95–65), and the 1997 Giants would have lost the NL West to the Braves (101–61). The 1996 Orioles were a wild-card team that would have finished behind both the Indians and Yankees in the old AL East. By contrast, four of the weak-hitting playoff participants from 1993–2003 would have won their division under the old playoff format (1996 Braves in NL West, 1996 Rangers in the AL West, 1998 Cubs in the AL East, and 2002 A's in the AL West). So, had we been using the old playoff format, the pre-1993 result would continue to hold — weak pitching teams still wouldn't have won any divisional titles, while some weak hitting teams would have.

And again, none of the four weak pitching teams won the World Series, although the 1997 Indians won the ALCS and came awfully close to winning the World Series, while the 1996 Orioles made it to the ALCS. As noted, however, two weak hitting teams have won the World Series since 1992 (the 1996 Yankees and 1997 Marlins). The bottom line is that, when you look at them closely, the lists in Tables 5.11–13 indicate that, despite being in an era of high offensive production, it remains more likely that a team must be strong relative to its league in pitching rather than in hitting to win any sort of meaningful title.

Conclusion

The basic argument is that above-average pitching is necessary but not sufficient in order to have a championship team, and, as demonstrated in the next chapter, pitching performance varies substantially from year to year. By contrast, above-average offensive production is neither necessary nor sufficient on a championship team, and hitting performance tends to be more stable from year to year. Because pitching, especially starting pitching, is more necessary and more variable than hitting, there is greater competitive balance in baseball than in other sports. In basketball, the most dominant player, say Michael Jordan or Kobe Bryant, plays every night, and team winning percentages are widely dispersed. In baseball, the most important player, say Pedro Martinez, Randy Johnson, or Roger Clemens, takes the hill every fourth or fifth day, and team winning percentages are much more compressed. Moreover, as demonstrated in the previous chapter, the draft has evolved into a reliable method for the equitable distribution of young pitching talent. Taken together, these results should offer some solace to fans that worry that their team will never be able to compete.

5
Pitching Variability

Heading into every season in the mid– to late 1990s, the Braves looked poised to become (or repeat as) champions in the National League and maybe the World Series as well. Theirs was a dynasty predicated on pitching excellence. How then can one possibly argue that pitching variability is a primary contributor to competitive balance in baseball? The short answer is that dominant, consistent staffs like the Braves' are quite rare, especially since the Marvin Miller Era. Dominance generally requires two or three of a team's pitchers to be among the best in the league. The data indicate that having three top pitchers on one team in any one year is difficult to do, to say nothing of doing it over a number of years.

PITCHING QUALITY ON DOMINANT TEAMS

Pitching performance and consistency since World War II is assessed by selecting those pitchers who finished in the top 25% of their league in wins in each year. Wins are, of course, a flawed measure of pitching performance because they are so heavily influenced by run support and defense. Here, however, the goal is to measure pitching consistency. To bias the analysis against the conclusion that pitching is highly variable, one of the key arguments in the book, wins is likely preferred to other measures because hitting and defense are relatively less variable. If pitching performance is found to be highly variable based on wins, therefore, it is likely to be even more so for other measures. After the main results are presented, more discussion and analysis is offered on why wins is a reasonable measure of pitching performance. In addition, similar qualitative results are derived regarding the relative consistency of pitchers versus hitters for alternative pitching measures such as ERA and WHIP (walks plus hits allowed per inning pitched).

The number of teams in each league is multiplied by five to determine the number of pitchers eligible to be among the leaders in wins at the beginning of a season. Although the five-man starting rotation is a relatively recent innovation, it seemed reasonable to assume that at the outset of a season there were probably five pitchers on each team who had a shot at winning a high number of games. So, for example, in 1950, when there were eight teams in the American League, the eligible pitching pool was 40. Any pitcher that finished in the top 10 in wins in 1950 was, therefore, included in the database. In those instances in which pitchers tied for the last spot among the leaders, the one with the lower earned run average is included in the database.

Before discussing the wins data, note that the last column in tables 5.1 and 5.2 provides data on the number of teams with winning percentages of .600 or better, and their share of the total teams in each league. This is the flip side of the data presented in the Introduction on sub–.400 teams. As in the case of sub–.400 teams, teams with .600 winning percentages have become rarer over time. In the American League (Table 5.2), the share declined from 17.6% in the Mantle Era, to 8.2% in the Aaron Era, to 8.1% in the Miller Era, and 7.8% in the recent era. In the National League (Table 5.1), the share was 13.7% in the Mantle Era, 7.2% in the Aaron Era, 5.0% in the Miller Era, and 8.4% in the recent era. The biggest drop in both leagues occurred after the Mantle Era, and the introduction of the amateur draft. Combining the data from both leagues, the shares were 15.6% for the Mantle era, 7.7%, 6.7%, and 8.1% for the Aaron, Miller, and recent eras, respectively. Although the share has crept up slightly in the recent era, it would be difficult to use those data to argue that competition has grown unbalanced.

The "top 25%" data demonstrate clearly that dominant teams often require at least three pitchers among the leaders in wins (Tables 5.1, 5.2). Among the 124 teams with winning percentages over .600 between 1945 and 2003, only 12 have had one or fewer pitchers among the league leaders in wins.[1] Can a championship team get by with only two pitchers among the league victory leaders? The National League data (Table 5.1) indicate that, with the exception of the Aaron Era, .600 teams were at least as likely to have three or more pitchers among the leaders in victories than they were to have two or fewer. For example, in both the Mantle and the recent eras, half of the dominant teams had three or more pitchers in the top 25%. In the Marvin Miller Era, six of nine had more than two pitchers among the leaders. The 1986 Mets, moreover, had five pitchers among the top 13 in victories—Dwight Gooden 17–6, Ron Darling 15–6, Bob Ojeda 18–5, Sid Fernandez 16–6, and Roger McDowell 14–9.

The Aaron Era is somewhat different; nine of 12 dominant teams in the NL had two or fewer pitchers among the league leaders in victories. Cincinnati's Big Red Machine teams (1972–76) make up five of the nine one- or two-pitcher teams. These were strange teams (Table 5.3). They never had a pitcher that won 20 games—Jack Billingham won 19 in 1973 and 1974. They also never had a year in which fewer than four pitchers had double-digit victories. In a typical year, five or six had at least 10 victories. In 1974, for example, they were an exceptionally balanced staff (Billingham 19–11, Don Gullett 17–11, Clay Kirby 12–9, Fred Norman 13–12, Pedro Borbon 10–7, and Clay Carroll 12–5). Although relatively few of their pitchers finished among the victory leaders, the Reds' balance and durability were remarkable during this span. Jack Billingham and

Table 5.1 — National League Teams with Winning Percentages over .600 (1945–2003) Categorized by Number of Pitchers in Top 25% in Wins

Era	Number of Pitchers in Top 25% of Wins						Total Teams
	(0)	(1)	(2)	(3)	(4)	(5)	
Mantle Era (45–62)	0	3	7	9	1	0	20 (13.7%)
Aaron Era (63–76)	0	2	7	3	0	0	12 (7.2%)
Miller Era (77–92)	0	1	2	5	0	1	9 (5.0%)
Recent Era (93–03)	0	1	6	4	2	1	14 (8.4%)
Total Teams	0	7	22	21	3	2	55

Note: The figures in parentheses in the last column reflect the percentage of teams that played during that era that had a winning percentage of at least .600.

Table 5.2 — American League Teams with Winning Percentages over .600 (1945–2003) Categorized by Number of Pitchers in Top 25% in Wins

Era	Number of Pitchers in Top 25% of Wins						Total Teams
	(0)	(1)	(2)	(3)	(4)	(5)	
Mantle Era (45–62)	0	2	9	13	2	0	26 (17.6%)
Aaron Era (63–76)	0	1	8	4	1	0	14 (8.2%)
Miller Era (77–92)	0	1	4	10	2	0	18 (8.1%)
Recent Era (93–03)	0	1	2	7	2	0	12 (7.8%)
Total Teams	0	5	23	34	7	0	69

Note: The figures in parentheses in the last column reflect the percentage of teams that played during that era that had a winning percentage of at least .600.

Don Gullett were a combined 147–89 from 1972 to 1976. With the exception of Gullett's 1972 record (9–10), neither had fewer than 11 wins or a losing record in those five years. Neither pitched fewer than 124 innings per campaign; they each averaged over 175 — 222 for Billingham, 178 for Gullett.

They had solid relief help from Pedro Borbon and Clay Carroll. Borbon posted a 42–22 record, never appeared in fewer than 62 games in a season, never pitched fewer than 121 innings, and never had an ERA above 3.35. From 1972 to 1975 (he went to the White Sox in '76), Carroll posted a 33–22 record, never appeared in fewer than 53 games, pitched fewer than 90 innings, or had an ERA above 3.69. His '72, '74, and '75 ERAs were 2.25, 2.14, and 2.95, respectively. When Gary Nolan was healthy ('72, '75–'76), he was outstanding: a 45–23

Table 5.3 — The Big Red Pitching Machine

	1972	1973	1974	1975	1976
Jack Billingham	12–12 218 IP 3.18 ERA	19–10 293 IP 3.04 ERA	19–11 212 IP 3.95 ERA	15–10 208 IP 4.11 ERA	12–10 177 IP 4.32 ERA
Don Gullett	9–10 135 IP 3.94 ERA	18–8 228 IP 3.51 ERA	17–11 243 IP 3.04 ERA	15–4 160 IP 2.42 ERA	11–3 124 IP 3.00 ERA
Pedro Borbon	8–3 122 IP 3.17 ERA	11–4 121 IP 2.15 ERA	10–7 139 IP 3.24 ERA	9–5 125 IP 2.95 ERA	4–3 121 IP 3.35 ERA
Clay Carroll	6–4 96 IP 2.25 ERA	8–8 93 IP 3.69 ERA	12–5 101 IP 2.14 ERA	7–5 96 IP 2.95 ERA	
Gary Nolan	15–5 176 IP 1.99 ERA	0–1 10 IP 3.48 ERA	DNP	15–9 211 IP 2.63 ERA	15–9 239 IP 3.46 ERA
Ross Grimsley	14–8 198 IP 3.05 ERA	13–10 242 IP 3.23 ERA			
Fred Norman		12–6 166 IP 3.30 ERA	13–12 186 IP 3.15 ERA	12–4 188 IP 3.73 ERA	12–7 180 IP 3.10 ERA
Clay Kirby			12–9 231 IP 3.27 ERA	10–6 111 IP 4.70 ERA	

record, no fewer than 175 innings in any year, and ERAs of 1.99, 2.63, and 3.46, respectively. Ross Grimsley or Fred Norman provided a capable fourth starter — Grimsley at the beginning of the period ('72-'73), Norman at the end ('73-'76). Out of that fourth slot, the Reds received at least 12 wins and 180 innings in each year. The combined Grimsley-Norman record was 76–47.

To argue that the Big Red Machine was a dynasty predicated on pitching might oversell the point a bit, but not by much. In 1977, when the Reds won fewer than 90 games for the first time since 1971, their bats were still dangerous. George Foster led the league in home runs (52) and in RBI (149). Foster, Dan Driessen, Pete Rose, and Ken Griffey all hit over .300. Joe Morgan (.288 BA, 22 HR, 78 RBI) and Johnny Bench (.275 BA, 31 HR, 109 RBI) had good years. As a result, the Reds ranked second in runs scored (behind the Phillies). Their pitching, however, slumped. The acquisition of Tom Seaver helped stem the decline, as he went 14–3 with a 2.34 ERA in 20 games. Fred Norman continued his steady performance, going 14–13 in 35 games and 221 innings pitched with an ERA of 3.38. The rest of the staff simply fell apart. Billingham went 10–10 with a 5.22 ERA. Gullett left the team for the Yankees (14–4, 3.89 ERA). Gary Nolan split his time with the Reds and Angels compiling a 4–4 record and a 6.16 ERA; he retired at the end of the year. Gullett's and Nolan's innings were picked up largely by the unremarkable Paul Moskau (6–6, 4.00 ERA, 108 IP) and Doug Capilla (7–8, 4.23 ERA, 106 IP). Within one year, the Reds lost production from three of their workhorses— Billingham, Gullett, and Nolan — and they finished 10 games behind the Dodgers.

The point behind this digression on the Reds (aside from pointing out that this wasn't some recreational softball team that won its games by outslugging opponents 15 to 14) is to indicate that the dominant National League teams of the Aaron Era, who, for the most part, had only a couple of pitchers among league victory leaders, had very balanced pitching staffs. As will be shown, this sort of balance is difficult to achieve and almost impossible to sustain.

Dominant American League teams exhibited similar pitching balance and, perhaps, greater durability than their National League counterparts (Table 5.2). Only five of the 69 AL teams with winning percentages over .600 had fewer than two pitchers among the league leaders in victories— none had less than one. The "one-pitcher" teams were, again, more balanced than these statistics suggest.

For example, the Yankees teams of '57 and '60 are quite similar to the Big Red Machine teams in balance if not durability. The '57 team had six pitchers with 10 or more victories, no pitcher with more than 16 — Tom Sturdivant (16–6, 2.54 ERA), Bob Turley (13–6, 2.71 ERA), Bobby Shantz (11–5, 2.45 ERA), Don Larsen (10–4, 3.74 ERA), Whitey Ford (11–5, 2.57 ERA), and Bob Grim (12–8, 2.63 ERA). The next year only Turley and Ford achieved double-digit victories, and the Yankees' winning percentage fell below .600. In 1959, Ford was the only one among the '57 group that achieved double-digit victories; and the Yanks finished third in the AL posting a 79–75 record.

Like the dominant teams of the National League, the majority in the American League had at least three pitchers in the top 25% in victories. Fifteen of the 26 teams of the Mantle Era had at least three; the same for 12 of the 17 teams in the Marvin Miller Era, and nine of the 12 teams from the recent era. Curiously, the Aaron Era is again different. Nine of its 14 dominant teams had only one or two pitchers among the victory leaders.[2] With the exception of the 1964 Yankees, however, each of those teams had at least four pitchers with 10 or more wins.

Although they may have had a little more star power in Vida Blue and Catfish Hunter, the '71, '72, and '75 A's teams— three of the nine one- or two-pitcher teams in the AL — are similar to the balanced Reds teams. The 1972 staff was typical: Blue, 24–9, 1.82 ERA; Hunter, 21–11, 2.96 ERA; Chuck Dobson, 15–5, 3.81 ERA; Diego Segui, 10–8, 3.14 ERA; and John "Blue Moon" Odom, 10–12, 4.28 ERA. Dependable relief pitching came from Rollie Fingers (4–6, 17 saves, 3.00 ERA), Bob Locker (7–2, 6 saves, 2.88 ERA), and Darold Knowles (5–2, 7 saves, 3.59 ERA). Despite having only a couple of pitchers among league leaders in victories, these too were balanced pitching corps.

PITCHING CONSISTENCY ON DOMINANT TEAMS

If one is concerned about competitive balance, the victory leader statistics provide some comfort. Dominant teams must have balanced pitching staffs, which in any given year often requires some of their pitchers to perform above expectations. To achieve such balance in one year is difficult; to sustain it over a number of years is exceedingly rare. The list of teams that (1) had a .600 winning percentage, (2) had three or more pitchers in the top 25% in wins, and (3) had at least three of those pitchers appear among the league victory leaders the year before, demonstrates just how rare (Table 5.4). Included are some of the great staffs of all time. The Indians of the early '50s appear three times ('51, '52, and '54). The 1954 staff was, perhaps, the best with Early Wynn (23–11, 2.73 ERA), Mike Garcia (19–8, 2.64 ERA), Bob Lemon (23–7, 2.72 ERA), Art Houtteman (15–7, 3.35 ERA), and Bob Feller (13–3, 3.09 ERA) who was in the twilight of his career. Also on the list are two of the outstanding Orioles teams of the early '70s. The 1971 team is, of course, the only team with four 20-game winners—Mike Cuellar (20–9, 3.08 ERA), Jim Palmer (20–9, 2.68 ERA), Pat Dobson (20–8, 2.90 ERA), and Dave McNally (21–5, 2.89 ERA).

Table 5.4 — Teams with .600 Winning Percentage, Three or More Pitchers in Top 25% in Wins, at Least Three of Whom Appeared Among League Leaders in Wins in Prior Year

Team	Pitchers in Top 25%	Percent of Those Pitchers Among League Leaders in Prior Year
'51 Indians	4	75%
'51 Yankees	3	100
'52 Indians	3	100
'54 Indians	3	100
'57 Braves	3	100
'62 Reds	3	100
'70 Orioles	3	100
'71 Orioles	4	75
'74 Dodgers	3	100
'89 A's	4	75
'93 Braves	4	75
'97 Braves	4	100
'98 Braves	4	75
'99 Braves	3	100
'02 A's	3	100

The most appearances are for the Braves teams of the 1990s. To illustrate how remarkable their accomplishments were, only three pitchers—Tom Glavine, Greg Maddux, and Andy Pettitte—finished among the top 25% in

5 — Pitching Variability

The 1971 Orioles are the only team with four 20-game winners — (left to right) Mike Cuellar 20–9 (3.08 ERA), Pat Dobson 20–8 (2.90 ERA), Dave McNally 21–5 (2.89 ERA), and Jim Palmer 20–9 (2.68 ERA). They were also one of only 15 teams since World War II to (1) have a .600 winning percentage, (2) have three or more pitchers in the top 25% of their league in wins, and (3) have at least three of those pitchers appear among the league victory leaders the year before.

wins in all six seasons from 1995 to 2000. Three others made the list five times, Kevin Brown, Pedro Martinez, and Charles Nagy. Ten pitchers made it four times, including Roger Clemens, Randy Johnson, Mike Mussina, and David Wells. Those are pretty dominant pitchers (and two are first-ballot Hall of Famers), and they made the top 25% in only four of six years. To repeat, only 16 pitchers made the list at least four times in those six years. When you consider that those 16 consistent winners had to be shared among 28–30 teams, there's just not a lot to go around.

Consistent winners are rare and yet the Braves had two of the three that made the list every year from 1995 to 2000. This is a big part of what makes the Braves one of the very best pitching staffs in major league history and why the Braves won their division in each of those years. From 1945 to 1992, only 10 teams satisfied the three criteria for inclusion in Table 5.4. Yet the Braves made the list four times in an eight-year span. And it's not just because of Glavine and Maddux. John Smoltz was among the top 25% in wins in four of six years from 1995 to 2000, and he won a Cy Young Award. In 1998, the Braves had a .654 winning percentage and *five* pitchers in the top 25% in wins. Glavine, Smoltz, and Maddux each had 17 or more wins. Kevin Millwood also had 17 and Denny Neagle chipped in 16.

The Braves do not, however, undercut the arguments presented here about parity and pitching variability. No other team from the 1990s appears on the list. The Braves are unique and therefore not reflective of any general trend. The Oakland A's staff of 2003 does make the list, but only time will tell whether Tim Hudson, Mark Mulder, and Barry Zito will have continued success, and whether they will remain together in Oakland. Given the A's limited financial resources, it seems unlikely that they will.

The other six teams on the list may not be quite as storied as the Atlanta Braves, Orioles and Indians staffs, but they're no slouches either. The 1957 Milwaukee Braves were led by three solid pitchers—Warren Spahn (21–11, 2.69 ERA), Lew Burdette (17–8, 3.72 ERA), and Bob Buhl (18–7, 2.74 ERA). Spahn's consistency is legendary, but Buhl and Burdette were also remarkably consistent in the '50s. From 1956 to 1960 Buhl compiled a 72–35 record, averaged 14.4 victories per year, and never had a winning percentage below .640 or an ERA above 3.45. Burdette was good over a longer period—from 1953 to 1961 he had a 157–95 record, an average yearly winning percentage of .628, and an average of 17.4 wins per year.

The 1951 Yankees team had three starting pitchers—Vic Raschi, Allie Reynolds, and Eddie Lopat—who were consistently good throughout the late '40s and early '50s. Raschi won 19 games in 1948, and 20 or more in '49, '50, and '51. From 1947 to 1952, Reynolds never won fewer than 16; his average record during that span was 18–8. Lopat went 87–51 from 1946 to 1951, never had fewer than 15 wins, and only once had a winning percentage below .600. They also received fine relief pitching from Joe Page, especially from 1946 to 1948 when he compiled 60 saves and a 34–24 record. Halberstam's *Summer of '49* makes it clear that these guys were a very tough staff, good enough to get past the Red Sox teams of Ted Williams, Dom DiMaggio, Johnny Pesky, and Bobby Doerr.

The 1962 Reds are the biggest surprise on the list. They had a solid, balanced staff led by Joey Jay (21–14, 3.76 ERA), Bob Purkey (23–5, 2.81 ERA), and Jim O'Toole (16–13, 3.50 ERA). In 1961, all three won more than 16 games, none had an ERA over 3.76, and the Reds went 93–61 to win the National League, only to lose the World Series to the Yankees in five games. A nice staff, but not exactly a bunch of Hall of Famers. Probably no simple statistical test will perfectly identify the best staffs of all time. By contrast, the 1974 Dodgers did have at least one Hall of Famer, if not a first-ballot nominee, in Don Sutton. They also had Tommy John, whose 288–231 lifetime record merited some consideration by those submitting ballots. They had a 20-game winner in Andy Messersmith, who was a fine pitcher until his arm blew out (130–99, lifetime record).[3] Mike Marshall provided superb relief help (15–12, 106 appearances, 208 innings pitched, 21 saves, 2.42 ERA), a young Doug Rau (13–11, 3.73 ERA), an aging Al Downing, and the ageless Charlie Hough rounded out the staff. Admittedly, few fans would rate the 1974 Dodgers among the top pitching staffs since World War II, but closer inspection indicates that they belong.

The 1989 A's are another staff that, at first glance, might not appear to belong among the very best. They were, however, quite dominant: four pitchers with at least 17 wins—Dave Stewart 21-9 (3.32 ERA), Mike Moore 19-11 (2.61 ERA), Bob Welch 17-8 (3.00 ERA), and Storm Davis 19-7 (4.36 ERA)— a 99–63 a record, and a four-game sweep of the Giants in the World Series. The year before, Stewart, Welch, and Davis had also appeared among the league leaders in victories. From 1990 to 1992, the A's won the division twice, and Stewart, Welch, and Moore appeared among league victory leaders often, each winning at least 10 games per year. Throw in Dennis Eckersly's masterful relief, and you have quite a staff. Why don't most fans remember them as such? Probably because of their upset losses in the World Series, to the Dodgers in '88 and the Reds in '90, and their AL Championship loss to the Blue Jays in '92. Had they won one additional World Series, they would probably be remembered differently. They were, however, among the most durable, talented pitching staffs of the post-war era.

The experiences of the great Braves, A's, Orioles, and Indians staffs suggest it unlikely that the league will be dominated by one team for an extended period. The Braves, A's and Indians won only one World Series each, and, although the Orioles won in both 1966 and 1970, only Jim Palmer and Dave McNally were mainstays of both staffs. So even the most durable and brilliant staffs haven't dominated baseball, at least not for more than a handful of years. Someone leaves for more money, someone gets hurt, someone has an off year and the staff begins slipping. The data on pitching variability that follow further underscore that point. From year to year a pitcher's performance, even a great one, is highly variable — probably as much as for any other type of professional athlete. Perhaps it's the physical toll that pitching exacts, or the mental strain that comes from being the focal point of the game. Whatever it is, pitching performance varies.[4]

YEAR-TO-YEAR VARIABILITY IN PITCHING PERFORMANCE

In any given year, only about 40% of the pitchers that appear among the top 25% in victories were also among the leaders in the prior year. In the National League there was no year from 1945 to 2003 in which more than 67%

of the pitchers on the victory leaders list appeared the year before; the lowest recurrence rate for any year was 20%. Similarly, in the American League, there was no year in which more than 70% of the pitchers repeated; as few as 15% repeated (in 1961). In the vast majority of years, 25%-50% of the top 25% in wins appeared on that list the year before (Table 5.5).

Table 5.5 — Percent of Pitchers Among League Victory Leaders Who Also Appeared in Prior Year, 1945–2003

Reappearance Rate	American League (Number of Years)	National League (Number of Years)
0–25%	2	3
26–50%	45	41
51–75%	12	15
76–100%	0	0

The names on that 1961 AL list are illustrative of the surprises on a typical victory leaders list. The two pitchers that appeared in the prior year were Chuck Estrada and Frank Lary. Among those that hadn't appeared in 1960, two were bona fide stars coming off bad years (Whitey Ford and Jim Bunning). The rest of the list included Steve Barber, Ralph Terry, Luis Arroyo, Don Mossi, Mudcat Grant, Don Schwall, Camilo Pascual, Bill Stafford, and Juan Pizarro. There were some decent pitchers on the list but no real stars— Barber, Grant, Lary, Mossi, Grant, and Pizarro all had lifetime winning percentages over .500 and won between 100 and 150 games; Pascual was 174–170 lifetime. Estrada, Schwall, and Stafford were relative flashes in the pan; none won more than 50 games in his career.[5]

For fans more comfortable with a recent example, only five of the 18 pitchers on the 2001 AL list also made the victory leaders list in 2000. They included Roger Clemens, Bartolo Colon, Andy Pettitte, and Aaron Sele, who had all appeared multiple times in the 1990s, and Tim Hudson, who was making just his second appearance. The nonrepeaters included four pitchers returning to the list after missing it in 2000: Jamie Moyer, Mike Mussina, Freddy Garcia, and Brad Radke. The remaining nine positions were taken by pitchers making their first appearance among the victory leaders. Some were rookies (or close to it), including Mark Mulder, Joe Mays, C.C. Sabathia, Barry Zito, and Mark Buehrle. Two others had been in the major leagues for a handful of years, namely Eric Milton in his fourth season and Cory Lidle in his fifth. The last two slots were filled by Steve Sparks, who had been in the majors since 1995, and Paul Abbott who was a rookie in 1990. Both the 1961 and 2001 AL lists underscore the hit-or-miss flavor of the victory leaders list in many years.

On teams that had winning percentages over .600, and had at least three pitchers among the league leaders in victories (top 25%), roughly half of these pitchers (51.2%) had not appeared among the victory leaders in the prior year.

Pitching success, even for the most dominant teams, is difficult to predict. On average, a team needs a pleasant surprise from one or two pitchers to achieve a .600 record. Even among great teams, the Garcia-Lemon-Feller-Wynn staffs are the exception, not the rule. Far more typical were the 1983 White Sox, whose winning percentage was .611. LaMarr Hoyt, at 19–15, had led the AL in victories in 1982, but neither Richard Dotson (11–15) nor Floyd Bannister (12–13, with Seattle) were particularly impressive in that year. However, in 1983 Bannister won 16, Dotson 22, and Hoyt 25.

Even the greatest pitchers find it difficult to remain among the league's elite year in and year out. From 1945 to 1992, only 19 pitchers appeared among the top 25% in victories at least 10 times (Table 5.6).[6] Seventy-one percent of their appearances on the victory leaders list were repeats; that is, the pitcher had also appeared the year before. Greg Maddux and Warren Spahn have the most impressive credentials on the list. Both appeared among victory leaders 16 times. Fifteen of Maddux's appearances were repeats, while 14 of Spahn's were. Maddux also appeared in an astounding 16 consecutive years, more than any other pitcher. By comparison, only nine of Tom Seaver's 14 appearances were repeats, and his longest consecutive streak was seven years. No pitcher other than Maddux appeared more than 12 times consecutively.

Table 5.6 — Pitching Consistency
Post–World War II Pitchers with at Least
10 Appearances Among Top 25% in Victories
(in alphabetical order)

Name	Appearances	Repeats	Longest Streak
Bert Blyleven	11	5	4 (84–87)
Steve Carlton	13	10	10 (74–83)
Roger Clemens	13	11	7 (86–92)
Whitey Ford	11	8	5 (61–65)
Tom Glavine	12	11	12 (91–02)
Fergie Jenkins	11	6	6 (67–72)
Greg Maddux	16	15	16 (88–03)
Dennis Martinez	11	6	5 (91–95)
Jack Morris	13	11	10 (79–88)
Mike Mussina	10	7	6 (92–97)
Phil Niekro	12	7	7 (74–80)
Jim Palmer	12	7	5 (69–73)
Gaylord Perry	12	9	10 (66–75)
Robin Roberts	10	7	8 (49–56)
Nolan Ryan	10	5	3 (72–74)
Tom Seaver	14	9	7 (67–73)
Warren Spahn	16	14	11 (53–63)
Don Sutton	15	11	10 (69–78)
Early Wynn	10	7	8 (50–57)

The list also contains mild surprises like Don Sutton and Jack Morris. Both had 10-year consecutive appearance streaks; only Maddux, Spahn, Tom Glavine, Gaylord Perry, and Steve Carlton did the same. Sutton ranks third in appearances with 15, Morris ties for fifth with 13. Along with Glavine, they tie for third in repeat appearances with 11.

Because Sutton had great difficulty making the Hall of Fame and Morris is still on the outside looking in, here is a quick sales pitch for each. Sutton had a 324–256 lifetime record, a .559 winning percentage, and a 3.26 ERA. As Bill James points out, in the minds of voters, Sutton had a minor flaw in that he never really had humongous years;[7] he won 21 games in 1976 and 19 a couple of times, but generally he kept chugging along at anywhere from 15 to 18 wins a year. While a manager loves a consistent winner like Sutton, the Baseball Writers of America prefer a little more flash in their Hall of Fame pitchers.[8] Hence, Nolan Ryan, he of the over 5,500 strikeouts and seven no-hitters, greased through the electoral process on the first ballot.[9] By contrast, Sutton had difficulty. He finally made it in 1998 on his fifth try. Had Sutton not made it in 1998, he probably would have had to wait at least until 2000, because Nolan Ryan's 1999 candidacy would have stolen votes from him. But Sutton was the better pitcher. Ryan was 319–287, had a .526 winning percentage, and a 3.17 ERA. True, Sutton played on somewhat better teams, but his career record is substantially superior to Ryan's. Their ERAs are essentially the same; and Sutton also struck out a few batters, 3,574 to be exact. The most notable difference, and the one that, perhaps, best explains the disparities in record, are Ryan's 2,755 walks as compared to Sutton's 1343.[10]

Morris had a 254–185 record, good for a .579 winning percentage, and a 3.90 ERA. Compare that with Don Drysdale: 209–166, .557 winning percentage, 2.95 ERA. Morris had three seasons with at least 20 victories, Drysdale had two. Both played on some good teams, yet Morris won 45 more games while compiling only 19 more losses. Drysdale's ERA was lower, but that's because he pitched his home games in Los Angeles while Morris pitched in hitters' parks like Tiger Stadium and the Metrodome. In the years that both Morris and Nolan Ryan were pitching (1979–92), Morris was by far the more dominant force. He had winning percentages over .500 in 12 of the 14 years, over .600 in eight of those years. He won at least 20 games three times and led the American League in victories twice. He won world titles wherever he went — Detroit, Minnesota, and Toronto. Ryan had winning percentages over .500 in 11 of the 14 years, over .600 in but five. In no year did he win 20 games or lead his league in victories. Ryan's '79 Angels and his '80 and '86 Astros played in the league championship series, but none advanced to the World Series. Had you polled general managers in each year from '79 to '92, an overwhelming majority likely would have wanted Morris on their teams before Ryan. Morris was clearly the better pitcher, probably the most dominant pitcher of the '80s, yet Nolan's longevity and blazing fastball have captured the fancy of fans and writers alike. Ryan went into

Warren Spahn was the most consistent winner of his day, finishing among the top 25% of National League pitchers in victories a remarkable 16 times. Only Greg Maddux rivals that level of consistency, with 17 appearances on the top 25% list from 1998 to 2004. In 2005, he missed the list with only 13 wins.

the hall with greater ease than either the still-waiting Morris or long-deferred Sutton. He shouldn't have, but he did.

Back to the business at hand. The average consecutive appearance streak is 7.9 years for the pitchers in Table 5.6. These are the aberrations—the most durable, successful pitchers since World War II—and they still tend to dominate baseball for less than a decade. The percent of repeat appearances figure (71%) also merits some discussion; it means that of their most productive years (in terms of wins), roughly one in three, was an improvement over the prior year. It does *not* mean that, on average, in more than two out of every three years, these guys appeared among the league leaders in victories. Table 5.6 considers only their very good years. Warren Spahn, for example, pitched as a regular for twenty years,[11] but appeared among the league leaders in victories in only 16 of those years. Steve Carlton pitched for 24 years, arguably 20 of them as a regular, and appeared 13 times among victory leaders. Nolan Ryan pitched in an astounding 27 seasons, had 20 or more appearances in 25 of them and was among the winningest pitchers only 10 times. On average, these pitchers spent closer to 50% of their careers among the league victory leaders.

The 71% repeat performance result indicates that, in the best years of their careers, even the most dominant pitchers of the postwar era experienced year-to-year variability. Whether it was due to injuries (as in the case of Palmer and Seaver) or hot and cold streaks (Ryan, Carlton, Blyleven), most managers had to worry a bit at the beginning of each season about how well his star pitcher would perform. By contrast, a manager probably had to worry somewhat less about his star position players. To illustrate, compare the most consistently dominant pitchers, Maddux and Spahn, with some of the best batsmen since 1945. From 1969 to 1983 Rod Carew appeared among the top 10 hitters in his league in batting average.[12] That's 15 straight years of batting averages over .300. Assuming that 10 players per team are eligible for the batting crown, there were about 125 batters that competed against Carew in any given year. He won the batting crown six times. He finished in the top five (or top 4%) 12 times,[13] eight consecutively. He finished in the top 12 (roughly the top 10%) in 13 consecutive seasons, 14 overall. In percentage terms, his 12 times in the top five in batting average would be akin to a pitcher finishing in the top two in victories for all the years during this span. Only Maddux and Spahn even come close to this, and no other pitcher compares with them. Spahn led his league in victories a remarkable eight times and finished second three times. In his other five appearances in the top 25%, he ranked no higher than third, just outside the top 5%. Spahn's longest streak of consecutive appearances among the top 5% was six (1956–1961), his longest streak among the top 10% was nine years (1953–1961). Maddux led the National League in victories three times, finished second twice and third twice. He finished in the top 5% in wins in eight of the 18 years in which he pitched (through 2003). His longest streak among the top 5% was four years (1997–2000), and his longest among the top 10% is his current streak of seven (1997–2003). The next best is Tom Seaver who finished first three times and second four times, a total of seven appearances in the top 5%. His longest consecutive appearance streak in the top two was but three years (1971–1973).

Whereas there are no pitchers similar to Spahn or Maddux, there are a number of hitters like Carew, some of them Carew's contemporaries. For example, Pete Rose hit over .300 in 15 of 17 years (1965–81), and won three National League batting crowns (1968, '69, and '72). Though his average was steady, his hit totals were even more impressive. He led the NL in hits seven times, finished second five times, and third once, and had at least 185 hits in every year from 1965 to 1981 except 1967 (he had 176) and 1981 (the strike-shortened season; he led the league with 140 hits). During that 17-year span, he never finished lower than ninth (top 8%) in hits; he finished out of the top five only three times. So, no pitcher since World War II except for Maddux has finished in the top 25% in victories for more than 12 consecutive years; Rose finished in the top 10% in hits for 17 consecutive years—in the top 5% for 14 consecutive years. And again Maddux's longest streak among the top 5% in victories was only four years.

Other Carew contemporaries put together at least 10 consecutive years in which they were well within the top 10% in hits or average: Wade Boggs batted over .300 in every year from 1982 to 1991, won batting titles in five of those years (four consecutive from 1985 to 1988), had over 180 hits in nine of those years, and over 200 in seven consecutive years. From 1964 to 1974, Lou Brock never had fewer than 180 hits, topping 200 four times, and 190 eight times. We could go on—Aaron, Clemente, and Mays all accomplished similar feats of sustained batting achievement. Going back further, Stan Musial and Ted Williams did the same. More recently, Kirby Puckett,[14] Edgar Martinez, and, of course, Tony Gwynn, each strung together multiple impressive seasons. Gwynn won the National League batting title in eight of the 16 years in which he had enough at-bats to be eligible. He batted over .300 an NL-record 18 straight years. In short, these data indicate that top hitting performance is easier to sustain than top pitching performance.

ARE WINS A LOUSY MEASURE OF PITCHING PERFORMANCE?

Some of you are still probably thinking that wins are a lousy indication of pitching performance. To a large extent, Rose's performance alone determined whether he'd be among the league leaders in hits. For his wins, Spahn needed run support from Aaron and Eddie Matthews, and excellent defense from the likes of Bill Bruton and Felix Mantilla. This could explain why great hitters appear to be more consistent than great pitchers, at least when pitching performance is measured by wins. However, if run support and defense are somewhat less variable than pitching performance, using wins as a measure of pitching success might overstate the level of pitching consistency.

To cite some examples of variability in the performance of the most consistent pitchers in Table 5.6 using earned run average, a more "clean" measure of pitching performance, in Spahn's nine-year run among the top 10% in victories (1953–1961), his ERA varied from a low of 2.10 in 1953 to a high of 3.50 in 1960. He led the league in ERA in 1953 and 1961, but he fell out of the top five in 1954 and 1960. His longest streak in the top 10% (fourth place or higher) was five years (1955–1959); he never put together two consecutive years in the top 5% (first or second place). Maddux has been a bit more consistent, finishing in the top five in ERA 10 times in his 18-year career including seven straight from 1992 to 1998. He also finished in the top two seven times, including a remarkable six consecutive appearances from 1993 to 1998.

Aside from Maddux, Sandy Koufax had the longest run among the top two in ERA. He won the National League ERA title an incredible five years in a row, 1962–1966; in three of those years his ERA was under 2.00. Koufax was a rarity. Only two other postwar pitchers—Roger Clemens and Maddux—have won as many as three ERA titles consecutively. Four others (Seaver, Ron Guidry, Randy Johnson, and Pedro Martinez) won two consecutive titles. Going back further, Cy Young, Christy Mathewson, Grover Cleveland Alexander, and Walter Johnson never won more than two consecutive ERA titles. Feller, Bob Gibson, Carlton, Ford, Palmer, and Ryan never won two in a row. To make yet another comparison with hitters, Carew won four consecutive batting titles (six of seven from 1972–78), Boggs and Gwynn also won four straight, and Musial won three straight. Ted Williams only won back-to-back titles—but he did it on three different occasions. Bill Madlock, Roberto Clemente, Tony Oliva, Tommy Davis, Pete Rose and Carl Yastrzemski won back-to-back titles. Pre–World War II, Ty Cobb won an amazing nine straight titles (12 of 13, from 1907 to 1918), Rogers Hornsby won six straight. Honus Wagner won four straight and seven of nine National League titles from 1903 to 1911.

For those who prefer some of the newer measures of pitching performance to ERA, conclusions regarding the relative consistency of pitchers and hitters are similar. For example, Greg Maddux ranked in the top five in WHIP (walks plus hits divided by innings pitched) 10 times in his career, including eight appearances in succession. He ranked in the top two eight times, including four times in a row from 1992 to 1995. These figures are remarkably similar to his ERA rankings. In short, because the goal was to demonstrate that top pitching performance is difficult to maintain, this analysis used wins—a less volatile measure than ERA—to bias the results against the desired conclusion. Had ERA or WHIP been selected, the consistency of hitters relative to pitchers would have been more pronounced.

In addition, the data indicate that wins aren't that bad a measure of pitching performance. On average, pitchers that win more games also tend to have lower ERAs (Table 5.7). Since World War II, the league leader in victories had an average ERA of 2.92. The fifth-place pitcher had an average ERA of 3.28; the 10th-place pitcher 3.49. The pattern becomes a bit less pronounced for places 11 through 15, but recall that when pitchers at the bottom of the list were tied in wins, the one with the lower ERA was selected for the victory leaders list. This introduces a downward bias in the ERA figures for those places. These general results also hold up when the data are broken down by era. It therefore seems safe to conclude that wins are a reasonably instructive measure of pitching performance. The next section examines whether pitching performance as measured by wins is becoming more variable over time. It if is, there is less reason to worry about competitive balance.

Table 5.7 — Average ERA of Victory Leaders Broken Down by Place, 1945–2003

Place (in Wins)	Average ERA
1st	2.92
2nd	3.05
3rd	3.04
4th	3.14
5th	3.28
6th	3.31
7th	3.34
8th	3.34
9th	3.36
10th	3.49
11th	3.46
12th	3.28
13th	3.38
14th	3.54
15th	3.44

ARE TODAY'S PITCHERS SOFT?

Greg Maddux could be an aberration. If the typical player today is so pampered that he is not motivated to produce Spahn-like consistency, one would expect additional variance in pitching performance, which could lead to more competitive balance. On the other hand, it seems unlikely that the best professional ballplayers now are any less dedicated or hungry than were their predecessors. Some players probably spend too much time on the disabled list, but for every one of those there's a Nolan Ryan, Cal Ripken, Tom Glavine, or Mike Mussina — guys who love(d) to play baseball, and who took (and take) off-season conditioning more seriously than the stars of yesteryear, which undoubtedly contributed to their remarkable consistency. True, today's players are paid obscene sums, which may cause complacency in some, but on average the improved training regimen of the modern star that large salaries permit probably more than makes up for any complacency born of a larger guaranteed salary.

Not everyone agrees that modern ballplayers have the same willingness to win that old-timers did. No less an authority than Mr. Consistency, Warren Spahn, held forth on the subject:

> We only had one year contracts in those days, so I'd go to spring training, knowing I had to earn my job every year. I never felt the security they have today and I didn't want it. I think I became a better pitcher without it. It kept me hungry.... It's that desire to be greater than the other guy that makes a person worth his salt,

whether he's a petroleum engineer or ballplayer or what, and I'm not sure the kids today have it the way we did. I'm not one of those guys who say everything was best in the old days. If there's a better way to do something, I want to learn it, but still, I'm not sure the kids now have the same dedication we did. We've gotten too lazy as a nation, too spoiled.[15]

It's clear that the recently deceased Spahn offered better curveballs than social commentary. Worker productivity, real gross domestic product, and the length of the work week have all been on the rise in this country. In short, his worries about national sloth are easily dismissed, but there may be some merit to his idea that the incentives faced by today's ballplayers could have an adverse impact on the game.

Note, however, that the list of the most consistent winners since World War II (Table 5.6) contained a number of pitchers from each of the four eras. From the Mantle Era there were Spahn, Roberts, Wynn, and Ford; from the Aaron Era, Perry, Niekro, Palmer, Seaver, and Jenkins; from the Marvin Miller Era there were Carlton, Ryan, Morris, Blyleven, and Sutton. Dennis Martinez and Roger Clemens spanned both the Miller and recent eras. Finally, the recent era contributed Maddux, Glavine, Mussina, Randy Johnson (nine appearances on the victory leaders list as of 2003) and Pedro Martinez (eight). Both Johnson and Martinez look likely to join the pitchers in Table 5.6. By Spahn's logic, pitchers with big multiyear contracts don't need to prove themselves from year to year. One might, therefore, have expected the most consistent winners to be clustered in the Mantle and Aaron eras. However, many of the players on the list played in the Miller and recent eras which suggests that, despite their large contracts, some pitchers have been able to sustain greatness.

Okay, there may be a few "throwbacks" in any era that play for the love of the game as opposed to the product endorsement, but what of the vast majority of today's pitchers? Table 5.8 shows that in each era, a little over 40% of the winningest pitchers appeared among victory leaders in the prior year. If Spahn were correct, we would expect that there would be fewer pitchers making repeat appearances among victory leaders. However, the percentage of repeat appearances has remained roughly constant, despite the escalation of major league salaries. The high- and low-water mark in each era has also remained relatively constant — around 20% to 30% in the lowest year, 60% to 70% in the highest. Actually, you could make the case that Spahn's contemporaries in the Mantle Era displayed the least consistency — in an average year 42% of their victory leaders were making a repeat performance and, in their low tide year, only 15% repeated. In the Aaron Era, about 46% of their pitchers repeated in a typical year, and in their least repetitive year that figure was 27%. The Miller Era average, 42%, ties the Mantle Era figure; its low, 20%, is somewhat higher. In the recent era, 42% of pitchers made repeat performances, and the low was 28%. Based on these data, Spahn couldn't possibly argue that the best pitchers in his era were any more consistent than the best pitchers in subsequent eras.[16]

Table 5.8 — Percentage of Pitchers in Top 25% in Victories That Also Appeared in Top 25% in the Prior Year

	Average	*High*	*Low*
Mickey Mantle Era (1945–1962)			
National League	41.9%	60.0%	20.0%
American League	41.9%	70.0%	15.4%
Henry Aaron Era (1963–1976)			
National League	47.6%	61.5%	26.7%
American League	45.0%	66.7%	30.8%
Marvin Miller Era (1977–1992)			
National League	39.2%	66.7%	20.0%
American League	45.5%	61.1%	27.8%
Recent Era (1993–2003)			
National League	40.8%	55.0%	27.8%
American League	42.9%	61.1%	27.8%

A corollary to the Spahn hypothesis—that financial security breeds complacency—might hold that the average age of the winningest pitchers would have decreased over time. In other words, the young multimillionaires of the Miller and recent eras might have had little incentive to pitch on into their 30s. The data, however, indicate otherwise (Table 5.9). The highest average age of the victory leaders was 29.58, for the recent era. In addition, the average age was second highest in the next most recent era, the Miller (29.49), followed by the Mantle Era (29.4) and the Aaron Era (28.24).[17] Despite the slightly higher averages for the recent eras, the most remarkable aspect of the age profile, like the repeat performance data in Table 5.8, is its consistency across eras.

In any era, the youngest pitcher to appear among the victory leaders is about 20, the oldest generally a little over 40. Three Mantle Era pitchers were over 40—Spahn appeared three times, Wynn and Gerry Staley each appeared once. Much of the over-40 club pitched in both the Aaron and Miller eras: Gaylord Perry, Steve Carlton, Jerry Koosman, Joe Niekro, Rick Reuschel, and Charlie Hough each appeared once. Seaver, Sutton, and Ryan appeared twice. Phil Niekro appeared among victory leaders a remarkable five times after the age of 40. In the recent era, Dennis Martinez appeared once, and in 2003 Jamie Moyer, David Wells, and Roger Clemens all made appearances on the victory leaders list. The majority of post–40 appearances are by pitchers who played after 1980. This likely is attributable to the improved conditioning of the modern ballplayer.

Of course, age might not be a perfect indication of tenure in the major

Table 5.9 — Age Profiles of Pitchers in Top 25% in Victories by Era

	Average	Youngest	Oldest
Mantle Era (1945–62)	29.40 (4.11)*	21	41
Aaron Era (1963–76)	28.24 (3.80)	19	42
Miller Era (1977–92)	29.49 (4.52)	20	46
Recent Era (1993–2003)	29.58 (4.13)	21	41
Total (1945–2003)	29.20 (4.20)	19	46

*The standard deviations in parentheses are measures of the typical dispersion about the mean value. Roughly two-thirds of the observed values for an era fall within the interval one standard deviation above and one standard deviation below its mean.

leagues. It might be that, lacking sufficient skill at an early age, the vast majority of modern pitchers reached the big leagues at a more advanced age than Mantle Era pitchers. Their careers may have been shorter than Spahn's contemporaries, but they became sufficiently rich in such a short time that it didn't matter. Again, however, this hypothesis is not supported by the data. There have been five pitchers that have appeared among league victory leaders by age 20 — Wally Bunker, Gary Nolan, Don Gullett, Bert Blyleven, and Dwight Gooden. That list suggests no bias in favor of the Mantle Era. In fact the Mantle and the recent eras are the only two not to have a pitcher 20 or younger among its victory leaders.[18]

In addition, the data on the average tenure of league victory leaders indicate that the typical modern leader had more major league experience than his Mantle Era counterparts (Table 5.10). The average pitcher from the recent era had 6.7 years of major league experience, which is second only to the Miller Era at 7.1 years of experience. Pitchers from the Aaron- and Mantle Era lists had roughly 6.25 years of experience. If Spahn is right, why did those modern ballplayers hang around so long? The list of pitchers who appeared among league victory leaders with at least 20 years of major league experience includes Spahn, Wynn, Phil Niekro, Sutton, and Ryan, which indicates no strong bias in favor of earlier eras. Moreover, 42-year-old Roger Clemens will join that list at the end of the 2004 season. Contrary to Spahn's assertions, the data indicate that the best modern pitchers are every bit as tough as he and his contemporaries were. The age profile and the average tenure of the typical victory leader, and the percent of victory leaders making repeat appearances has remained remarkably consistent over time.

In some ways, pitching has changed — albeit slightly. For example, the move to a five-man rotation and the increased reliance on relief pitching in the

Table 5.10 — Tenure Profiles of Pitchers in Top 25% in Victories by Era (Years of Major League Experience as of Appearance Among Victory Leaders)

	Average	High	Low
Mantle Era (1945–62)	6.26 (4.15)*	20	0
Aaron Era (1963–76)	6.24 (3.60)	21	0
Miller Era (1977–92)	7.11 (4.63)	24	0
Recent Era (1993–2003)	6.66 (4.09)	19	0
Total (1945–2003)	6.61 (4.20)	24	0

*The standard deviations in parentheses are measures of the typical dispersion about the mean value. Roughly two-thirds of the observed values for an era fall within the interval one standard deviation above and one standard deviation below its mean.

modern era has over time reduced the average number of wins that it takes to appear among the top 25% in victories (Table 5.11). That number was 17.7 in the Mantle Era, 16.6 for the Miller Era, and 16.2 for the recent era (strike years excluded).[19] Spahn's contemporaries, however, were again outpaced by pitchers from the Aaron Era; the typical top 25% pitcher in that era averaged 18.2 victories. The data indicate that, in some additional respects, the Mantle and Miller eras were substantially similar; the winningest Mantle-Era pitcher was Robin Roberts with 28 wins in 1952, the winningest Miller-Era pitcher was Bob Welch with 27 in 1990. The lowest victory total ever to appear among league leaders during the Mantle Era was 13; the lowest total among the Miller and recent-era pitchers was 12. Admittedly, these are a bit misleading because teams played only 154 games in the Mantle Era, while in the Miller Era and in much of the Aaron Era teams played 162 games. Miller- and recent-era win totals should therefore be slightly greater than Mantle-Era totals. The additional games, no doubt, explain at least some of the disparity between the Mantle- and Aaron-era pitchers.

In light of the additional games, the slight disparity between the Mantle- and Aaron-era averages is probably small enough to ignore, but David Halberstam offered one additional hypothesis to explain at least a small part of the discrepancy. He suggests that, in those years during the Mantle Era when a Yankees pitcher closed in on 20 wins, if the team had already clinched the pennant, General Manager George Weiss and manager Casey Stengel (and later Ralph Houk) might skip his turn in the rotation, or field a weak lineup:

> It was better to let them win fifteen or, at most, eighteen, which meant that the team could still win the pennant, but management would retain maximum lever-

Table 5.11— Average Wins of Pitchers in Top 25% in Yearly Victories by Era

	Average	High	Low
Mantle Era (1945–62)	17.7 (2.94)*	28	13
Aaron Era (1963–76)	18.2 (2.98)	31	13
Miller Era (1977–92)	16.6 (2.49)	27	12
Recent Era (1993–2003)	15.6 (2.72)	24	9
Recent Era, Strike Years excluded	16.2 (2.46)	24	12

*The standard deviations in parentheses are measures of the typical dispersion about the mean value. Roughly two-thirds of the observed values for an era fall within the interval one standard deviation above and one standard deviation below its mean.

age in negotiations in the following year. That was as much a part of Yankee tradition as winning the pennant and the World Series.[20]

Allie Reynolds' statistics are certainly provocative; he never won more than 20, had 19 wins once, and often had fewer starts than contemporaries like the Indians' Bob Lemon and Bob Feller. In 1947, for example, Reynolds' 19 wins earned him second place in the American League behind Feller who had 20 wins. Feller appeared in 42 games and started 37; Reynolds appeared in 34 games, starting only 30. In 1948, a similar situation occurred. Vic Raschi led the Yankees in victories with 19. Hal Newhouser of Detroit led the league with 21 wins. The Indians' Bob Lemon and Gene Bearden tied for second with 20 wins. Raschi had 36 appearances and 31 starts; Newhouser had 39 appearances, 35 starts, Lemon had 43 and 37, Bearden had 37 appearances (but did have two fewer starts than Raschi). In 1952, Reynolds finally won 20 games. He did it in 35 appearances with only 29 starts. Mike Garcia, who won 22 games that year, led the league in starts with 36. Jim Bouton, however, ended up with 18 wins in 1964 while leading the league in games started with 37.[21] Of course, he had already won 21 games in 1963 — the need to depress his win totals for contract purposes might have lapsed. The data are hardly conclusive, but, if the best team in baseball were artificially depressing its pitchers' wins totals, this may have had a slight dampening effect on the average wins of the top 25% pitchers in the Mantle Era. Probably too slight an effect to be important, but worth the insight into the cynically parsimonious Yankees management of those times.

There is one last way that pitching in the Miller Era differed from pitching in other eras. Pitchers switched teams a lot more frequently (Table 5.12). Sixty-six percent of the pitchers on the top 25% lists from the Mantle Era had played their entire careers with one team. For the Aaron Era, that figure remained high, at 63%; in the Miller Era, it dropped to 52%, and in the recent era it declined even further to 44%. Twenty-four percent of the Miller-Era pitchers had played for at least three teams, while almost a third had done so in the recent era. In the Mantle and Aaron eras that figure was 12% and 14%, respectively. The most traveled pitcher that appeared among victory leaders in the Mantle and Aaron eras was James Wilson who had played for six different teams when he won 15 games for the White Sox in 1953. In the Miller Era Doyle Alexander had played on eight teams when he won 17 games for the Blue Jays in 1987. In the recent era, the Yankees were David Wells' seventh team when he won 19 games in 2002.

Table 5.12 — Number of Teams Played For, Pitchers in Top 25% in Victories Broken Down by Era

Teams	Mantle Era	Aaron Era	Miller Era	Recent Era
One	65.6% (244)	63.1% (250)	52.3% (276)	44.4% (181)
Two	22.3% (83)	22.7% (90)	24.1% (127)	23.3% (95)
Three	8.1% (30)	9.6% (38)	10.4% (55)	16.7% (68)
Four	3.2% (12)	3.8% (15)	6.6% (35)	8.1% (33)
Five	0.5% (2)	0.8% (3)	4.2% (22)	3.9% (16)
Six	0.3% (1)	—	1.7% (9)	2.9% (12)
Seven	—	—	0.4% (2)	0.7% (3)
Eight	—	—	0.4% (2)	—

One worry was that free agency would make it easier for a handful of richer, large-market teams to warehouse pitching talent, leading to less competitive balance. However, while it may overstate the point to say that free agency *caused* the competitive balance exhibited in the Miller Era, it is true that both coexisted. It cannot, therefore, be argued (as some owners have) that free agency destroys competitive balance. For the reasons outlined in the first and second chapters, greater movement of veteran players did occur, but it has not helped the winning percentages of large-market teams that much.

CONCLUSION

It is baseball's good fortune that good pitching rather than hitting is a necessary condition for a champion. Because there is more variability in pitching performance, baseball will continue to be unpredictable — probably less predictable than other professional sports, with the possible exception of football. It seems odd, therefore, when sportswriters worry more about competitive balance in baseball than in basketball or football. In part, this could be because baseball's commissioner misses no opportunity to assert that the competition is hopelessly unfair to small-market teams like his Milwaukee Brewers. However, from the 1978 Yankees to the 1992 Blue Jays, baseball had no repeat champions. During that same span, basketball and football had plenty. Basketball had the Pistons, Lakers, and Bulls. Football had the Steelers and 49ers (Table 5.13).

Table 5.13 — Champions During the Marvin Miller and Recent Eras, 1977–2003

Year	Baseball	Football	Basketball
Miller Era			
1977	Yankees	Raiders	Trailblazers
1978	Yankees	Cowboys	Bullets
1979	Pirates	Steelers	Sonics
1980	Phillies	Steelers	Lakers
1981	Dodgers	Raiders	Celtics
1982	Cardinals	49ers	Lakers
1983	Orioles	Redskins	Sixers
1984	Tigers	Raiders	Celtics
1985	Royals	49ers	Lakers
1986	Mets	Bears	Celtics
1987	Twins	Giants	Lakers
1988	Dodgers	Redskins	Lakers
1989	A's	49ers	Pistons
1990	Reds	49ers	Pistons
1991	Twins	Giants	Bulls
1992	Blue Jays	Redskins	Bulls
Recent Era			
1993	Blue Jays	Cowboys	Bulls
1994*	No Champion	Cowboys	Rockets
1995	Braves	49ers	Rockets
1996	Yankees	Cowboys	Bulls
1997	Marlins	Packers	Bulls
1998	Yankees	Broncos	Bulls
1999	Yankees	Broncos	Spurs
2000	Yankees	Rams	Lakers
2001	Diamondbacks	Ravens	Lakers
2002	Angels	Patriots	Lakers
2003	Marlins	Buccaneers	Spurs

*Strike-shortened season

From 1977 to 1992, 13 different franchises won World Series, only seven won Super Bowls, and eight won NBA titles. During that span, only three baseball teams won more than one World Series, compared to four multiple-year winners in basketball and five in football. During the Miller Era, no baseball team won as many as three series; the Redskins, Raiders, 49ers, Lakers and Celtics all won at least three titles.

The tables seem to have turned in recent years. From 1993 to 2003, eight different teams won Super Bowls, while only six teams won World Series, and four won NBA championships. However, had the 1994 season been completed, it is possible, or even likely, that baseball would have had seven different champions. Moreover, in the 27 years of the Miller and recent eras, baseball has crowned 17 different champions, while football has had 13. In basketball, the figure is only 10.

The recent concerns about competitive balance in baseball are largely attributable to one team, the Yankees. As of January 2001, they had won three World Series in a row, and four of the last five. The Bulls and then the Lakers had similar strangleholds on the NBA, so not much had changed in basketball, but in football there were some changes. Although many different teams won Super Bowls, especially toward the end of the era, the Dallas Cowboys won three of four from 1993 to 1996, and the Denver Broncos won back-to-back Super Bowls in 1998 and 1999. Based solely on repeat champions, it isn't clear that football is more competitive than baseball.

But the champions metric, which is what a lot of commentators and fans use to compare competitive balance across sports, is not the right one to use. It is the overall narrowing of winning percentages, and the rarity of sub–.400 teams, as described in Chapters 1 and 2, that make it clear that baseball is growing increasingly balanced. Yes, the Yankees had a remarkable five-year run, but their clutch performances in the playoffs and World Series do *not* nullify the data for the league as a whole. As Marvin Miller is quick to point out, since the dawn of free agency baseball has enjoyed remarkable competitive balance. On that score, at least, we should listen to him. The data indicate that, due to pitching variability, baseball has always been difficult to dominate, and that the player movement associated with free agency has, if anything, only exacerbated that difficulty.

6

The Wild Card

INTRODUCTION

This chapter evaluates the wild-card playoff format adopted in 1995 in terms of the number of teams it keeps in contention throughout the season and the quality of the eventual playoff participants. It also evaluates fans' response to the races under the new format in the years just after its adoption. Because those years came on the heels of the strike, fans were likely less willing to attend games. The reader should therefore consider the attendance results at the end of the chapter a sort of lower bound on the appeal of the new format.

On September 1, 1996, the new format was probably keeping fan interest alive in many teams that otherwise would have been out of the race. In the American League, for example, the White Sox, Orioles, Mariners, Red Sox, and Twins were all within five and a half games of the wild-card lead (Table 6.1).[1] At various times after the July All-Star break, both the Brewers and the A's had also crept within striking distance of the wild-card leader (six or seven games). Although the White Sox had clawed to within two games of Cleveland at the All-Star break, the Indians appeared to have the Central Division well in hand by September. The Rangers, who battled with the Mariners and A's early in the season, had established some control in the West. Only the East remained interesting due to a late charge by the Orioles coupled with an August swoon on the part of the Yankees. On the whole, despite the relatively weak races in the Central and West, the new playoff format seemed to be working: as late as Labor Day, eight American League teams had a legitimate shot to be in the playoffs.

Under the old playoff format, which was in place from 1969 to 1993, only the division champions (East and West) in each league made the playoffs. Had it been used in 1996, on September 1 the Indians and the Rangers would have had relatively comfortable leads in their respective divisions (Table 6.2). No team would have been within three games of either of them, and only the Yankees (four games back in the East) and the White Sox (five games back in the West) would have been within five games of the division leaders. The Mariners and Orioles would have been within 10 games of the division lead. At eight games back, the Orioles would have had little hope of overtaking both the Yankees and Indians in their remaining 27 games. The Mariners would have been

Table 6.1—American League Standings September 1, 1996

Team	Record	Pct.	Games Back
EAST			
New York Yankees	76–59	.563	—
Baltimore Orioles	72–63	.533	4
Boston Red Sox	69–67	.507	7.5
Toronto Blue Jays	63–73	.463	13.5
Detroit Tigers	49–87	.360	27.5
CENTRAL			
Cleveland Indians	80–55	.593	—
Chicago White Sox	73–64	.533	8
Minnesota Twins	67–69	.493	13.5
Milwaukee Brewers	66–71	.482	15
Kansas City Royals	62–75	.453	19
WEST			
Texas Rangers	77–58	.570	—
Seattle Mariners	70–65	.519	7
Oakland A's	66–72	.478	12.5
California Angels	62–74	.456	15.5
WILD-CARD RACE			
Baltimore Orioles	72–63	.533	—
Chicago White Sox	73–64	.533	—
Seattle Mariners	70–65	.519	2
Boston Red Sox	69–67	.507	3.5
Minnesota Twins	67–69	.493	5.5
Milwaukee Brewers	66–71	.482	7
Oakland A's	66–72	.478	7.5

in a position very similar to the Orioles. In short, the division races would not have been significantly improved under the old format. Indeed, the best race was in the AL East under the new format — importantly, given the Indians' outstanding record, the Orioles-Yankees tussle would have been meaningless under the old format. Under the old format, therefore, only six teams would have had any shot at the playoffs, and the Mariners and Orioles would have been long shots. Under the new format, eight teams were in closer contention for the playoffs than either the Orioles or Mariners would have been under the old format. In terms of widespread fan appeal, therefore, it is difficult to argue that in 1996 the new format did not outperform the old.

In the National League, the results were substantially similar. Although the Braves had a big lead in the East, the West and the Central were quite competitive. Three teams (the Cardinals, Cubs, and Reds) were within six games of the Central-leading Astros. The Dodgers and Rockies were within six games of West leader San Diego. Admittedly, the Rockies, Cubs, and Reds were more

Table 6.2 — Hypothetical American League Standings Under the Old Playoff Format September 1, 1996

Team	Record	Pct.	Games Back
EAST			
Cleveland Indians	80–55	.593	—
New York Yankees	76–59	.563	4
Baltimore Orioles	72–63	.533	8
Boston Red Sox	69–67	.507	11.5
Milwaukee Brewers	66–71	.482	13
Toronto Blue Jays	63–73	.463	17.5
Detroit Tigers	49–87	.360	31.5
WEST			
Texas Rangers	77–58	.570	—
Chicago White Sox	73–64	.533	5
Seattle Mariners	70–65	.519	7
Minnesota Twins	67–69	.493	10.5
Oakland A's	66–72	.478	12.5
California Angels	62–74	.456	15.5
Kansas City Royals	62–75	.453	16

than five games off the pace in their respective divisional races—with fewer than 30 games remaining, a division championship was probably a long shot. The wild-card, however, had the Rockies within five games of the playoffs and had a good young Expos team within a game and a half. Under the new format, then, there were seven teams within five games of a playoff berth, and 10 teams within 10 games.

Under the old format, far fewer NL teams would have been in contention as of Labor Day (Table 6.4). The Expos and Braves would have led their respective divisions. No team in the NL West would have been within five games of the Braves. The Padres would have been the closest at nine games back. The Cubs and the Cardinals would have been the only NL East teams within five games of the Expos. That would have made only four teams within at least five games of a playoff berth, only seven teams within 10 games. In short, the wild-card format had far more cities involved in playoff races in 1996 than would have contended under the old format.

On the other hand, the Expos would have fared better under the old format than the new. Presumably, one of the reasons the wild-card was put in place was to give weaker teams (often from "small" markets like Montreal) a better chance to make the playoffs. This, of course, has prompted purists to indict the new format for watering down the quality of playoff teams. However, Montreal, a team with a worse record than the Dodgers, Astros, and Padres, would have made the playoffs under the supposedly more restrictive old for-

Table 6.3 — National League Standings September 1, 1996

Team	Record	Pct.	Games Back
EAST			
Atlanta Braves	84–51	.622	—
Montreal Expos	72–62	.537	11.5
Florida Marlins	65–71	.478	19.5
New York Mets	60–76	.441	24.5
Philadelphia Phillies	54–82	.397	30.5
CENTRAL			
Houston Astros	74–63	.540	—
St. Louis Cardinals	71–65	.522	2.5
Chicago Cubs	67–67	.500	5.5
Cincinnati Reds	67–68	.496	6
Pittsburgh Pirates	56–79	.415	17
WEST			
San Diego Padres	76–61	.555	—
Los Angeles Dodgers	74–61	.548	1
Colorado Rockies	70–67	.511	6
San Francisco Giants	58–75	.436	16
WILD-CARD			
Los Angeles Dodgers	74–61	.548	—
Montreal Expos	72–62	.537	1.5
St. Louis Cardinals	71–65	.522	3.5
Colorado Rockies	70–67	.511	5
Chicago Cubs	67–67	.500	6.5
Cincinnati Reds	67–68	.496	7
Florida Marlins	65–71	.478	9.5

mat; had the season ended on Labor Day, the best team in the National League would have faced the team with the *fifth* best record in the league. As demonstrated later in the chapter, moreover, this type of result was by no means rare under the old format. In short, the data indicate that the old format was no less capricious than the new in the way it selected its playoff teams. The team quality argument does not, therefore, tip clearly in favor of the old format as some would have us believe.

However, many self-described purists still question the legitimacy of a team entering the playoffs via the wild-card:

> Why play a season? Why bother to determine which team has the talent, the fortitude, the ability to endure and play at a high level through injuries, mind-numbing road trips, slumps, the "dog days" of August and come out on top, a winner? Then play other winners (of divisions) for the league championship and ultimately the World Series. Why not put all teams in the league in the playoffs (*e.g.* hockey) and call the season an exhibition?
>
> Norbert Kraich (fan)[2]

Table 6.4 — Hypothetical National League Standings Under Old Playoff Format September 1, 1996

Team	Record	Pct.	Games Back
EAST			
Montreal Expos	72–62	.537	—
St. Louis Cardinals	71–65	.522	2
Chicago Cubs	67–67	.500	5
Florida Marlins*	65–71	.478	8
New York Mets	60–76	.441	13
Pittsburgh Pirates	56–79	.415	16.5
Philadelphia Phillies	54–82	.397	19
WEST			
Atlanta Braves	84–51	.622	—
San Diego Padres	76–61	.555	9
Los Angeles Dodgers	74–61	.548	10
Houston Astros	74–63	.540	11
Colorado Rockies*	70–67	.511	15
Cincinnati Reds	67–68	.496	17
San Francisco Giants	58–75	.436	25

*Although neither team existed under the old playoff format, the hypothetical standings presented here assume that the Marlins would have been placed in the NL East, the Rockies in the NL West. In its infinite wisdom, the league had, however, placed the Atlanta Braves in the NL West, so who knows for sure where Colorado and Florida would have ended up.

To argue that the wild-card makes the regular season meaningless is ridiculous. The wild-card team endures a 162-game season, just as did division winners under the old format. More importantly, the data (presented below) indicate that, in many cases, the wild-card would have had a better record than did one of the division champions under the old format. Witness the plight of the '96 Dodgers or Padres had the old format been in place. How rational is a playoff scheme that often excludes the second best team in the league?

Kraich takes the wild-card to its logical end, and argues that baseball will soon become like hockey, where the season is more exhibition than endurance contest because most teams make the playoffs. Such reasoning by false analogy, while somewhat entertaining, is also silly. There is little chance that baseball will expand the playoff format any time soon — and it will never be expanded so much that most teams make the playoffs. Why not? Because the average fan, like Mr. Kraich, wouldn't be that interested in an expanded format. The wild-card and divisional races would mean less under too-inclusive a playoff format, and the results would likely be that overall attendance (regular season plus playoffs) would suffer, despite additional rounds of playoffs.

Even baseball management Neanderthals have to respond to a market demand curve (one hopes).

What is frustrating about purists is that, while they can readily recognize that there might be too many teams in the playoffs, they are unwilling to explore the possibility that there could be too few. In hockey and basketball, over half of the teams in the league make the playoffs; in football, 12 of 31, or roughly 40% of teams, get into the postseason. Under the old divisional format in baseball, four of 28 teams (14%) made the playoffs. This format limited the number of teams in contention, and thus had an adverse effect on attendance (as indicated by the regression results in the Introduction). Under the wild-card format, eight teams (29% of the total) made the playoffs in 1996. With the addition of two new expansion teams, it became eight of 30 teams in 1998, or a little over one-quarter of the total — a figure substantially lower than for the other major sports. Baseball executives, although clearly shortsighted in other respects (witness work stoppages, or their inability to televise all playoff match-ups in 1995), have struck the appropriate balance with the wild-card: baseball maintains some selectivity when it chooses playoff participants, but more cities and teams remain in contention late in the season. In short, Kraich's notion that baseball will become like hockey is unfounded (at least for now), and his implication that the present wild-card system admits weak sisters to the playoff dance is not well supported by the data (as you'll see in a moment).

So what motivated baseball executives to adopt the supposedly abominable wild-card? Kraich's editorial goes on to argue that it's simple greed on the part of the owners. But, like it or not, this is a market economy. There are two (or more) parties to every transaction and, to the extent possible, each tries to get a deal that it finds acceptable. So the overpriced tickets, fat payoffs from television networks, and extra corporate sky boxes that Kraich goes on in his rather lengthy editorial to attribute to the wild-card will occur only if fans express sufficient interest. If ticket prices are too high, or fans really don't find the first round of the playoffs interesting, then the wild-card will be a flop, no matter how greedy the owners are. The 1995–96 experiences suggest that the average fan is, however, interested in the expanded playoffs. At best, Kraich's is a well-meaning but overly sentimental viewpoint.

THE DATA

For the wild-card format to be a success, it needs to produce more positive outcomes, on average, than did the divisional format. Positive outcomes may depend on your point of view, but there are a few criteria that we might employ. First, the format should bring more teams into contention than did the old format. If the wild-card waters down the quality of playoff teams, as its detractors assert, without generating fan interest in additional cities, then it should be judged a failure. Second, we do need to examine the wild-card detrac-

Table 6.5 – Results Summary, American League Playoff Races Under Wild-Card Format, 1977–1992

Year	Teams, Old Format*	Teams, New Format*	Wild Card Win. Pct.	Weak Div. Champ (New Format)	Wild-Card Winning Margin	Actual Weak Divis. Champ	Win. Pct.
1977	5	6	.602	.580	0	Yankees	.617
1978	7	7	.611	.537	7	Royals	.568
1979	6	8	.569	.543	2	Angels	.543
1980	3	4	.617	.512	14	Royals	.599
1982	6	7	.556	.574	1	Angels	.574
1983	5	9	.568	.475	1	Orioles	.605
1984	7	12	.549	.500	2	Royals	.519
1985	5	5	.602	.556	12.5	Royals	.562
1986	6	9	.556	.519	3	Angels	.568
1987	11	10	.593	.500	7	Twins	.525
1988	6	9	.543	.549	1	Red Sox	.549
1989	7	8	.562	.549	4	Blue Jays	.549
1990	5	10	.531	.543	3	Red Sox	.543
1991	7	11	.537	.525	3	Blue Jays	.562
1992	6	6	.556	.568	1	A's	.593
AVG.	6.1	8.1	.570	.535	4.1		.560

*The number of teams within 10 games of a playoff berth.

Note: Strike-shortened 1981 season not included because divisional playoff format was altered.

tors' principal claim — that, on average, the new format diminishes the quality of the average playoff team. As the Dodgers-Padres experience of 1996 indicates, the new format could actually improve the average quality of playoff teams by including those with the second and third best records in the league — teams that would have spent October in front of the television under the old format. In this sense, the new format might conceivably right some of the wrongs that occurred under the old, especially when one division was especially weak in comparison with the other (witness the 1973 Mets or the 1987 Twins). Finally, in those years when the new format actually does degrade the quality of the average playoff team, to what extent does it do so? In a year when the new format corrected an injustice perpetrated under the old system and involved additional cities in the playoff chase, reasonable minds might agree that it was a success—provided that none of the playoff participants were embarrassingly weak teams that *would not have made it under the old format*. In some years, however, a lousy team would make the postseason under either format, so it's unfair to judge the wild-card a failure for an outcome shared by its predecessor.[3]

Because the American League did not expand from 1977 to 1992, all the playoff races during that span can be recomputed as they would have occurred under the new format.[4] To see whether the new format would have included additional teams in the playoff chase, Table 6.5 compares the number of teams within ten games of a division championship under the old format with the number within 10 games of a playoff berth (division championship or wild-card) under the new.[5] In 11 of the 15 years, at least one additional team would have been in contention under the wild-card format. In seven years, two or more additional teams would have been contenders. When the individual races are described in more detail below, it becomes apparent that, in at least one of the four years when the wild-card format would not have kept additional teams in the race, the new format would have produced more satisfying races and higher quality playoff teams than the divisional format. In short, it can be safely concluded that, in the vast majority of years, the wild-card would have kept fans' interest alive in more cities than the division format.

Of course, involving additional teams in the playoff race is a necessary but hardly sufficient condition for the wild-card to be judged a success. To assess the *quality* of the playoff teams under either format, Table 6.5 shows what the winning percentages of the wild-card team and the weakest division winner would have been under the new format, and compares them to that of the weaker division winner under the old format. The average wild-card team would have had a .570 winning percentage (about a 92–70 record). In four of the 15 years, the wild-card would have been a .600 team. The weaker division winner under the old format had a winning percentage of .560; in only two of the 15 years did the weaker division champ have a .600 record. These figures suggest that the quality of the wild-card teams would have been somewhat higher than that of one of the teams that we actually watched in the AL playoffs. Why weren't purists griping more loudly about the lousy teams in the playoffs?

Perhaps the strength of the wild-card teams should come as little surprise. After all, the wild-card can come from any division, and thus is not constrained by the way that baseball's divisions have been crafted. Unless the division winners have the top three records in the league, which is unlikely, the wild-card is bound to have the second or third best record. Under the old format, there was no assurance that the weaker division winner would have one of the league's top three records. In some years this did occur, but in others it didn't. As a result, the wild-card team would have been a more worthy playoff participant, on average, than the weaker division champion.

The potential Achilles' heel for the new playoff format, however, is not the wild-card team but the weakest division champion. As presently crafted, one division (the AL West) has only four teams. From 1977 to 1992, that division would have produced weak champions on multiple occasions, especially in the early '80s (Table 6.5). The Rangers, for example, would have won the division in 1983 with only a .475 winning percentage. On two other occasions (1984 and '87) the AL West Champion A's would have had a .500 winning percentage. With only five teams in the AL Central and AL East, those divisions also would have been capable of producing relatively weak champions. Yet, the East would have produced no truly weak champions, while the Central would have produced only a couple, each with 84–78 records (a .519 winning percentage). Despite these notable failures, the weakest division champ would have had an average winning percentage of .535 (87–75 record).

If you take out the three horrendous AL West Champs, the weakest champion would have had a .546 average winning percentage. One can't completely ignore these failures, but it is interesting that they all would have come out of the division with only four teams. To the extent that reorganization of the divisions might eventually ameliorate those problems, the eventual lower bound on quality might be somewhere near the weakest AL Central Champs (84–78, .519 winning percentage). Note also that the average of the records of the wild-card and the weakest division champions (minus the three awful years) would have been .560—*identical* to that of the weak division champ under the old format. In other words, for 12 of the 15 years, the new format would have produced wild-cards and weak division champions whose average quality matched that of the weak champ under the old format. The wild-cards would have been a little better, the weak champs a little worse, but the average quality of the additional teams in the playoffs would have been roughly the same as one of the teams we actually watched. However, those three awful years would weigh heavily on the minds of detractors, as they probably should. Reorganization could make this outcome less likely, but it can't completely eliminate it. On average, however, the data indicate that the wild-card format will not significantly degrade the quality of the teams in the playoffs.

There is one final thing that might rightfully be expected of the wild-card format—a genuine race. The criterion for a contender used to this point (within 10 games of a playoff berth) is probably a little weak. It could be the case that the wild-card brings additional teams within eight or nine games of the playoffs, but that the race isn't really close. To be sure that this wouldn't have been so, Table 6.5 also provides information on the average margin of victory in the wild-card race. In two years, the races would have been runaways. The 1985 Yankees (97–64) would have won by 12.5 games; the 1980 Orioles (100–62) would have won by a whopping 14 games. Despite these two years, the average victory margin would have been only 4.1 games. In four years, the wild-card team would have won by a single game. In 1977, Baltimore and Boston would have played a one-game playoff to determine the wild-card. If the two runaway years are excluded, the average winning margin drops to 2.7 games. On average, therefore, the wild-card race would have been a good one.

In almost every year from 1977 to 1992 the wild-card format would have (1) brought additional teams into AL races, or (2) not permitted a weak team to enter the playoffs, or (3) generated a close race, although a purist might expect it to accomplish all three in the same year before conceding that the format was a success. It seems reasonable that the wild-card format could accomplish only two of these objectives and, depending on the circumstances, rightly be considered a success, but others might disagree. To help convince the curmudgeons, a more difficult test of the format was created. On the positive side, the wild-card format received a checkmark if it included at least one additional team in the playoff race, generated a wild-card race whose outcome was decided by five or fewer games, and "righted a wrong" by including the team with the second best record, one that would otherwise have been left out of the playoffs.

This stricter test also requires the wild-card format to avoid awful outcomes. In two of 15 years from 1977 to 1992 the old format produced AL division champs with winning percentages below .530; in two others a division champ was only slightly better (88–74, .543 winning percentage). In other words, in 27% of the years considered, the old format produced a playoff team of roughly comparable quality to an 87–75 team. This would seem a good lower bound, and a fair definition of a weak playoff team. For that reason, our wild-card test penalized the wild-card format if it made a playoff team out of any division winner or wild-card that did not win 12 more games than it lost (87–75, .537 winning percentage).

In a perfect year, therefore, the wild-card had to do five things—bring at least one additional team into a race, produce a wild-card winner with at least an 87–75 record, a weakest division winner that also met the 87–75 criterion, a wild-card champ that won by no more than five games, and, finally, right a wrong by including the team with the second best record (who otherwise would have been left out). This is a pretty tall order. In five years (1977, 1983, 1986, 1991, and 1992), the old format selected the two teams with the best records,

Table 6.6 — Wild-Card Performance Score

Year	Add'l Teams	Wild-Card 12 over .500	Weak Champ 12 Over .500	Wild-Card Race w/in Five Games	Right a Wrong—Permit 2nd Best to Enter Playoffs	Total Score
1977	X	X	X	X		4
1978		X	X		X	3
1979	X	X	X	X	X	5
1980	X	X			X	3
1982	X	X	X	X	X	5
1983	X	X		X		3
1984	X	X		X	X	4
1985		X	X		X	3
1986	X	X		X		3
1987		X			X	2
1988	X	X	X	X	X	5
1989	X	X	X	X	X	5
1990	X		X	X	X	4
1991	X	X		X		3
1992		X	X	X		3
Total	11	14	9	11	10	3.73

so it seems a little unfair to penalize the wild-card for also including those two teams in the playoffs. On the other hand, purists probably want to see evidence of clear improvements over the old system and, by including, say, the third and fourth best teams in the playoffs, the new system would have lowered the average quality in those five years. Note also that the other conditions are difficult to satisfy jointly. For example, in years when the wild-card and the weakest division champion are strong teams, it's probably more difficult to incorporate additional teams in the playoff chase. Also, when the wild-card is especially good, it decreases the likelihood of a close wild-card race. In short, this is a pretty stringent joint test of the new format.

Despite the test's stringency, the wild-card format scores a perfect five in four of 15 years (Table 6.6). Even purists have to agree that the new format was clearly superior to the old in these years (don't they?). In only one year would the wild-card have accomplished fewer than three of the five objectives—and that was 1987, the year the .525 Twins won the World Series. While neither format would have produced perfectly satisfying races in that year, the wild-card would have been a pretty dismal failure. In the remaining nine years, the wild-card would have accomplished at least three or four of the five objectives—the overall average was 3.73 objectives accomplished per year. Had the average fan been given a list of the five criteria and told that a little under four of them would be accomplished in a typical year, he would have been glad to dump the old format. Of course, the data may not convince those who subscribe to the "lies, damn lies, and statistics" view of empirical analysis. To help persuade them, the next section examines the individual races in detail. In a majority of years, the wild-card clearly would have outperformed the divisional format. In a handful of years, reasonable minds might disagree about the preferred format. However, in only **four or five** of 15 years would the divisional format clearly have outperformed the wild-card.

THE PENNANT RACES

Two simple things are to be expected from a format: exciting, broadly based races and balanced playoff matchups between capable teams. This section uses three questions to determine which format would have better achieved these objectives. First, which one would have produced closer races? Second, which format would have involved more franchises in a playoff race? An interesting race can involve only a couple of teams, but a more heated race would involve three or more. Those given to nostalgia might disagree. Granted, there is something stark and straightforward about two superior teams battling to the wire in a 162-game season. Take, for example, the 1980 American League East race in which the Yankees (103–59) held off the Orioles (100–62) by only three games. To be sure, it was a good race between two very good teams, but no other team in the East was within 16 games of the Yankees. In the AL West, the Royals (97–65) cruised past second-place Oakland by 14 games. So, only two teams in the American League were involved in a race in September. Although Yankees and Orioles fans might remember that race fondly, it can't be good for baseball when so few late-season games have an impact on the playoffs. To argue otherwise is selfish. In short, a perfect race will involve a lot of teams, and its outcome will be in question until the last days of the season. But we're not done there. It is possible to have a close, heated race between a bunch of mediocre teams. At various times in the '80s, for example, the AL West was a wild scramble between a pack of .500 teams. While this type of race can be fun, it is preferable to watch the best teams in the playoffs. The third question we're entitled to ask of a format, therefore, is whether it delivers the teams with the highest winning percentages. That's three simple criteria: (1) close races that (2) involve many teams, and (3) yield the best available playoff participants.

An additional factor that will be taken into account is what Bob Costas has referred to as the "integrity of the pennant race." During game four of the Orioles-Yankees 1996 American League Championship Series, Costas stated that under the new format "all attention shifts to the wild-card race" which undermines the integrity of the division races. In particular, he was referring to the last series of the 1996 season between the Dodgers and Padres, in which the winner became the NL West champion, while the loser entered the playoffs as the wild-card team. While Costas was correct that the series meant less than it would have had the loser been left out of the playoffs, it's not clear that this outcome recommends the divisional format over the wild-card. Costas, generally a careful analyst, didn't construct the appropriate counterfactual in this instance. Assuming the old divisional format had been in place, the Braves would have already won the NL West, and thus the Dodgers-Padres series would have meant nothing. So, while the integrity of the pennant race argument will be taken into account, the wild-card format will not be penalized for outcomes that would have been worse (or the same) under the old format. In the end, a race whose integrity is somewhat undermined is far better than no race at all.

Costas' claim that all attention shifts to the wild-card race from the division races is also a bit overblown. As you will see, many contenders would have been keenly aware of *both* races under the wild-card format. In addition, in a few instances, division races of substantial "integrity" would have persisted long after the wild-card race was no longer in doubt. We examine in greater detail the races in the American League from 1977 to 1992, a period when the number of teams and the composition of the divisions remained the same. We also know what the divisions would have looked like under the wild-card format for the American League because these same teams were in fact reassigned to three divisions when the new format was adopted in 1993. As noted above, we can therefore compare outcomes under the two formats during this period. By contrast, in the National League the adoption of the format coincided with the arrival of two new teams, making such comparisons problematic — absent those two teams, it is difficult to know what the three divisions would have looked like.

1977

Under either format, the 1977 races would not have involved that many teams (Table 6.7). As it was, there was a great three-team race in the East with the Orioles and Red Sox just two and a half games behind the Yankees. In the West, the Royals cruised to an eight-game victory over the Rangers. The wild-card format would have brought only one additional team, the White Sox, within 10 games of a playoff berth. All of the division champions under the new format would have been quite solid representatives — the weakest would have been the Rangers at 94–68 (.580). The wild-card would have been either the Orioles or the Red Sox. Both had excellent 97–64 (.602) records. However, both teams played only 161 games, and thus would have had to make up one game to help determine the wild-card. Had the teams remained tied after the make-up game, fans would have seen a one-game playoff. On the Wild-Card Scoreboard of Table 6.6, therefore, 1977 was a good year. The new format would have brought an additional team into the race, the weakest division champion and the wild-card would have had very good records, and the wild-card race would have been incredibly close. The only thing the new format couldn't do was to right a wrong because, under the old format, the teams with the best two records — the Yankees and Royals — actually met in the playoffs. Of course, the same result was entirely conceivable under the wild-card format as well.

Costas might argue that the existence of the wild-card would have undermined the integrity of the race in the East. Instead of three teams battling for one playoff berth, we would have watched them battle for two. Of course, that wouldn't necessarily have made the race any less exciting or the individual games any less important to the players and fans of the teams involved. As long as the number of teams in the race exceeds the number of available playoff spots, the race will be interesting. Had it been only a two-team race in the East, it obviously would have been cheapened by the wild-card. As it happened, there were three, so the integrity of the race critique of the wild-card isn't valid for 1977.

Fans might also like to know what the matchups would have looked like under the new format. Of course, with all the crazy rules that initially governed who played whom (*e.g.*, the AL West Champ plays the wild-card every third year provided the wild-card isn't also from the West), that would have been impossible to know. Both the matchups and home field advantage should have been determined by record. That is, the team with the best record should play the team with the weakest record, the team with the second best record should play the team with the third best record, and the top two should enjoy home field advantage in the first round. In this way, teams that play best during the regular season are rewarded for their efforts. When this chapter was first written in 1997, the format was really screwed up. Since then, baseball did actually come close to adopting the preferred playoff format. The best team now meets the worst, provided they are not in the same division.

Table 6.7 — Divisional Versus Wild-Card Format, 1977

Divisional Format			Wild-Card Format		
Team	Record	Games Back	Team	Record	Games Back
			EAST		
			NYY	100–62	—
			BAL	97–64	2.5
EAST			BOS	97–64	2.5
			DET	74–88	26
NYY	100–62	—	TOR	54–107	45.5
BAL	97–64	2.5			
BOS	97–64	2.5	CENTRAL		
DET	74–88	26			
CLE	71–90	28.5	KCR	102–60	—
MIL	67–95	33	CHW	90–72	12
TOR	54–107	45.5	MIN	84–77	17.5
			CLE	71–90	30.5
WEST			MIL	67–95	35
KCR	102–60	—	WEST		
TEX	94–68	8			
CHW	90–72	12	TEX	94–68	—
MIN	84–77	17.5	CAL	74–88	20
CAL	74–88	28	SEA	64–98	30
SEA	64–98	38	OAK	63–98	30.5
OAK	63–98	38.5			
			WILD-CARD		
			BAL	97–64	—
			BOS	97–64	—
			CHW	90–72	7.5

In the first year of the wild-card format, baseball executives likely would have said, for scheduling reasons, or because of their television contracts, they needed to prespecify the matchups. That was baloney, however. The best teams should have been rewarded. The fans prefer it, and the networks have an incentive to televise the matchups that maximize ratings. As far as scheduling, while it is true that some teams share a field with a football team, the vast majority do not. Most of the teams in the 1996 playoffs, for example, played in parks devoted solely to baseball (Orioles, Rangers, Yankees, Indians, Dodgers, Braves, and Cardinals). Only the Padres — who shared Jack Murphy Stadium with the

Chargers—would have had a potentially serious scheduling problem. There was simply no excuse for the initial arrangement.

The matchups are evaluated under the wild-card format, therefore, under the assumption (perhaps heroic) that baseball executives might eventually adopt playoff matchups based solely on merit. That is, the best team plays the fourth best, while the second best squares off against the third seed, regardless of whether that would pit division rivals against one another in the first round. In 1977, therefore, the Royals (102–60) would have been the top seed and would have faced the fourth-seeded Rangers. The Royals teams of the late '70s had relatively well-known players like George Brett, Hal McRae, and Frank White. Their pitching, which included Dennis Leonard (20–12, 3.04 ERA), Jim Colborn (18–14, 3.62 ERA), and Paul Splittorff (16–6, 3.69 ERA), was also quite good. The '77 Rangers, however, are probably not as well remembered. Their position players were dependable (including Mike Hargrove, Toby Harrah, Bert Campaneris, and Jim Sundberg), although none of them hit over .305 or had more than 87 RBI.[6] Their starting pitching, by contrast, was a bit more flashy. The staff included Gaylord Perry (15–12, 3.37 ERA), Doyle Alexander (17–11, 3.46 ERA), Bert Blyleven (14–12, 2.72 ERA), and Doc Ellis (10–6, 2.91 ERA). It would have been a good matchup.

In the #2–#3 matchup, the Yankees would have met either the Orioles or the Red Sox. Enough has been written about the Jim Palmer-Brooks Robinson-Earl Weaver Orioles teams and the Carl Yastrzemski-Jim Rice-Fred Lynn Red Sox teams, that they needn't be discussed in detail here. Suffice it to say that Reggie Jackson, Ron Guidry, and the rest of Billy Martin's Yankees would have been in a dogfight either way. Some might argue that, had the Yankees played either the Red Sox or Orioles in the first round of the playoffs, the regular season race in the AL East would have been meaningless. However, the regular season would have been played to (a) eliminate a very good team in either the Red Sox or Orioles and (b) determine that the Yankees deserved home field advantage in the first round.

In sum, the wild-card format would have been better than the divisional format in 1977. You do give up a little in terms of the Royals' race—they go from defeating the Rangers by eight games to defeating the White Sox by 12—but in return you get an additional team within 10 games of the playoffs, you maintain an excellent race in the East and, quite possibly, you get a dramatic one-game playoff between the Orioles and Red Sox to determine the wild-card. Jim Palmer vs. Luis Tiant, perhaps? To be fair, the races would have been pretty similar under either format, but the wild-card would have been slightly better.

1978

Had the wild-card format been in place, Boston Red Sox fans would remember 1978 quite differently (Table 6.8). Rather than be eliminated from the playoffs by Bucky Dent's dramatic home run in a one-game playoff with the Yankees, the Red Sox would have entered the playoffs as the wild-card. Here, Costas is right — the wild-card would have very much undermined the integrity and the drama of the AL East race. We would, however, have received very interesting races in the AL Central and AL West as compensation. The Brewers, six games back of the Red Sox and Yanks under the old format, would have held off the Royals by a single game. As far as righting wrongs goes, therefore, the new format would have been quite effective. That is, the playoffs would have included the second and third best teams in the league (the Red Sox and Brewers) while the Royals, with the fourth best record in the league, would have stayed home.

Table 6.8 — Divisional Versus Wild-Card Format, 1978

Divisional Format			Wild-Card Format		
Team	Record	Games Back	Team	Record	Games Back
			EAST		
			NYY	99–63	—
			BOS	99–63	—
EAST			BAL	90–71	8.5
			DET	86–76	13
NYY	99–63	—	TOR	59–102	39.5
BOS	99–63	—			
MIL	93–69	6	CENTRAL		
BAL	90–71	8.5			
DET	86–76	13	MIL	93–69	—
CLE	69–90	28.5	KCR	92–70	1
TOR	59–102	39.5	MIN	73–89	20
			CHW	71–90	21.5
WEST			CLE	69–90	22.5
KCR	92–70	—	WEST		
TEX	87–75	5			
CAL	87–75	5	CAL	87–75	—
MIN	73–89	19	TEX	87–75	—
CHW	71–90	20.5	OAK	69–93	18
OAK	69–93	23	SEA	56–104	30
SEA	56–104	35			
			WILD-CARD		
			BOS	99–63	—
			KCR	92–70	7
			BAL	90–71	8.5

Of course, there still would have been a bit of arbitrariness in determining playoff participants under the wild-card system. Either the Rangers or the Angels, teams that tied for the sixth best record in the league, would have won the AL West. At 87–75, neither team was terrible, and the division winner would have been determined in a one-game playoff. The aces of the staffs were Fergie Jenkins (18–8, 3.04 ERA) for the Rangers and Frank Tanana (18–12, 3.65 ERA) for the Angels. It would have been an interesting game.

On the Wild Card Scoreboard test (Table 6.6), 1978 is a mixed bag. The new format would have righted wrongs and thus improved the average winning percentage of the teams in the playoffs. In addition, neither the wild-card nor the weakest division champion would have been bad teams—the Red Sox at 99–63 would have been a very strong wild-card, while the Rangers or Angels would have been marginally acceptable division champions. On the negative side, the new format would not have included any additional teams in the race and would not have produced a close wild-card race. The format choice comes down to this: you undermine one of the most dramatic divisional races since 1969, and in return you get three very close division races. One race (East) isn't all that dramatic because the Red Sox will enter as the wild-card; another (West) pits two teams that can only be described as above average; and the third (Central) is both dramatic and involves strong teams, the Brewers and Royals. The season would have been far more interesting in places like Milwaukee, California, and Texas under the new format, but even nonpurists would agonize over undermining that Yankees-Red Sox race. It could reasonably be called a tie. So let's start two tallies: one for the more open-minded and another for purist curmudgeons. On the open-minded, the wild-card format is 1–0–1 through 1978. The purist's scorecard reads 1–1–0.

1979

This was one of those years where, because the AL East was a lot better than the West, the wild-card format would have vastly improved the quality of teams in the playoffs. As it was, the 102–57 Orioles faced the Angels (87–75), bearers of only the fifth best record in the league. Under the wild-card format, the Angels would have still made the playoffs and faced the Orioles. The Brewers, champions of the Central division, would have enjoyed home field advantage against the wild-card entry, the Red Sox. The divisional races wouldn't have been outstanding under either format. The Orioles won the East by eight; and, in a somewhat congested race between four better-than-average teams in the West, the Angels eclipsed the Royals by three games, the Rangers by five, and the Twins by six. Had the new format been in place, the Orioles and Brewers would have won their divisions by more than 10 games, but the margin in the West would have been only five games, and the wild-card race would have been quite close with the Red Sox edging the Yankees by two games.

As far as the Wild-Card Scoreboard in Table 6.6 goes, 1979 would have received passing grades in all areas: the Red Sox, Yankees, and Tigers would have been added to the playoff race; the wild-card race would have been close; the new format would have righted some wrongs by including teams with the

Table 6.9 — Divisional Versus Wild-Card Format, 1979

| *Divisional Format* | | | *Wild-Card Format* | | |
Team	Record	Games Back	Team	Record	Games Back
			EAST		
			BAL	102–57	—
			BOS	91–69	11.5
EAST			NYY	89–71	13.5
			DET	85–76	18
BAL	102–57	—	TOR	53–109	50.5
MIL	95–66	8			
BOS	91–69	11.5	CENTRAL		
NYY	89–71	13.5			
DET	85–76	18	MIL	95–66	—
CLE	81–80	22	KCR	85–77	10.5
TOR	53–109	50.5	MIN	82–80	13.5
			CLE	81–80	34
WEST			CHW	73–87	21.5
CAL	88–74	—	WEST		
KCR	85–77	3			
TEX	83–79	5	CAL	88–74	—
MIN	82–80	6	TEX	83–79	5
CHW	73–87	14	SEA	67–95	21
SEA	67–95	21	OAK	54–108	34
OAK	54–108	34			
			WILD-CARD		
			BOS	91–69	—
			NYY	89–71	2
			DET	85–76	6.5
			KCR	85–77	7
			TEX	83–79	9
			MIN	82–80	10
			CLE	81–80	10.5

second and third best records; and both the wild-card and the weakest division champion would have had respectable records, better than or equal to the *actual* AL West champion Angels. And all of this would have been accomplished without diminishing the average quality of the races. Reasonable minds can't disagree on this one. The wild-card format would have been far better than the divisional format. That makes the new format 2–0–1 on the open-minded scorecard, 2–1–0 on the curmudgeon's.

1980

It certainly wasn't great under the divisional format, but 1980 would have been an unmitigated disaster under the wild-card format. The East did produce another great two-team race with the 103–59 Yankees outlasting the 100–62

Orioles. In the West, the 97–65 Royals won the division by 14 games. The new format would have righted a wrong in that the Orioles would have been in the playoffs. However, their inclusion would have greatly cheapened the East race. Costas's integrity of the race critique of the wild-card is especially valid for 1980. The additional races that would have been created, moreover, would have been awful. In the Central, the Royals would have beaten the Brewers by 11 games; in the West, a mediocre A's team (83–79) would have cruised past a woeful Rangers team by 13.5 games; and, in the wild-card race, no team would have been within 14 games of the Orioles.

Table 6.10 — Divisional Versus Wild-Card Format, 1980

Divisional Format			Wild-Card Format		
Team	Record	Games Back	Team	Record	Games Back
			EAST		
			NYY	103–59	—
			BAL	100–62	3
EAST			BOS	83–77	19
			DET	84–78	19
NYY	103–59	—	TOR	67–95	36
BAL	100–62	3			
MIL	86–76	17	CENTRAL		
BOS	83–77	19			
DET	84–78	19	KCR	97–65	—
CLE	79–81	23	MIL	86–76	11
TOR	67–95	36	CLE	79–81	17
			MIN	77–84	19.5
WEST			CHW	70–80	26
KCR	97–65	—	WEST		
OAK	83–79	14			
MIN	77–84	19.5	OAK	83–79	—
TEX	76–85	20.5	TEX	76–85	13.5
CHW	70–90	26	CAL	65–95	17
CAL	65–95	31	SEA	59–103	24
SEA	59–103	38			
			WILD-CARD		
			BAL	100–62	—
			MIL	86–62	14

On the Wild-Card Scoreboard, 1980 also wouldn't have fared well. The new format would have brought one additional team within 10 games of a playoff berth. Unfortunately, that team would have been the 83–79 A's. Although the wild-card entry would have been a very good team, it would have been small compensation for undermining the AL East race, and, as already noted, the wild-card race itself would have been a joke. 1980 would have received a three out of five on the scoreboard, but that's misleading — the wild-card would have made things far worse. Yes, it would have been a kick to watch Billy Martin's A's against his old Yankees team in the first round. Moreover, given the way Martin worked his pitching staff and supposedly blew out so many of their young arms, it would have been a bit of poetic justice to see Rick Langford (19–12, 3.26 ERA), Mike Norris (22–9, 2.54 ERA), Matt Keough (16–13, 2.92 ERA), and Steve McCatty (14–14, 3.85 ERA) in the playoffs just once. Fun? Yes. Sufficient compensation? Not at all. On the open-minded scorecard that makes it 2–1–1 in favor of the wild-card. On the curmudgeon's it's all even at 2–2.

1982

Because the playoff format was changed dramatically, we skip over the strike-shortened 1981 season, and proceed directly to 1982, another year that's a bit of a mixed bag. Because the divisions were well balanced, the new format wouldn't have done much to correct injustices. As it was, the AL West champion Angels had the third best record in the league, just a game behind the Orioles' 94–68. Under the new format, the teams with the four best records would have made the playoffs, and their average winning percentage would have been the same as the average of the actual division champions. So, more cities would have been involved in the playoffs without diminishing the quality of the competition.

As far as the races go, a definitive analysis is difficult. As it was, the races were quite good: the Brewers beat the Orioles in Earl Weaver's last game as O's manager (before his improvident 1986 return) to win the division by a game, and the Angels beat the Royals by three. Under the wild-card, the East and the Central would have been less tight, but not dramatically so. The Orioles would have beaten the Red Sox by five games; the Brewers would have enjoyed the same winning margin over the Royals. The wild-card race would have been very close. The Royals would have beaten the Red Sox by a single game. The White Sox would have trailed by three; the Tigers would have been within seven. The West, however, would have been a slaughter — the second-place Mariners trailed the Angels by 17 games. Essentially we would have exchanged one one-game race for another, the actual AL East divisional race in return for the wild-card. Provided one doesn't get too prickly about it being a wild-card race, that trade shouldn't matter much. In addition, we would have replaced a three-game race in the AL West with two five-game races — in the East and the Central.

Over the course of a season, it's not clear that one three-game race is always worth more than two five-game races in terms of excitement. The wild-card would have also brought an additional team, the Tigers, within 10 games of a playoff berth. In the final analysis, it seems that one might be willing to

Table 6.11—Divisional Versus Wild-Card Format, 1982

Divisional Format			Wild-Card Format		
Team	Record	Games Back	Team	Record	Games Back
			EAST		
			BAL	94–68	—
			BOS	89–73	5
EAST			DET	83–79	11
			NYY	79–83	15
MIL	95–67	—	TOR	78–84	16
BAL	94–68	1			
BOS	89–73	6	CENTRAL		
DET	83–79	12			
NYY	79–83	16	MIL	95–67	—
TOR	78–84	17	KCR	90–72	5
CLE	78–84	17	CHW	87–75	8
			CLE	78–84	17
WEST			MIN	60–102	35
CAL	93–69	—	WEST		
KCR	90–72	3			
CHW	87–75	6	CAL	93–69	—
SEA	76–86	17	SEA	76–86	17
OAK	68–94	25	OAK	68–94	29
TEX	64–98	29	TEX	64–98	33
MIN	60–102	33			
			WILD-CARD		
			KCR	90–72	—
			BOS	89–73	1
			CHW	87–75	3
			DET	83–79	7

exchange the races we had for the races we would have had, *plus* the additional team in the race.

With regard to other criteria on the Wild Card Scoreboard, 1982 also does well. As noted, the wild-card race was especially close and the team with the second best winning percentage, the Orioles, who were passed over under the divisional format, would have been a playoff team. In addition, neither the wild-card nor the weakest division champion would have been bad teams. That's a perfect five on the scoresheet, although the comparison between formats is less clear-cut than that statistic would indicate. Truth is, the divisional format also did a good job in 1982. All else was close to equal, and the wild-card format brought an additional team into the race. On that basis, the open-minded scorekeeper gives the new format the nod. The curmudgeon calls it a push. That makes it 3–1–1 in favor of the wild-card on the open-minded sheet, 2–2–1 on the curmudgeon's.

1983

This one's tough. Under the divisional format, the races weren't very good. In the East, the Orioles beat the Tigers by a comfortable six games; the White Sox won the West by 20. The wild-card format certainly would have kept fans interested in a higher number of cities. While the White Sox still would have won the Central easily, and the Orioles would have enjoyed the same six-game cushion in the East, the wild-card and the West races would have been close.

The wild-card race would have been indisputably good. Four teams with records of 87–75 or better — the Tigers, Yankees, Blue Jays, and Brewers — finished within five games of one another. The Tigers would have held on by one game over the Yankees for the playoff berth. As none of these teams were really close enough to threaten the Orioles late in the season under the old format, the new one would have been a clear improvement with respect to the AL East.

Table 6.12 — Divisional Versus Wild-Card Format, 1983

| Divisional Format | | | Wild-Card Format | | |
Team	Record	Games Back	Team	Record	Games Back
			EAST		
			BAL	98–64	—
			DET	92–70	6
EAST			NYY	91–71	7
			TOR	89–73	9
BAL	98–64	—	BOS	78–84	20
DET	92–70	6			
NYY	91–71	7	CENTRAL		
TOR	89–73	9			
MIL	87–75	11	CHW	99–63	—
BOS	78–84	20	MIL	87–75	12
CLE	70–92	28	KCR	79–83	20
			CLE	70–82	29
WEST			MIN	70–92	29
CHW	99–63	—	WEST		
KCR	79–83	20			
TEX	77–85	22	TEX	77–85	—
OAK	74–88	25	OAK	74–88	3
CAL	70–92	29	CAL	70–92	7
MIN	70–92	29	SEA	60–102	17
SEA	60–102	39			
			WILD-CARD		
			DET	92–70	—
			NYY	91–71	1
			TOR	89–73	3
			MIL	87–75	5

Unfortunately, the new format would have brought not only the strong Eastern teams into closer contention for the playoffs but also the hapless teams of the West. The 77–85 Rangers would have eclipsed the A's by three games and the Angels by seven. As noted above, had the AL West been comprised of five teams instead of four, this outcome would have been far less likely. In addition, this is the *only year* in which the new format would have produced a playoff team with a sub–.500 record. All that said, however, placing this Ranger team in the playoffs would have been an abomination. Buddy Bell led the team with a .277 batting average (14 HR, 77 RBI). Rick Honeycutt came over from the Dodgers in midseason to have a very nice year (14–8, 2.42 ERA), but, at the outset, the ace of the staff was the workman-like Charlie Hough (15–13, 3.18 ERA). There's a very good chance we would have seen Mike Smithson (10–14, 3.91 ERA) for at least one start against the White Sox. Cranky purists would have been outraged, and rightfully so.

So, where should one come down on the format decision? On the scoreboard, '83 is another mixed year. Under the old format, only five teams were within 10 games of a playoff berth; under the new, there would have been nine. The wild-card team would have been very solid, and the race would have been very close. On the negative side, the new format would have corrected no injustices because the old format selected the teams with the top two records. As a result, the average quality of the teams in the playoffs would have been diminished—greatly diminished due to the Rangers. In the end, although that wild-card race would have been enjoyable, even the open-minded scorekeeper can't give the nod to the new format. And, of course, the purist rates it a failure. Indeed, the true purist would cite 1983 as prime evidence that the new format would be an unmitigated disaster. That makes it 3–2–1 for the wild-card on the open-minded scoresheet; an ugly 2–3–1 on the curmudgeon's.

1984

The purist might argue that 1984 would have been nearly as great a disaster as 1983. The 81–81 Angels, a team only marginally better than the '83 Rangers, would have won the West. In addition, the 84–78 Royals would have won the Central. These mediocre playoff participants are a sure indictment of the new format, right? Well, not really. This is another case where the wild card should not be blamed for sins also committed under the old format. The playoffs we actually watched pitted the Tigers—the team with the league's best record—against the Royals, bearers of only the sixth best record in the league. It is true that under the new format the Angels, three games worse than the Royals, with only the seventh best record in a league of fourteen, would have also made the playoffs. However, the inclusion of the mediocre Angels must be balanced against the inclusion of Toronto, the league's second winningest team. If the Royals were going to make it under either format, it's not that big a deal to include the Angels. The Royals' winning percentage, after all, was only .519. You can argue that the inclusion of the Angels would have diminished the quality of the playoffs, but it's clear that we already had quality problems under the divisional format.

Table 6.13 — Divisional Versus Wild-Card Format, 1984

Divisional Format			Wild-Card Format		
Team	Record	Games Back	Team	Record	Games Back
			EAST		
			DET	104–58	—
			TOR	89–73	15
EAST			NYY	87–75	17
			BOS	86–76	18
DET	104–58	—	BAL	85–77	19
TOR	89–73	15			
NYY	87–75	17	CENTRAL		
BOS	86–76	18			
BAL	85–77	19	KCR	84–78	—
CLE	75–87	29	MIN	81–81	3
MIL	67–94	36.5	CLE	75–87	9
			CHW	74–88	10
WEST			MIL	67–94	16.5
KCR	84–78	—	WEST		
CAL	81–81	3			
MIN	81–81	3	CAL	81–81	—
OAK	77–85	7	OAK	77–85	4
SEA	74–88	10	SEA	74–88	7
CHW	74–88	10	TEX	69–92	11.5
TEX	69–92	14.5			
			WILD-CARD		
			TOR	89–73	—
			NYY	87–75	2
			BOS	86–76	3
			BAL	85–77	4
			MIN	81–81	8

This is another of those years in which additional cities are brought into the races without significantly diminishing the quality of the playoff participants. In some sense, these are the easiest ones to call. Not surprisingly, these years tend to do well on the Wild Card Scoreboard, and 1984 is no exception. The new format scores four out of the possible five. The races would have involved additional teams, and the wild-card race would have been close, producing a good playoff participant in Toronto, whose inclusion would have corrected an injustice perpetrated under the old system. The only black eye is the two mediocre division champions, but the old system was nearly as culpable on that score. On the open-minded scoresheet, therefore, 1984 is a clear win for the new format. However, a curmudgeon would focus excessively on the Angels, and so we will let him call it a tie. That makes it 4–2–1 in favor of the wild-card on the open-minded sheet, 2–3–2 on the curmudgeon's.

1985

On the heels of the weak division champions from the West in the prior two years, 1985 would have been a field day for purists. Although the new format would have corrected an injustice by including the 97–64 Yankees in the playoffs, it would have done so by undermining the integrity of the AL East race. Costas would have been right to complain as the wild-card would have greatly cheapened the race between the Blue Jays and Yankees. To add further insult, by splitting the Royals and Angels apart, the new format would have ruined what was a great one-game race in the West. In addition, the wild-card race would have been a joke — New York by 12.5 games. There would have been no silver lining. The year does score a three on the scoresheet on the basis of a strong wild-card, strong division champions, and inclusion of the league's second winningest team. But these minor achievements would have come at the expense of two great races. It's an easy call. That makes the new format 4–3–1 on the open-minded scoresheet, 2–4–2 on the curmudgeon's.

It is interesting to note that, had the lords of baseball passed judgment on the new format just eight years into the experiment, they might have found it wanting. While an attempt has been made to give the curmudgeon any conceivable reason to choose the old format over the new, many purists would have thought the same way, and so the 2–4–2 record to this point should not be easily dismissed. The hue and cry that would have gone up after the West produced such pathetic champions in '83 and '84, and after divisional races were eviscerated in '85, might have been enough to cause baseball people to reconsider their decision. Very few pundits, moreover, would have constructed the appropriate counterfactual (that is, comparing outcomes under the new format with those that would have obtained under the divisional format) in their stories. Nope, the new format would have been roundly vilified. This all would have been unfortunate because, as you will see, the wild-card was just suffering from growing pains. The second half of the period would have been quite different. That is why thoughtful fans should evaluate new innovations over longer time frames. People in the media have to come up with a new story every day, so it's hard to begrudge them their focus on time periods insufficient to produce definitive analysis. People who don't operate under deadlines, however, might be willing to wait 10 or so years. If one cares about the game, the only criterion by which to judge an innovation is whether, on average over sufficiently long time periods, it produces outcomes superior to the status quo.

Table 6.14 — Divisional Versus Wild-Card Format, 1985

Divisional Format			Wild-Card Format		
Team	Record	Games Back	Team	Record	Games Back
			EAST		
			TOR	99–62	—
			NYY	97–64	2
EAST			DET	84–77	15
			BAL	83–78	16
TOR	99–62	—	BOS	81–81	18.5
NYY	97–64	2			
DET	84–77	15	CENTRAL		
BAL	83–78	16			
BOS	81–81	18.5	KCR	91–71	—
MIL	71–90	28	CHW	85–77	6
CLE	60–102	39.5	MIN	77–85	14
			MIL	71–90	19.5
WEST			CLE	60–102	31
KCR	91–71	—	WEST		
CAL	90–72	1			
CHW	85–77	6	CAL	90–72	—
MIN	77–85	14	OAK	77–85	13
OAK	77–85	14	SEA	74–88	16
SEA	74–88	17	TEX	62–99	27.5
TEX	62–99	28.5			
			WILD-CARD		
			NYY	97–64	—
			CHW	85–77	12.5

1986

Things start to get a little better for the wild-card in '86. Under the existing format, both divisions were decided by at least a five-game margin, so there wasn't much to lose in terms of races. True, some might argue that the wild-card would have undermined the integrity of the Yankees-Red Sox race, but that was hardly a two-team race and, as noted, it wasn't that close. And again, as long as there are more teams in contention than there are playoff spots, the race has integrity. The East had four teams within 10 games of one another scrambling for two spots (the division championship and the wild-card). Under the new format, the division would have been conceded to the Red Sox early on, but there would have been a very tight wild-card race. That race would have seen the Yankees, Tigers, Blue Jays, and Rangers finish within four games of each other, a race clearly superior to the ones we had.

Purists, however, might have objected to one of the playoff teams under the new format. Would you believe it? The 84–78 Cleveland Indians would have won the Central by six and a half games. Before anyone becomes too indig-

Table 6.15 — Divisional Versus Wild-Card Format, 1986

Divisional Format			Wild-Card Format		
Team	*Record*	*Games Back*	*Team*	*Record*	*Games Back*
			EAST		
			BOS	95–66	—
			NYY	90–72	5.5
EAST			DET	87–75	8.5
			TOR	86–76	9.5
BOS	95–66	—	BAL	73–89	22.5
NYY	90–72	5.5			
DET	87–75	8.5	CENTRAL		
TOR	86–76	9.5			
CLE	84–78	11.5	CLE	84–78	—
MIL	77–84	18	MIL	77–84	6.5
BAL	73–89	22.5	KCR	76–86	7.5
			CHW	72–90	12
WEST			MIN	71–91	13
CAL	92–70	—	WEST		
TEX	87–75	5			
KCR	76–86	16	CAL	92–70	—
OAK	76–86	16	TEX	87–75	5
CHW	72–90	20	OAK	76–86	16
MIN	71–91	21	SEA	67–95	25
SEA	67–95	25			
			WILD-CARD		
			NYY	90–72	—
			DET	87–75	3
			TEX	87–75	3
			TOR	86–76	4

nant, we should remember that just two years prior we had an *actual* AL West Champion with the identical record. In the subsequent year, the AL West champion Twins were only one game better. So, the old format produced playoff participants a lot like the '86 Indians. For sheer novelty, a 1980s Indians playoff appearance would have been a nice by-product of the new format. What's more, this team wasn't really that bad. Pat Tabler, Tony Bernazard, Julio Franco, and Joe Carter all batted over .300. Bernazard, Carter, Brooks Jacoby, Mel Hall, Andre Thornton, and Cory Snyder all had at least 17 home runs. Carter led the league in RBIs with 121. The pitching was interesting; it included starters Tom Candiotti (16–12, 3.57 ERA), Phil Niekro (11–11, 4.32 ERA), and Ken Schrom (14–7, 4.54 ERA). A couple of crazy knuckleballers like Candiotti and Niekro in a short series against Roger Clemens and the Red Sox? It certainly would have been watchable. The format should, of course, be downgraded for admitting Cleveland, but only slightly.

On the Wild Card Scoreboard, 1986 offered mixed results. Two additional cities were drawn into the races, the wild-card race was close, and its champion was a respectable playoff participant. One of the division winners was a bit weak, and no injustices were corrected because the divisional format had already selected the two winningest teams. This means that the average quality of the playoff teams would have been diminished, but not too dramatically. Under the old format, the playoff teams had a combined .577 winning percentage (93–69 record). Under the new, the teams would have had a .557 winning percentage (90–72). The trade then is a little bit of quality for interest in additional cities, a great wild-card race, and the novelty of the Indians in the playoffs. It's not that difficult a call for the open-minded scorekeeper. For the curmudgeon, the Indians would have presented a problem, but it's a little unfair to let him rule in favor of the old format based on only one small gripe. He can call this one a tie, but the next one like this will have to go in favor of the new format. That makes it 5–3–1 in favor of the new format on the open-minded scoresheet, 2–4–3 on the curmudgeon's.

1987

Neither format would have offered fully satisfactory results in 1987 but, on balance, most would agree that the old would have outperformed the new. While it looks pretty bleak for the wild-card at this point, things get a lot better from here. Anyway, there was a two-game race between the Tigers and the Blue Jays that would have been cheapened by the wild-card. The West was a bit of an embarrassment under either format: that screwy Twins team (85–77) held on by a few games in another mad scramble between mediocre teams. Every team finished within 10 games of them. For that reason, the new format would have allowed *fewer* teams within 10 games of the playoffs than did the divisional format. This is the only year in which this occurs, which indicates that things have to be a bit strange before the wild-card does not deliver on its promise to be at least as inclusive as the old format. In any event, the new format would have had 10 teams within 10 games of a berth; the old one had *11*. Both were awfully inclusive. The new format would have been slightly more discriminating, however. The White Sox (77–85) would have been dropped from the list of contenders.

As often happens in years when the two divisions are so dramatically unbalanced, the new format would have corrected some injustices and improved the average quality of the teams in the playoffs. The Blue Jays and the Brewers, teams with the league's second and third best records, respectively, would not have been passed over under the new format. Of course, you correct some injustices, you create some others. The A's, owners of the league's seventh best record, would have been a playoff team. Still, the average winning percentage of playoff teams under the new format would have been .565, identical to that under the old format.

Table 6.16 — Divisional Versus Wild-Card Format, 1987

Divisional Format			Wild-Card Format		
Team	Record	Games Back	Team	Record	Games Back
			EAST		
			DET	98–64	—
			TOR	96–66	2
EAST			NYY	89–73	9
			BOS	78–84	20
DET	98–64	—	BAL	67–95	22.5
TOR	96–66	2			
MIL	91–71	7	CENTRAL		
NYY	89–73	9			
BOS	78–84	20	MIL	91–71	—
BAL	67–95	31	MIN	85–77	6
CLE	61–101	37	KCR	83–79	8
			CHW	77–85	14
WEST			CLE	61–101	30
MIN	85–77	—	WEST		
KCR	83–79	2			
OAK	81–81	4	OAK	81–81	—
SEA	78–84	7	SEA	78–84	3
CHW	77–85	8	CAL	75–87	6
TEX	75–87	10	TEX	75–87	6
CAL	75–87	10			
			WILD-CARD		
			TOR	96–66	—
			NYY	89–73	7
			MIN	85–77	11

On the scoresheet, 1987 was an abysmal failure. Fewer teams were involved in races, the quality of the weakest division winner was low, and the wild-card race wasn't very close. Most importantly, to create that lame wild-card race, the integrity of a great AL East race would have been undermined. The wild-card Blue Jays were a good team and their inclusion in the playoffs did correct an injustice, but that is small compensation for the format's glaring failures. Needless to say, the curmudgeon agrees. That makes it 5–4–1 in favor of the new format on the open-minded sheet, 2–5–3 on the curmudgeon's. It's always darkest before the dawn.

1988

Finally, an easy win for the new format. The divisional format produced a great race in the East between five good teams. The 89–73 Red Sox behind Roger Clemens (18–12, 2.93 ERA) and Bruce Hurst (18–6, 3.66 ERA) held off the Tigers, Blue Jays, Brewers, and Yankees who were all within four games. By contrast, the West was a blow-out as the A's cruised past the Twins by 13 games. Under the new format, the Twins, Brewers, and Royals would have had a nice race in the Central, with the Twins beating the Brewers by four and the Royals by six and a half. Despite the Brewers' absence, the race in the East still would have been a good one. Moreover, with four teams competing for no more than two playoff spots, the integrity of the East race would not have been in jeopardy. And it was not at all clear that the wild-card spot would go to an Eastern division team. In essence, we would have had seven teams from the East and Central divisions competing for three playoff berths. At season's end, five teams would have been separated by three and a half games in their quest for the wild-card. It would have been great. Of course, the West would have been a bust, but to some extent, that was also true under the old format. In terms of races, the new format would have beaten the old one handily.

Table 6.17 — Divisional Versus Wild-Card Format, 1988

Divisional Format			*Wild-Card Format*		
Team	Record	Games Back	Team	Record	Games Back
			EAST		
			BOS	89–73	—
			DET	88–74	1
EAST			TOR	87–75	2
			NYY	85–76	3.5
BOS	89–73	—	BAL	54–107	34.5
DET	88–74	1			
TOR	87–75	2	CENTRAL		
MIL	87–75	2			
NYY	85–76	3.5	MIN	91–71	—
CLE	78–84	11	MIL	87–75	4
BAL	54–107	34.5	KCR	84–77	6.5
			CLE	78–84	13
WEST			CHW	71–90	19.5
OAK	104–58	—			
MIN	91–71	13	WEST		
KCR	84–77	19.5			
CAL	75–87	29	OAK	104–58	—
CHW	71–90	32.5	CAL	75–87	29
TEX	70–91	33.5	TEX	70–91	33.5
SEA	68–93	35.5	SEA	68–93	35.5
			WILD-CARD		
			DET	88–74	—
			MIL	87–75	1
			TOR	87–75	1
			NYY	85–76	2.5
			KCR	84–77	3.5
			CLE	78–84	10

The new format also would have selected the four teams with the best winning percentages for the playoffs. On this score, the old format did not perform poorly, however, as it identified the first and third best teams in terms of winning percentage. As a result, the average winning percentage of playoff teams under the new format would have been a bit lower than under the old. But that's only because we're adding two teams to the calculation that had records almost identical to the Red Sox. The lower bound on the quality of the playoff teams, therefore, would have diminished by only a game. It would be difficult for purists to argue that the new format had admitted substantially inferior teams relative to the old.

It's no surprise that 1988 also does well on the Wild Card Scoreboard. In fact, it scores a perfect five. The Twins and Royals would have been brought into a race. Neither the wild-card nor the weakest division champion would have been bad teams. The wild-card race would have been incredibly close. An injustice would have been corrected in that the Twins, the second winningest team in the league, would have been included in the playoffs. Incidentally, under the wild-card format you'll notice that the "right" Twins team would have made the playoffs, not the mediocre '87 team. What can one say? In some years, the gods would have smiled on the wild-card format. That makes it 6–4–1 in favor of the new format on the open-minded card, 3–5–3 on the curmudgeon's.

1989

A little less resounding, but still a clear victory for the new format. The race in the East was a bit less cramped than it had been in the prior year, but it still saw four teams within eight games of each other at season's end. In the West, the A's won by seven games, a pretty substantial margin, if somewhat smaller than the thumping they put on the division in the prior year. Under the new format, neither of these races would have been greatly perturbed. The Blue Jays would have won the "new" East by two over the Orioles. One might argue that the wild-card would have undermined this race, but that conclusion is tenuous. First, the Red Sox were just six back of the Jays, which means that, had the wild-card gone to an East team, three teams would have battled for two spots throughout most of the year. More importantly, however, the Angels would have won the wild-card by four games, which means that the East teams would have been playing for only one playoff berth (as they did under the old format). So the East race would not have been cheapened by the new format.

The remaining division races would have been lousy but, as noted, so was the West race under the existing format. Oakland would have won the West by eight games over the Angels; Kansas City would have won the Central by 11 over the Brewers. One might argue that the Angels-A's race would have been undermined by the presence of the wild-card, but there wasn't much of a race to undermine. On balance, the division races would have been no less com-

Table 6.18 — Divisional Versus Wild-Card Format, 1989

| Divisional Format | | | Wild-Card Format | | |
Team	Record	Games Back	Team	Record	Games Back
			EAST		
			TOR	89–73	—
			BAL	87–75	2
EAST			BOS	83–79	6
			NYY	74–87	14.5
TOR	89–73	—	DET	59–103	30
BAL	87–75	2			
BOS	83–79	6	CENTRAL		
MIL	81–81	8			
NYY	74–87	14.5	KCR	92–70	—
CLE	73–89	16	MIL	81–81	11
DET	59–103	30	MIN	80–82	12
			CLE	73–89	19
WEST			CHW	69–92	22.5
OAK	99–63	—			
KCR	92–70	7	WEST		
CAL	91–71	8	OAK	99–63	—
TEX	83–79	16	CAL	91–71	8
MIN	80–82	19	TEX	83–79	16
SEA	73–89	26	SEA	73–89	26
CHW	69–92	29.5			
			WILD-CARD		
			CAL	91–71	—
			BAL	87–75	4
			BOS	83–79	8
			TEX	83–79	8
			MIL	81–81	10

pelling under the new format. In addition, we would have received a mildly interesting wild-card race. The Angels' four-game margin over the Orioles suggests that the race would have merited watching until late in the season. The Red Sox and Rangers, mediocre teams to be certain, would have lingered eight games back of the Angels. It wouldn't have been the most riveting wild-card race ever, but it wouldn't have been awful either. Given that the division races wouldn't have suffered under the new format, the wild-card race tips the balance in favor of the new format.

The quality of the teams in the playoffs would also have been as high under the new format as the old. The old format produced a matchup between the first and fourth best teams (in terms of winning percentage). The new format would have included the second and third best teams—the Royals and the Angels. Because those two teams had only slightly better winning percentages than the Blue Jays (the actual Eastern Division champion), the average winning percentage of playoff teams under the new format would have been slightly lower than it was under the old. However, the lower bound on the quality of playoff teams would have remained unchanged. In short, the new format could not have been blamed for diminishing the quality of the teams in the playoffs in 1989.

The races would have been slightly better and the quality of the playoff teams would not have been diminished, so it's not surprising that 1989 is also a good year on the Wild Card Scoreboard. Another perfect five for five. The wild-card race was relatively close and it produced a good playoff participant. The weakest division champion was not a bad team (indeed, it was the same weak champion that the old format produced). The Rangers were brought into a race and, as noted, an injustice was corrected with the inclusion of the Royals. There's not much to quibble about here — the new format wins. That makes it 7–4–1 in favor of the wild-card on the open-minded card and 4–5–3 on the curmudgeon's.

1990

This year is a close call but the balance tips in favor of the wild-card. As it was, we had a good two-team race in the East and another Oakland blowout in the West. These are exactly the sort of conditions under which the wild-card is most likely to undermine the integrity of a race and, to some extent, that also would have occurred here. The Red Sox, with Clemens at his most dominant (21–6, 1.93 ERA), held off the Blue Jays by two games. Had there been a wild-card, Toronto would have won it, which would have an adverse effect on the Eastern race. That said, the Blue Jays would not have coasted to their wild-card berth. The Rangers would have been but three games behind. Until the last weeks of the season, therefore, the Red Sox, Blue Jays, and Rangers all would have been unsure about which two of them would enter the playoffs. Again, as long as there are more teams competing than there are available spots, the race is a good one. Nor would this arrangement have shifted all focus to the wild-card. For Red Sox and Blue Jay fans, their focus would have been pretty evenly split between the wild-card and the East. Even those who cling to the notion that division races are somehow inherently superior to wild-card races must admit that the tarnished East race would not have been a clash of the Titans. Neither the 88–74 Red Sox nor the 86–76 Blue Jays stirred up the drama that, say, the Orioles and Yankees—each winners of 100 games—did in 1980. With the Orioles so far in front of the wild-card field in that year, that East race really would have lost something due to the wild-card. This one would have lost much less.

On the positive side, whereas the divisional format was again unable to produce the top two teams in terms of winning percentages, the new format would have again correctly identified the league's top four teams. The second

Table 6.19 — Divisional Versus Wild-Card Format, 1990

Divisional Format			Wild-Card Format		
Team	Record	Games Back	Team	Record	Games Back
			EAST		
			BOS	88–74	—
			TOR	86–76	2
EAST			DET	79–83	9
			BAL	76–85	11.5
BOS	88–74	—	NYY	67–95	21
TOR	86–76	2			
DET	79–83	9	CENTRAL		
CLE	77–85	11			
BAL	76–85	11.5	CHW	94–68	—
MIL	74–88	14	CLE	77–85	17
NYY	67–95	21	KCR	75–86	18.5
			MIL	74–88	20
WEST			MIN	74–88	20
OAK	103–59	—			
CHW	94–68	9	WEST		
TEX	83–79	20			
CAL	80–82	23	OAK	103–59	—
SEA	77–85	26	TEX	83–79	20
KCR	75–86	27.5	CAL	80–82	23
MIN	74–88	29	SEA	77–85	26
			WILD-CARD		
			TOR	86–76	—
			TEX	83–79	3
			CAL	80–82	6
			DET	79–83	7
			CLE	77–85	9
			SEA	77–85	9
			BAL	76–85	9.5

winningest team in the league was the White Sox, who hadn't really challenged the A's throughout the season. They were, however, six games better than the Red Sox and eight games better than the Jays. If the postseason is really supposed to reward the best teams, it was an injustice to have jilted the White Sox. Yes, the inclusion of the White Sox and the Blue Jays would have lowered the average winning percentage of the playoff teams slightly (.590 to .573), and the lower bound would have been two games worse than under the old format. Diminished quality would not, however, have been a major problem.

In addition to correcting the injustice perpetrated against the White Sox, the new format would have produced a good wild-card race that would have involved a bunch of additional teams. A lot of these teams were pretty lousy, but the eventual winner of the race would not have been terrible. Although on the scoreboard 1990 is marked down because the wild-card team was only 10 games above .500, the Blue Jays were only two games worse than the Red Sox, who were actually in the playoffs. To some extent, therefore, the new format is being held guilty of a sin that the old one also committed. As the weakest division champion under the new format, the Red Sox did make it over the quality threshold for Table 6.5, which gives the year a commendable score of four out of five. In sum, the balance of the evidence tips in favor of the new format. One race would have been undermined, but only slightly, and the quality of playoff participants would have diminished, but almost imperceptibly. In return for these minor defects, we would have received a number of additional cities in the playoff hunt, correction of an injustice, and a pretty good wild-card race. It is difficult to see how anyone could call this a victory for the old format. Not even the curmudgeon should be allowed to call it a tie. It is true that there would have been some trade-offs here, but the new format deserves a win on both cards. That makes the wild-card 8–4–1 on the first card, and 5–5–3 on the curmudgeon's.

1991

The year only scores a three on the Wild Card Scoreboard, but that's a little misleading. The new format couldn't right a wrong because the old one correctly identified the top two teams in terms of winning percentage. The new format also lost a point because the weakest division champ, the Rangers, wouldn't have been 12 games over .500. At 85–77 they weren't awful, however, and under the new format the West would have been a great race between four teams at or above .500. All of them would have been within four games of the Rangers. Under the old format, none of these teams would have been closer than 10 games behind the Twins.

In return for a pretty good race in the West, little would have been sacrificed. As it was, the East was decided by seven games and the West by eight. Under the new format, the East still would have been decided by seven, as the 91–71 Blue Jays would have held on against the Red Sox and Tigers, each 84–78. The Twins would have won the Central by the same eight-game margin by which they won the West under the old format. So, had the wild-card race been lousy, the races still would have been better under the new format. The wild-card race, however, would have been a good one. At season's end, *seven* teams would have been within six games of the 87–75 White Sox. While none of these teams were overpowering, all were at least .500. With this many teams in the race, there was little cause for concern regarding the integrity of any race. Of course, under the old format, there weren't really any races that could have been cheapened by the wild-card. In short, it's clear that the races would have been far more interesting under the new format.

Because the divisional format did identify the top two teams, the average

Table 6.20 — Divisional Versus Wild-Card Format, 1991

Divisional Format			Wild-Card Format		
Team	Record	Games Back	Team	Record	Games Back
			EAST		
			TOR	91–71	—
			BOS	84–78	7
EAST			DET	84–78	7
			NYY	71–91	20
TOR	91–71	—	BAL	67–95	24
BOS	84–78	7			
DET	84–78	7	CENTRAL		
MIL	83–79	8			
NYY	71–91	20	MIN	95–67	—
BAL	67–95	24	CHW	87–75	8
CLE	57–105	34	MIL	83–79	12
			KCR	82–80	13
WEST			CLE	57–105	38
MIN	95–67	—	WEST		
CHW	87–75	8			
TEX	85–77	10	TEX	85–77	—
OAK	84–78	11	OAK	84–78	1
SEA	83–79	12	SEA	83–79	2
KCR	82–80	13	CAL	81–81	4
CAL	81–81	14			
			WILD-CARD		
			CHW	87–75	—
			BOS	84–78	3
			DET	84–78	3
			OAK	84–78	3
			MIL	83–79	4
			SEA	83–79	4
			KCR	82–80	5
			CAL	81–81	6

quality of the playoff teams would have been diminished under the new format. Again, however, the new format would have correctly identified the top four teams in the league. What's more, because the White Sox and Rangers were both within six games of the Blue Jays, the average winning percentage of playoff teams would not have dropped too dramatically. Under the old format the average winning percentage was .574; under the new it would have been .552. Relative to the benefits that the new format would have produced, this drop in quality should be a minor concern.

The scoreboard summarizes well the new format's potential benefits in 1991. It earns one point for increasing the number of teams within 10 games of a playoff berth from seven to 11; only 1984 and 1990 would have seen larger jumps in the number of teams in contention. It earns an additional two points because the wild-card champion White Sox would have been 12 games over .500, and that race would have been close. As noted, the format loses a point because there were no injustices to correct since the divisional format correctly identified the teams with the highest winning percentages. It loses another because the Rangers, the weakest division champ, were only eight games over .500. Given the improved races, these seem to be only minor blemishes. Table 6.6 scores 1991 only three, but it's a strong three. Reasonable minds could not disagree that the new format would have outperformed the old. That makes the wild-card 9–4–1 on the open-minded scoresheet, 6–5–3 on the other.

1992

The 1992 results also favor the new format. As it was, the races were good but not great. The Blue Jays beat the Brewers by four games in the East, and the A's resumed their dominance in the West defeating the Twins by six. Under the new format, the Jays would have beaten the Orioles by seven in the East; the Brewers would have defeated the Twins by two in the Central; and the A's would have won the West in another laugher — only the Rangers would have been within 20 games of them. So, the Central race would have been two games closer than was the East under the old format, and the East would have been one game wider than was the actual West. Ignoring the wild-card race, some might trade the races under the old format for those under the new. Throwing the wild-card race into the calculation, however, tips the balance clearly in favor of the new format. That one would have been a close three-team race between the Twins, Orioles, and White Sox. In the end, the Twins would have outlasted the Orioles by a single game. With the White Sox lurking within the division, and with the Orioles making it unclear whether a Central division team was actually going to win the wild-card, the Twins and Brewers would have felt that the Central division race was one of substantial integrity. The Costas critique would not, therefore, apply in this year. On the whole, the races would have generated more interest under the new format.

The quality of the playoff teams under the new format would have been high as it would have again correctly identified the top four winningest teams in the league. All four would have had at least 90 wins. However, because the old format correctly identified the top two teams, the average winning percentage among playoff participants would have been lower under the new format, but not substantially so (.593 under the old; .577 under the new). Most fans would have gladly traded the small drop-off in quality for the improved races.

The year 1992 is also a pretty good one on the Wild Card Scoreboard. The format scores points for producing a close wild-card race, a good wild-card team, and good division winners. It loses points because there were no injus-

Table 6.21— Divisional Versus Wild-Card Format, 1992

Divisional Format			Wild-Card Format		
Team	Record	Games Back	Team	Record	Games Back
			EAST		
			TOR	96–66	—
			BAL	89–73	7
EAST			NYY	76–86	20
			DET	75–87	21
TOR	96–66	—	BOS	73–89	23
MIL	92–70	4			
BAL	89–73	7	CENTRAL		
NYY	76–86	20			
CLE	76–86	20	MIL	92–70	—
DET	75–87	21	MIN	90–72	2
BOS	73–89	23	CHW	86–76	6
			CLE	76–86	16
WEST			KCR	72–90	20
OAK	96–66	—	WEST		
MIN	90–72	6			
CHW	86–76	10	OAK	96–66	—
TEX	77–85	19	TEX	77–85	19
KCR	72–90	24	CAL	72–90	24
CAL	72–90	24	SEA	64–98	32
SEA	64–98	32			
			WILD-CARD		
			MIN	90–72	—
			BAL	89–73	1
			CHW	86–76	4

tices to correct, and because it brought no additional teams within 10 games of the playoffs. That last failing is, however, due to the rather arbitrary 10-game contention standard. Under the old format, only one team (the Brewers) was within five games of a division champion. Under the new, the Twins, Orioles, Brewers, and White Sox all would have been within four games of a playoff berth. The new format, therefore, would have drawn teams further into the races. Had the within-contention criterion been constructed a little differently, the format would have scored a four in 1992. In any event, this is another year that tips in favor of the new format. Better races, more cities truly in contention, with only slightly diminished quality among playoff teams—the choice isn't difficult. That makes the final score 10–4–1 in favor of the new format on the open-minded sheet; 7–5–3 on the curmudgeon's. The curmudgeon was given every opportunity to choose the old format over the new, and still the new one came out ahead. One would have to be an incredibly stubborn traditionalist to look at all of this evidence and conclude that, on average, the wild-card will *not* be an improvement over the old divisional format. Of course, there is little doubt that such traditionalists exist.

ONE REMAINING PROBLEM

Recall that the analysis of the wild-card was motivated by results from the Introduction that indicated that competitive balance, as represented by the number of teams within 10 games of a playoff berth, had a substantial impact on attendance. To the extent that the new format brings additional teams into the races, therefore, it can be considered a success—or so the reasoning went. Actually, it might not be so simple. Fans might not respond to the wild-card races and the new division races in the same way that they did the old division races. If, for example, fans perceive the wild-card race to be but a sideshow for mediocre teams, it might not produce much additional attendance. It was for this reason that in this chapter the new format was evaluated not only in terms of the number of teams that it would have brought into the race, but also with respect to the quality of its playoff teams. Although the data clearly indicate that the races would have been better under the new format, and that, on average, the quality of playoff participants would have been only slightly diminished (and in some cases improved), it was not a certainty that fans would view these races as legitimate. The previous descriptions of what the races would have looked like from 1977 to 1992 inspire confidence that these races will be the type that should generate fan interest but, as they say, there is no accounting for taste—especially if the typical fan is bombarded by pundits who question the integrity of those races.

At least initially, the wild-card data was difficult to interpret because attendance was somewhat depressed by the labor strife of the mid–90s. But even the earliest indications were that during the course of the season attendance remained highest in those cities that were involved in a race—either wild-card or divisional. In their October 3, 1995, edition, *Baseball Weekly* (*BW*) offered data suggesting that, even in the year just after the strike, fans responded positively to the races under the new format (Table 6.22). Among those 12 teams that remained within five games of a playoff berth as of September 25, average attendance during their most recent homestands was 27.4% higher than during the season as a whole. For a team that was averaging 30,000 per game, a 27.4% increase meant 8,220 additional people in the seats.[7] Admittedly, there are some problems with these data. First, *BW*'s data covered a weekend series, while the average season attendance was computed over both weekday and weekend series. To some extent, therefore, the increased attendance in Table 6.22 is the product of higher draws on weekends. In addition, one could argue that, over the course of the season, fan attitudes toward baseball were gradually improving, and that the attendance increases largely reflect these improved attitudes. While these two effects likely contributed to the improved attendance, it is unlikely that the 139% increase in Seattle's attendance or the 46% increase in the Yankees' didn't have something to do with the races. Interestingly, rather than focus on the increased fan interest that the races appeared to spawn, *BW* used the figures to point out that, despite being in contention, Kansas City and Houston still could not fill even half of their stadiums. Yet, one could just as easily argue that low attendance figures as a percentage of capacity were to be expected just after the strike, and that those figures were not good indicators of fans' reactions to the new format (as the *BW* analysis seemed to imply).

Table 6.22 — Attendance of Teams in Playoff Contention October 1, 1995

Team	Most Recent Series Avg. Attendance	As share of Capacity	Season Avg. Attendance	% Difference
American				
Boston	28,843	.852	30,198	-4.5%
California	31,055	.898	24,112	28.8%
Cleveland	41,774	.975	39,965	4.5%
Kansas City	19,218	.473	17,803	8.0%
New York	35,934	.618	24,361	45.9%
Seattle	50,934	.861	21,307	139.1%
Texas	28,653	.581	27,908	2.7%
National				
Atlanta	46,002	.873	35,582	29.3%
Cincinnati	33,038	.624	25,967	27.2%
Colorado	48,027	.957	47,028	2.1%
Los Angeles	48,615	.868	38,058	27.7%
Houston	22,877	.425	19,461	17.6%

Sources: Baseball Weekly and Elias Sports Bureau.

Table 6.23 offers alternative measures to test whether fans were responding positively to races under the new format which indicate that the results that *BW* reported were a bit misleading, at least as regards fans' affinity for the races. As noted, the weekend attendance as a percentage of yearly average attendance that *BW* reported for September was largely capturing the "day of the week" effect, not fan interest in races. As also noted, most teams, whether they're in a race or not, draw more fans on Saturdays than on an average day, even in September. To provide a better indication of whether additional fans would pay to witness the new races, Table 6.23 expands *BW*'s analysis to include not only contending teams, but also those that were out of it. To conclude that the races are captivating fans in September, contending teams must have higher weekend to average attendance ratios than do the also-rans.

Table 6.23 — Attendance: July and September, 1996

Team	July GB div	July GB wc	Sept. GB div	Sept. GB wc	Sept. % of Avg. (Mon.–Sat.)	Sept. % of Avg. (Tues.–Sat.)	Sept. % of Avg. (Sat.)	% chg. (Tues.)	% chg. (Sat.)
	(1)	(2)	(3)	(4)	(5)	(6)	(7)	(8)	(9)
Group I Stayed									
Yankees	0	0	0	0	-	-	93.8	-	-
Indians	0	0	0	0	-	100.5	100.6	-	-0.5
Wh. Sox	4	0	7	0	126.3	99.1	133.0	-	-12.5
Rangers	0	0	0	0	-	102.9	127.1	-18.1	-0.3
Mariners	3	1	5	3.5	-	-	-	-	-
Braves	0	0	0	0	-	-	131.6	-	27.5
Expos	7	0	4.5	0.5	-	94.4	87.8	-	-41.9
Cards	0	0	0	0	-	103.2	132.3	-	-15.0
Astros	3	2.5	3	1.5	104.6	102.3	152.6	-	-25.1
Dodgers	0	0	0	0	93.4	92.3	112.9	-47.2	-18.0
Padres	0	0	0.5	0	75.8	75.8	93.4	-	-54.2
Rockies	3.5	2.5	5.5	5	100.1	100.1	100.2	.03	0.3
Group II Arrived									
Orioles	9	5	4	1	99.6	100.4	104.6	-5.5	1.5
Group III Hovered									
Cubs	7	6	8	5	106.8	110.7	127.6	0.7	-7.6
Reds	5.5	4.5	6.5	5	-	85.0	93.1	-19.4	-29.0
Group IV Improved									
Red Sox	14	9	9.5	6	94.8	91.5	111.4	-40.9	-5.2
Twins	13.5	10.5	15.5	7	-	77.0	100.2	-47.7	-42.9
Group V Dropped									
Brewers	10.5	7.5	16	9	-	87.3	112.3	-15.0	-35.0
A's	9.5	8.5	12.5	8.5	-	86.4	91.8	-23.6	-21.5
Angels	9.5	8.5	14.5	10.5	-	-	-	-	-
Marlins	13.5	5.5	18	10	-	93.4	115.8	-0.5	3.9
Mets	13.5	5.5	19.5	15.5	92.9	92.3	112.2	-20.2	-16.6
Giants	8.5	10	22.5	22	45.0	44.9	57.6	-	-68.6
Group VI Never in Contention									
Blue Jays	16	11	17.5	14.5	116.3	110.3	137.3	-	19.8
Tigers	29.5	25.5	34	30.5	-	91.6	106.6	-	-7.7
Royals	16.5	13.5	21	12.5	94.8	82.7	95.7	-25.9	-32.3
Phils	20.5	13	29	21	-	75.4	78.0	-	-
Pirates	10.5	10	-	-	-	-	-	-	-

Notes: Column (1) and column (2) are games back in the division and wild-card races, respectively, just after the All-Star break. The data come from Saturday, July 13, or July 20, if the team did not play at home on the 13th. If a team did not play at home on either of those dates, Tuesday, July 16, was used. Column (3) and column (4) also measure games back. Data are for Saturday, September 14. If data were unavailable for the 14th, the 7th was used. Columns (5), (6), and (7) measure September attendance relative to average attendance. Column (5) has the average attendance between a Monday and a Saturday in its numerator,

(continued on page 194)

(Notes to Table 6.23 —*continued*)

average home attendance for the year in its denominator. Data are from Monday, September 16. If data for the 16th were unavailable, the 9th was used. Saturday data are for the 14th; if unavailable, the 7th was used. Column (6) has the average attendance between a Tuesday and a Saturday in September in the numerator, average home attendance in the denominator. September Saturdays were selected as described above. Column (8) is the percentage change in attendance from a Tuesday in July to a Tuesday in September. September Tuesdays were selected as described above. July data are for the 16th. Column (9) is the percentage change in attendance between a July Saturday and a September Saturday. July data are for the 13th, or, if data for the 13th were unavailable, the 20th. Source: Baseball Weekly.

Teams are grouped into six categories in Table 6.23: (1) stayers—those that were in a race (within five games) at the All-Star break and in September, (2) arrivers—those that weren't within five games of the playoffs at the break, but were in the race by September, (3) hoverers—those that were never quite in the race (five to eight games back) in July and September, (4) improvers—those that were well out of the race at the break (nine to 15 games back) that improved enough to get into the hoverer category in September, (5) droppers—hoverers at the break that were nine to 20 games off the playoffs in September, and (6) non-contenders—those that didn't even hover in July or September. If the new races were holding fans' interest we would expect the stayers and the arrivers to have higher weekend-to-average attendance ratios than the other groups in September.

To test that proposition, attendance data was collected for one home game for each team on a Saturday in the first two weeks of September.[8] Monday and Tuesday data were also collected for as many teams as possible. Although there was not much Monday data available for this period, the Tuesday and Saturday data make it clear that, on average, stayers and arrivers had higher September-to-average attendance ratios than the others. Although Tuesdays appear to be relatively slow nights for baseball, more than half of the stayers and the arrivers (six of 10) drew better than average crowds (see column 6). Only two of the 13 teams in groups 3–6 (for which the data were available) drew above average crowds on September Tuesdays. The average for groups 1–2 was 97.1% of their average crowd, for 3–6 it was 86.8%. Similar results obtain for the Saturday data: nine of the 12 stayers and arrivers drew better than average crowds (column 7). Eight of the 13 hoverers, improvers, droppers, or noncontenders did the same. All teams in groups 1–2 had ratios of at least 87.8% (Expos); the lowest values overall were for a dropper (Giants, 57.6%) and a noncontender (Phillies, 78%). The average Saturday-to-average ratio among stayers and arrivers was 114.2%; among the others it was 103.0%. On average, therefore, fans of contending teams do appear to attend September games more frequently than other fans, even after controlling for the day of the week. Admittedly, this is a weak test of the new format's popularity, but one that it passes nonetheless. These attendance improvements will be put in better perspective shortly.

First, however, a small aside: notice that if the Blue Jays are removed from the noncontenders, the average Saturday-to-average attendance ratios decline in an orderly fashion from groups 1–2 to 6: stayers and arrivers 114.2%, hoverers 110.4%, improvers 105.8%, droppers 97.9%, non-contenders 93.4%. This may be more statistical fluke than anything else, but it does inspire a bit of confidence in the way teams were grouped, and it does suggest that, in September, attendance was increasing in the extent to which a team was (or had been) involved in the race.

Of course, that result only works if you eliminate the Blue Jays, which brings up another important point—in some cases, the attendance figures in Table 6.23 are especially dependent on the game that was sampled. As you might expect, attendance depended not only on how well the home team was playing, but also on who their opponents were and how they were playing. The Jays, for example, drew especially well on Saturday, September 14, because they were playing the Yankees (the team with the second best average road attendance in the AL at 28,186 per game) and because their starting pitcher, Pat Hentgen, needed a few more wins to notch the Cy Young Award. Now there's no good way to also control for opposition effects with the available data, and opposition effects or no, the average figures in Table 6.23 provide a pretty reliable indication that contending teams do outdraw the others in September, even under the new format.

In column eight, Table 6.23 presents the percentage change in home attendance between a Tuesday just after the All-Star break and one in early September. Column nine contains the same information for Saturday attendance. These figures are probably less reliable than the average attendance ratios (columns 5, 6, and 7) because, whereas the ratios compared attendance on one or two September days to a "reliable" season average, columns 8 and 9 compare attendance between two games. Opposition effects, or weather, or some other peculiarity could have a large impact on either game used in the comparison. So, for example, columns 8 and 9 indicate that the Dodgers and especially the Padres experienced large attendance drop-offs in September, despite being in the race. However, on the September day sampled, both were playing outside their division—the Padres had the Reds and the Dodgers hosted the Cardinals. By contrast, in July, each played a division rival and drew especially well. The Padres drew 55,046 for a Saturday game against the Rockies; the Dodgers 54,226 for a game against the Giants. Had they played out of their division in both the July and September games sampled, we would have a more reliable indicator of the popularity of the races, although their attendance ratios (columns 5–7) do suggest that Southern Californians were a bit underwhelmed by them.

Despite the extreme sensitivity of these figures to opposition effects, the percentage changes in attendance also indicate that contending teams outdrew also-rans in September. The Saturday data (column 9) are substantially more complete than the Tuesday data. If the Blue Jays' game is again excluded from the calculation, on average the arrivers and stayers outperformed the other groups: arrivers and stayers–12.6% (-7.3%, if the Dodgers and Padres are excluded), -18.3% for hoverers, -24.1% for improvers, -27.6% for droppers, and–20.2% for noncontenders. The noncontenders probably would have been much worse had the Phillies and Pirates been playing at home during the September weeks sampled. The data also illustrate a more general point. In September, contending teams don't experience attendance explosions. Rather, they appear to be the teams best able to maintain attendance at July levels. The *BW* data suggested that playoff races *increased* attendance in September.

This probably seems like a lot of work to prove something that is pretty obvious. Moreover, to establish that fans like the new format, it is necessary but *hardly sufficient* to demonstrate that contenders outdraw the others as the season winds down. It must also be demonstrated that contenders outdraw others by as much as they did under the old format. Toward that end, Table 6.24 offers data from 1992. Again, home attendance data was used for each team for which it was available from one Saturday in early July and another in early September. The results were substantially similar to those for 1996 (column 3). The ratio of September Saturday attendance to the year's average was 114.1% for those teams in the race (stayers and arrivers) — almost identical to the 1996 figure (114.2%). As in 1996, the 1992 figures for droppers and noncontenders were lower than for contenders (109.4% and 101.5%, respectively). The hoverers didn't perform as well in 1992 as they did in 1996 (90.5% versus 110.4%), but that 1992 figure was driven by San Diego's low September attendance, a franchise whose attendance patterns defy explanation. On the whole, however, the Saturday-to-average attendance ratios tell a consistent story across the two years.

The percentage change in attendance from the July Saturday to the September Saturday (column 4) is also consonant with the 1996 data. Almost everyone lost attendance relative to their July levels, but contenders lost less than others. The average change for stayers and arrivers was–6.3%. For droppers it was–21.0%; for non-contenders–25.9%. The same pattern occurred in 1996. Admittedly, in 1992, the hoverers screw things up a bit (+7.5), but again that's due to San Diego whose 1992 data are strange. They stayed about six to seven games back throughout much of the season. On Saturday, July 11, they drew 11,777. On Saturday, September 12, they drew 15,879, which suggests, perhaps, that their fans became more interested as they lingered on the outskirts of the race. However, in each of those games the Padres drew less than their season average, which suggests that, at some point in the season, fans were substantially more interested than at the end. Maybe it was the weather, maybe it was opposition effects. Based on the box scores, it is difficult to know. Suffice it to say that, aside from San Diego, the attendance patterns exhibited by contenders and noncontenders were substantially similar in 1992 and 1996.

Table 6.24 — Attendance: July and September 1992

Team	Games Back 7/12 (1)	Games Back 9/5 (2)	% of Season Avg. (3)	% Change (4)
Group I Stayed				
Blue Jays	0	0	101.4	0.0
Orioles	4	0.5	104.0	0.0
A's	2	0	105.9	-21.5
Twins	0	4.5	78.9	-42.4
Pirates	0	0	183.4	25.9
Expos	4	4	136.6	19.1
Braves	3	0	88.8	-
Group II Arrived				
Brewers	7.5	4.5	-	-
Group III Hovered				
White Sox	8.5	6.5	106.3	-19.8
Padres	6.5	7	74.7	34.8
Group IV Improved				
-				
Group V Dropped				
Rangers	5.5	13.5	100.1	-17.8
Cubs	7.5	10.5	126.1	-9.4
Cardinals	3.5	12	111.9	-
Mets	6	16.5	-	-
Reds	0	6.5	99.4	-35.9
Group VI Never in Contention				
Red Sox	11	14.5	107.8	-1.6
Tigers	13	15	124.9	-43.7
Yankees	11	15	97.1	-47.0
Indians	18.5	15.5	74.6	-
Angels	18	18.5	87.8	-28.6
Royals	19	16	116.4	-7.4
Mariners	18	23.5	-	-
Phillies	12	24	96.1	-32.6
Astros	12	15.5	122.4	-23.0
Giants	9.5	19.5	-	-
Dodgers	14	25.5	86.3	-23.0

Notes: Column (1) is games back in the division race after the games on Saturday, July 11. Column (2) is games back as of Saturday, September 5. In column (3), the numerator is attendance on a September Saturday. The denominator is average attendance for the year. September Saturday data comes from September 5. If data for the 5th were unavailable, the 12th was used. Column (4) measures the percentage change in attendance between a July Saturday and a September Saturday. July data are for the 11th or, if data for the 11th were unavailable, the 18th. September Saturdays were selected as described above.

Recall that in 1996 contenders could have been vying for either division or wild-card titles, and many were in far closer contention in the wild-card race. In other words, the September attendance data is similar for 1992 division contenders and 1996 wild-card contenders. Although there is substantial variability within categories—among '92 contenders, for example, the September-to-average ratio ranged from 79% to 183%—the September attendance data do indicate that fans responded to the earliest races under the new format much as they did those under the old.

Of course, given the variability within the categories in Tables 6.23 and 6.24, some might need something more than the average figures to be persuaded. Fortunately, there were seven teams that had substantially similar seasons in 1992 and 1996 (Table 6.25). These seven help to control for quirky attendance differences between franchises that might account for the wide variation within categories in the previous tables. For example, the Cubs—a team that tends to draw well and thus inflates the September attendance figures for its category—were 6–10 games back at the All-Star break in each year. In September, they lingered five to seven back in both seasons. Their 1992 September-to-average attendance ratio was 126.1%. Their 1996 figure was 127.6%. The Orioles were four to five games back at the break in both years. In September, they were within a game, and their September-to-average ratio was 104% in both years. The Reds and Phillies also had similar ratios in both years, although both their ratios and their average attendance figures were a bit lower in 1996 reflecting, perhaps, fans' lingering post-strike antipathy toward the game—at least with respect to those teams that were out of contention by September. The only teams in Table 6.25 that didn't display similar attendance figures in both years were the Braves and Expos. Of course, the Braves' September ratio was much higher in '96 than in '92 indicating that fans weren't any less interested in the new NL East race than the one in the old NL West. For the Expos, the 1996 figures were worse than those for 1992 but, given the murmuring that had already begun about whether Montreal was a city deserving of a major league franchise, that might not be so surprising. In non-French-speaking cities, anyway, fans of teams that were in similar positions in '92 and '96 responded the same way in both years. In short, based on the available data from 1992 and 1996, it appears highly unlikely that fans will be any less interested in the new races than they were in the old ones.

THE RECENT EXPERIENCE UNDER THE WILD-CARD FORMAT

Perhaps such comparisons started to appear in print earlier, but it was in 1998 that there was a proliferation of brief articles, especially in *Baseball Weekly*, about what lousy races would have been taking place under the old playoff for-

Table 6.25 — Attendance: Teams in Similar Situations 1992, 1996

Team	July GB92 (1)	July GB96 (2)	Sept. GB92 (3)	Sept. GB96 (4)	Sat./Avg. Sept. 92 (5)	Sat./Avg. Sept. 96 (6)	Avg. Att. 92 (7)	Avg. Att. 96 (8)
Braves	3	0	0	0	88.8	131.6	37993	35818
Expos	4	0	4	0.5	136.6	87.8	20606	19982
Orioles	4	5	0.5	1	104.6	104.0	44047	45024
Cubs	10.5	6	7.5	5	126.1	127.6	26256	28450
Reds	0	4.5	6.5	5	99.4	93.1	28592	24492
Mets	6	5.5	16.5	15.5	-	112.2	21970	20363
Phillies	12	13	24	21	96.1	78.0	23796	23098

Notes: Column (1) is games back in the division race on July 11, 1992. Column (2) is games back in either the wild-card or division race (whichever was lower), on July 13, 1996. Column (3) is games back on September 5, 1992. Column (4) is games back in either the division or wild-card race as of September 14, 1996. Column (5) is the September Saturday-to-average ratio in 1992. Column (6) is the same ratio for 1996. The ratio and the way September Saturdays were selected are described in Tables 6.23 and 6.24. Column (7) is average attendance in 1992. Column (8) is average attendance in 1996.

mat. By now, so much has been written and said about the benefits of the new wild-card format that little space is devoted to it here, except to present a little evidence from 1998. Comparisons between the two formats for the American League in 1998 appear in Table 6.26.[9]

Things look a bit different from the previous tables because the Tampa Bay Devil Rays replaced the Milwaukee Brewers in the American League after a minor realignment, and the California Angels (CAL) changed their name to the Anaheim Angels (ANA). Neither of those changes invalidates the format comparison, at least not in any obvious way. Recall that for the new format to be deemed an unqualified success there were five requirements—(1) at least one additional team within 10 games of a playoff berth, (2) a wild-card champ with a record at least 12 games over .500 (87–75), (3) all division champions with records at least as good as 87–75, (4) a relatively close wild-card race (meaning at least one contender within five games), and (5) a playoff berth for the team with the second best record in the league (if that team would not have made it under the old divisional format).

The new format met all five requirements in 1998 in the American League. Under the old system, the Yankees juggernaut would have made for a stultifyingly boring season in the East. It was clearly a much better summer in Boston, Cleveland, and Toronto than it would have been. The old format would have produced a race between Texas and Anaheim in the West, but that race also occurred under the new format. It's little wonder that fans and analysts alike had only plaudits for the new system. However, the data indicate that the day will come when what would have been a gripping two-team divisional race is cheapened by the wild-card, or when the weakest divisional champion has a record at or below .500. When that day does come, remember years like 1998,

Table 6.26 — Divisional Versus Wild-Card Format, 1998

Divisional Format			Wild-Card Format		
Team	*Record*	*Games Back*	*Team*	*Record*	*Games Back*
			EAST		
			NYY	114–48	—
			BOS	92–70	22
EAST			TOR	88–74	26
			BAL	79–83	35
NYY	114–48	—	TAM	63–99	51
BOS	92–70	22			
CLE	89–73	25	CENTRAL		
TOR	88–74	26			
BAL	79–83	35	CLE	89–73	—
DET	65–97	49	CHW	80–82	9
TAM	63–99	51	KCR	72–89	16.5
			MIN	70–92	19
WEST			DET	65–97	24
TEX	88–74	—	WEST		
ANA	85–77	3			
CHW	80–82	8	TEX	88–74	—
SEA	76–85	11.5	ANA	85–77	3
OAK	74–88	14	SEA	76–85	11.5
KCR	72–89	15.5	OAK	74–88	14
MIN	70–92	19			
			WILD-CARD		
			BOS	92–70	—
			TOR	88–74	4
			ANA	85–77	7

and remember that, on average, the data indicate that the new format outperforms the old by a substantial margin.

CONCLUSION

The data in this chapter make it clear that, had it been used from 1977 to 1992, the wild-card format would have delivered on its promise to provide more interesting races that incorporated additional teams. Purists will also be glad to know that the average quality of the playoff participants would not have been dramatically diminished under the new system. In some cases, quality actually would have improved. Moreover, the data indicate that fans have responded positively to the new races—as positively as they responded to races under the old format.

However, the data also indicate that there will come a year when one of the division winners is not a .500 team, or when the existence of the wild-card undermines the integrity of a two-team race that would have been riveting under the old system. When that day comes, purists will complain long and loud. That's fine, but they should keep in mind that, at times, the results were no less arbitrary under the divisional format, and that on average the new format appears to produce better races. They won't keep those things in mind, but they should.

Within the context of the other chapters, this one provides additional reasons not to worry too greatly about competitive balance. Like pitching variability and the draft, the wild-card will be an additional equalizer. First, there is the direct effect of permitting additional teams in the playoffs. There will, no doubt, be years in which a weak division champion or the wild-card wins the league championship, or the World Series (the wild-card Florida Marlins in 1997 and then again in 2003, for example). It seems likely that pitching variability and a well-functioning amateur draft would have sufficed to preserve competitive balance — at the least, we would never have returned to the lopsided competition of the '50s. The format change will, however, sometimes provide a direct avenue for less dominant teams to enter the playoffs. A more subtle effect of the new format could be the additional revenue it produces for marginal teams. If fans continue to respond to these races as they have, teams that would not have been in contention under the old format may be able to stay in it longer, and thus maintain relatively high attendance late into the season. If they make the playoffs, they will enjoy the revenue stemming from additional sold-out games and higher ticket prices. Provided they use this revenue well, they may be able to compete for free agents on a more equal footing — with or without the revenue sharing that they might receive. Moreover, as described in the first few chapters, the distortions and uncertainties in the market for players make it unlikely that an organization can sustain itself merely by spending money.

7

Conclusions

There are a number of results in this book that could strike many fans as counterintuitive, if not flat-out wrong. This is due in no small part to the way a number of events in baseball are covered by the press, and to the tendency of MLB's top brass, especially its commissioner, Bud Selig, to make disparaging remarks about its own product. This chapter discusses a few of those events, and how one might view them in light of the evidence presented here. It closes by discussing Commissioner Selig's views of recent events. Needless to say, the data do not support many of his conclusions.

SUB–.400 TEAMS, 1998

As noted in Chapter 1, the average share of teams with winning percentages below .400 remained around (or above) 15% from World War II until the inception of the draft in 1965. From that point it declined to about 5% in the early 1990s. The argument presented here was that, along with the draft, this decline might have something to do with the results of Zimbalist and Scully who found that free agents in the last half of their careers tend to be overpaid (relative to their level of production). So Marvin Miller might have been right — free agency, ridiculous salaries and all, may actually have an equalizing effect on baseball.

On the basis of past experience, one would expect that as an expansion year 1998 would have brought with it a host of sub–.400 winning percentages as the new teams struggled to become competitive. The 1998 season thus offered an opportunity to compare the number and share of lousy teams with past expansion years, many of which occurred prior to free agency. Table 7.1 presents those figures, along with the winning percentage of the worst team in the league in each of those years — an indication of how overmatched were the weakest of the weak. Not only the share, but also the number of teams below .400 was lowest for 1998 in comparison with other expansion years. The next closest year was 1993. One could argue that a full-blown free agent market did not arrive until the late '70s, and that the 1977 expansion year, therefore, should be grouped with '61, '62, and '69 as pre-free-agent expansion years. Indeed, the share of teams below .400 in 1977 (19.2%) resembles that for the earlier expansion years. However years are grouped, the bottom line is that in 1993 and 1998 a much lower share of total teams had winning percentages below .400. Based on that statistic it would be difficult to argue that baseball is growing less competitive and that the league's weakest teams are falling further behind the best ones.

Table 7.1 — Sub-.400 Teams in Expansion Years

Year	#Sub-.400	Teams	Share of Total Teams	Lowest
1961	3	18	16.7%	.305 (Phillies)
1962	3	20	15.0%	.250 (Mets)
1969	5	24	20.8%	.321 (Expos) (Padres)
1977	5	26	19.2%	.335 (Blue Jays)
1993	3	28	10.7%	.364 (Mets)
1998	2	30	6.7%	.333 (Marlins)

Tracking teams that are playing around the .400 mark can actually be quite interesting, if only because many of these teams are often much more competitive than one might expect. By August of 1998, it was pretty clear that the self-destructive impulses that drove owner Wayne Huizinga to decimate his 1997 Marlins championship team had ensured that they wouldn't reach .400. But the Expos, Tigers, Diamondbacks, and Devil Rays all hovered tantalizingly close to the .400 mark. In the end, the Diamondbacks, Expos, and Tigers all put on late mini-surges to secure winning percentages just over .400.

One could argue, however, that the sub-.400 result was merely attributable to a rather arbitrary standard. While it is true, for example, that had the standard been 70 wins in a season (a .431 winning percentage) instead of 65, 1998 would have had five "lousy" teams, yielding a share of 16.7%. That new standard would also, however, mean one additional lousy team in 1961 and 1962 and two additional teams in both 1969 and 1977. The shares for those years would all be between 20% and 30%. Under either a 65- or 70-win standard, the share of lousy teams was higher in the pre-free-agent years than in the 1990s.

Another indication that the weakest teams are not falling further behind strong ones is the winning percentage of the worst team in an expansion year. The lowest figures are for the 1961 Phillies (.305) and the fabled 1962 Mets (.250).[1] The next lowest is the .321 winning percentage shared by both the Expos and Padres in 1969. The next best are the '98 Marlins' .333 winning percentage and the '77 Blue Jays' .335. The best is the '93 Marlins at .364. As with the decline in the share of lousy teams, the gradual improvement in the winning percentage of the league's weakest team in expansions years (at least through 1993) indicates that competition is growing more, rather than less, balanced.

The one possible exception is the '98 Marlins, a team that was deliberately destroyed by its owner in an effort to cut costs to attract a buyer. Despite his efforts, the Marlins still posted a winning percentage higher than any of those posted by the worst team in any of the expansion years of the 1960s, a figure almost identical to the 1977 Blue Jays.[2]

Finally, the expansion-year results could be partially attributable to the improved terms on which new owners can now enter the league. However, the data on sub–.400 teams in the Introduction, which included nonexpansion years, also indicated that the gap between weak and strong is narrowing. The results presented in this chapter, therefore, cannot be entirely attributable to the terms on which new owners now enter the league.

SOMEBODY FINALLY NOTICED

For those concerned about competitive balance, the narrowing of winning percentages and the declining share of sub–.400 teams are arguably the most important facts about baseball over the past 30 years. They provide compelling summary statistics to indicate that, despite all the handwringing, baseball is growing increasingly competitive. And they are such simple statistics that one might expect that they would receive more attention in the popular press. Yet they tend not to be emphasized unless something strange happens, which was the case in 2000.

In 1999, three teams finished under .400. The Florida Marlins, Kansas City Royals, and Minnesota Twins all flirted with .400, but each finished just below that line. Truth is, 1999 could have easily produced no sub–.400 teams, but it didn't, and so again the year slipped by without anybody realizing how good baseball's worst teams actually are. It really wasn't a bad year in terms of the competitive balance. The share of sub–.400 teams was 10%, a little high for the '90s, but within the 5% to 10% range that has become common. But still, the 1999 figures weren't eye-catching, and so they weren't discussed much.

All that changed in 2000. On Sunday, September 17, in an article entitled "Standings Closer than Ever," Murray Chass of the *New York Times* reported that 2000 might be the first season in major league history in which no teams finished with a winning percentage lower than .400 or higher than .600. Chass also mentioned a few seasons that provided near misses:

> The major leagues came closest to the .400 to .600 range in 1958, when only the Washington Senators among the 16 teams finished out of that range. With a .396 percentage in the 154-game season, the Senators could have joined the other 15 teams if they had gained one additional victory, finishing with 62 instead of 61.
>
> Four other seasons ended with one team beyond the .400 to .600 range, the White Sox in 1959, the Detroit Tigers in '68 and '84, and the Oakland Athletics in '90.

7—Conclusions

Chass was prescient. In 2000, the winningest team in baseball, the Giants, finished 97–65 (.599). The losingest teams, the Cubs and the Phillies, were the Giants' mirror image 65–97 (.401). So the secret was out, and everybody would realize that baseball was remarkably competitive. Right? Well, not really. Opposition to Chass's views came from at least one surprising source, Rob Neyer, a former researcher for (and current coauthor of) Bill James. Neyer, who writes an excellent column on ESPN.com, is careful with data, writes well, and has a good sense of humor. But, on this issue, he whiffed badly. On September 18, 2000, he noted:

> To his credit, Chass did some research ... he just didn't take it the one extra and necessary step. If this season's parity is the result of some fundamental change in the game, then shouldn't we expect this parity to continue forward? Because if there's a fundamental change, the effects should show up in more than one season.

A fair point. So, what kind of research did Neyer do? He produced a table similar to the one that appears here as Table 7.2 on the number of teams falling outside the .400-.600 band in the near-miss years identified by Chass ('58, '59, '68, '84, '90, and 2000). He also listed the number of teams outside the band in the year before and the one just after the near-miss year. His hypothesis was that, if parity were really on the rise, it should also be reflected in the before and after years, not just the near-miss ones.

Table 7.2 — Number of Teams Outside .400 to .600 Range

	Prior Year	Near-Miss Year	Subsequent Year
1958	4	1	1
1959	1	1	5
1968	3	1	5
1984	3	1	2
1990	3	1	2
2000	6	0	5

Neyer looked at the data in Table 7.2 (except for 2001, which wasn't yet available), could find no discernable pattern, and concluded that there hasn't been any fundamental change in competitive balance. He then went a step further, crediting Commissioner Bud Selig with having the most realistic view on this issue:

> As Commissioner Bud said—and this might be the first time I've ever quoted Selig with approval—"There may be an aberration from time to time."

Rob, you didn't have to quote him with approval this time, either. Had Neyer done a little more research, and included more years in his analysis, he too would have shown that the share of sub-.400 teams has gone down over the past 40 years, and that the biggest declines coincided with the introduction of the amateur draft and free agency.

1997 FLORIDA MARLINS

One could argue that the team that most undermines the main arguments put forth here is not the 1998 Marlins but the 1997 edition of that team. Bobby Bonilla, Moises Alou, Kevin Brown, and Gary Sheffield were all high-priced mercenaries brought together in an effort to "buy" a championship. That's true, as far as it goes, but it ignores a couple of the other main arguments put forth here. The first is that the most important player on the '97 Marlins was not a major league veteran but Livan Hernandez, a rookie pitcher from Cuba. Hernandez won 11 games after the All-Star break and was the Marlins' key starting pitcher throughout the playoffs and World Series. Without him, they would have been hard pressed to win. Had he gone through the amateur draft, he likely would not have ended up a Marlin. As noted in Chapter 3, this is one area where change should be advocated — the draft must apply to *all* entering players, not just natives of the U.S. (and a few other places).

A second point regarding the 1997 Marlins is that, in the end, "buying" a championship proved to be a financial blunder. As discussed in Chapter 2, because free agents (especially those in the latter stages of their careers) tend to receive salaries that exceed their productivity levels, owners who use this method to build their teams are likely to take a financial bath. It was priceless to hear Wayne Huizinga whine throughout the 1997 season that he had spent millions and millions to provide a first-rate product to the citizens of Miami, and that they did not sufficiently appreciate it. The Marlins' experience suggests that overpaying for free agents in a market like Miami might not be a sustainable strategy for an owner concerned about both profits and wins. By contrast, the 2003 Marlins showed that there was a way to win without overpaying.

1998 YANKEES

Of course, Miami isn't New York, and some might argue that the '98 Yankees are the team that most undermines the arguments put forth here. Given their market size, and the passion of their owner, the Yankees could overpay for free agents indefinitely. Yet, the '98 Yankees, for all their dominance, also benefited substantially from two foreign pitchers, Hideki Irabu of Japan and Orlando "El Duque" Hernandez of Cuba (Livan's half-brother). Irabu went 13–9 with a 4.09 ERA. Hernandez was even better, 12–4 with a 3.13 ERA, and also performed well in the postseason.

Neither of these guys should have ended up with the Yankees. True, the rights to Irabu were originally assigned to the Padres, but Irabu made it clear from the start that he would stay in Japan rather than play anywhere but New York. That left San Diego in a very weak bargaining position, and little choice but to trade his rights to the Yankees (or maybe Mets). After defecting from

Cuba, Hernandez went first to a different country before entering the United States in an effort to escape the amateur draft. These signings violate the spirit, if not letter, of the draft rules. Without their combined 25–13 record, the Yankees would never have been as dominant. They also ate up 314 innings, which has obvious benefits for the rest of the staff. In a pitching-scarce world, it's an atrocity that they ended up with the pitching-rich Yankees.

There is an opposing viewpoint, one offered frequently by agents of foreign players. Joe Cubas, an early agent to a number of Cuban players, would probably argue that these guys are at a more advanced stage in their careers, and thus they should receive free agent status, as would any veteran major league player. Without the ability to negotiate with all teams, the salary received by these foreign players would be unjustly low; so low, in fact, that they might prefer to stay in their home countries. Why face the perils of defecting from Castro's regime if you're only going to be compensated like some kid who had a good College World Series?

There is some logic to the argument, and it is natural to feel sympathy for some of these players. However, Major League Baseball officials should view this issue from the point of view of its effect on the talent pool, not from the entering player's viewpoint. Some, or even many, of these foreign players have enough talent to make an immediate impact on the league. If we were once worried enough about teams like the Dodgers and Yankees stockpiling all of the best talent from U.S. high schools to implement a draft, how much more worried should fans be about them gobbling up established foreign stars? These are such "can't miss" prospects that, if we care about competitive balance at all, we should be *especially* concerned with how they are distributed throughout the league.

If they want to enter the league, they should have to make themselves eligible for the amateur draft. The analysis in Chapter 3 strongly indicates that the draft has been the key equalizing force in baseball over the past 30 years. To undermine it now would be to take a big step backward. Skirting the draft, moreover, has now become an American as well as a foreign pastime. "Superagent" Scott Boras mounted a significant recent challenge to the draft. He argued that his client, J.D. Drew of Florida State, should have been given the right to negotiate with other teams because the Phillies, who had drafted Drew, were unwilling to pay him his market value. This value had supposedly been determined in Boras' informal conversations with other clubs. Boras' cheek in this matter would have been humorous had it not been so potentially damaging to the game.

As it happened, Drew sat out the year and re-entered the draft. He was again picked in the first round, this time by the St. Louis Cardinals, but after nearly 10 other teams had passed on him, presumably to avoid the problems encountered by the Phillies. In an ESPN interview with Drew during his sit-out, he solemnly explained that he took his stand in defense of a principle. He probably believes it, but the principle has no more intellectual merit than it did when Buzzie Bavasi was railing against the draft as a socialist restraint of trade in the 1960s (see Chapter 3). The more important principle is competitive balance, and that's why each of these players—including Drew, Irabu, and the Hernandez brothers—should have been allowed to negotiate only with the team that drafted him. Under the new labor agreement, the compensation picks in the next draft for unsigned first- and second-round picks (as described in Chapter 3) are a step in the right direction, but still not enough.

It would be tempting to prevent such players from re-entering the draft after they sit out a year. If they honor their draft right and play out their first contracts reasonably well, they'll receive their so-called market value soon enough. In fact, the Scully-Zimbalist results suggest they will receive more than their market value in the latter stages of their careers. Moreover, in their first contracts all first-round picks tend to receive compensation well in excess of the league minimum, and it's not as if players who make the league minimum starve. It's very hard to have any sympathy for someone like Drew. For the Cubans, it is easier. Theirs has been a tough road. In the end, however, an equitable distribution of all new talent that comes into the league is the most sensible way to ensure competitive balance.

COSTAS ON THE WILD CARD

Just when it looked like the wild-card debate had been more or less settled, Bob Costas came out with a book on how to "fix" baseball, including changes to the playoff format.[3] Referring to the 1999 season, he wrote:

> And there are people who think the simple fact that the Mets, a wild-card team, made such a dazzling show of the National League Championship Series somehow justifies the wild card, proves the point that it's good for the game. But this small-sample lapse of logic is all wrong, a bit like saying that your four-pack-a-day uncle Louie, who lived to 90, proves that cigarette smoking isn't harmful.... Here are some hard truths you can't get past: Pennant races are the lifeblood of baseball's history. Wild cards are the product of modern times. And in baseball, you have to choose one or the other. You can't have them both. The two things are mutually exclusive. It is that understanding, that simple regard for common sense, rather than an excessive regard for tradition that accounts for my opposition to it. (Costas, 2000, pp. 124–26)

As to "small-sample logic," where is Costas's sample? In evaluating what the wild card would have meant over an extended period (1997–1992), the evidence in Chapter 6 suggested that it would have been an improvement on the old two-division format.

As it turns out, however, the wild-card results aren't the most compelling ones in this book. The draft, pitching variability, and compensation structures are what drive competitive balance, not the playoff format. And Costas has a proposal for a new playoff format that probably wouldn't be so bad, either. He suggests eliminating the wild card and just having three division champions in each league. The team with the best record would get a bye in the first round of the playoffs. So the point is not to make a strong a defense of the wild card here, because it's not central to the argument. But, when one looks at the evidence, it becomes difficult to conclude that the wild card will be terrible for baseball. It hasn't been to date, and it wouldn't have been if it had been adopted earlier. Why should the future be different?

Costas does try to provide some evidence that the wild card doesn't, in fact, help the small-market teams it was supposedly designed to assist. And in doing so, he illustrates why he should stick to broadcasting. Table 7.3 lists the wild-card winners in each league from 1994 to 1999.[4] Of that list Costas writes in *Fair Ball*, "Where, pray tell, are the small- and middle-market teams? ... The evidence is clear: The wild card offers a helping hand for the haves, not the have-nots."

Table 7.3 — Wild-Card Teams, 1994–99

	American League	*National League*
1994	Cleveland	Atlanta
1995	NY Yankees	Colorado
1996	Baltimore	Los Angeles
1997	NY Yankees	Florida
1998	Boston	Chicago Cubs
1999	Boston	NY Mets

This is a misleading bit of evidence. Places like Denver, Cleveland, Atlanta, and Miami aren't large-markets in any statistical sense. More importantly, it's not fair to look only at the wild-card teams to evaluate the playoff format. The Montreal Expos, for example, were leading the National League East in 1994. There was a good chance they would have been either the division champion or the wild card had the season been completed. The San Diego Padres, Cincinnati Reds, Oakland A's, and the Seattle Mariners each won at least one division title from 1995 to 2000, and each of them is also supposed to be a small-market have-not.

If we, like Costas, assume that the teams that were leading in 1994 would have made the playoffs, then over the 10-year period from 1994 to 2003 only seven of the league's 30 teams would not have seen playoff action. Of those seven, two played in large-markets (Philadelphia and Detroit). The remaining five were Kansas City, Milwaukee, Pittsburgh, Tampa Bay, and Toronto. Toronto, Philadelphia, and Pittsburgh each made the playoffs in 1992 or 1993 or both. So that really leaves four teams with no recent success, and one of them, Detroit, is a large-market team. This is not to suggest that Milwaukee and Kansas City don't face big obstacles to success. However, over three-quarters of the league has seen playoff action since 1994, including teams from cities of similar size. By listing only the wild-card teams from 1994 to 1999, Costas gave a pretty misleading picture of the current playoff format.

BUD SELIG

As demonstrated in Chapter 3, the draft has been the key to supporting increased competitive balance in baseball. So, do the lords of baseball focus on preserving the integrity of the draft? No, of course not. Rather than understanding the factors that have brought about competitive balance, and then protecting them, they have instead granted Commissioner Bud Selig wide powers to "fix" a game that really isn't broken. His view of the "problems" that need fixing is, at best, muddled:

> [Money is] the biggest problem. There's no question. A lot of people will say, "Well, there's always been disparity. The Yankees won 19 out of 22 years." I talked to a lot of old baseball people and I looked at a lot of numbers. And the difference is in the '30s and '40s, '50s and even in the '60s, competence was the most critical factor. If you look at the economics, you'd say "God, I'm amazed." There wasn't that disparity even between the New York Yankees and the St. Louis Browns, because there was no money. DiMaggio drove in 140 runs and they wanted to cut him by $5,000. So it was competence. Even the Milwaukee Braves were in trouble, desperate trouble, but they were able to have a great farm system and keep their players. They had Hank Aaron coming on. Eddie Matthews and [Warren] Spahn. And they picked up [Lew] Burdette. The whole team stayed together. But you can't do that today. Today it's about money. There's no sense hiding that [*Baseball Weekly*, February 9, 2000, p. 10].

Bud Selig — Baseball's commissioner wants to fix a game that's not really broken through revenue sharing. The results here cast doubt on whether that step is necessary.

As the reader will quickly realize, none of the numbers presented in this book support Selig's opinions. Competence was the most important thing? Today it's only about money? Chapter 1 demonstrated that there is no strong causal link between team payrolls and winning percentages. Further, there was a positive relation between market size and winning percentage only in the early decades that Selig extols. After the introduction of the draft in 1965, that link disappeared (Chapter 2). Moreover, there is less dispersion in winning percentages now than in the years when, in Selig's world, competence was king. There are also far fewer teams (as a percentage of the league) with winning percentages below .400. Everything in his statement is false. It's maddening.

And it gets worse. When *Baseball Weekly* pointed out that attendance figures indicate that baseball has never been healthier, Selig responded:

> But we're not fooling anybody. In the midst of this incredible renaissance, we have a paradox of disparity. I mean, I could sit here and deny and say we're in this great renaissance and we have some minor problems, but I can't do that. I keep saying to clubs, a fan has two things. He has hope and faith. And for us to deny hope and faith in Minneapolis, Pittsburgh, San Diego, Seattle, Milwaukee, Detroit, Houston, San Francisco, Oakland — and we could go on and on — isn't right [*Baseball Weekly*, February 9, 2000, p. 10].

Detroit, Houston, and the San Francisco–Oakland metropolitan areas rank in the top 10 markets in terms of population. Since 1995, San Diego, Seattle, Houston, Oakland, and San Francisco have all made the playoffs. San Diego and San Francisco went to the World Series in 1998 and 2002, respectively. Houston, Oakland, and Seattle have each made multiple playoff appearances since 1995.[5] In 2001, moreover, Seattle won more games than any other team in the history of baseball, save the 1906 Cubs. What is he talking about? Lost hope? A lack of faith? Hey, Bud, try rooting for the large-market Cubs.

Of course, the writers at *Baseball Weekly* aren't idiots, and so they asked whether Cincinnati's relatively small payroll, their 96–66 record in 1999, and their near miss of the playoffs undercut his basic argument. Selig's response in the February 9, 2000 issue:

> No, it was an aberration. And I talked about this with our (economic) task force at the time. There will always be the aberration. We haven't had an aberration. I wish we had one. But as (Reds general manager) Jim Bowden was saying himself the last three weeks — and he was absolutely right — when he said, "Where are we going to be next year? We have to get rid of some guys." And sure enough, (Greg) Vaughn is gone, and a bunch of people are gone. And in the end, they failed, too. We'll have an aberration every four, five, six years, but it all comes down to hope and faith. If you've got four or five clubs playing by a different set of rules than everyone else, that's not good.

Uh, Mr. Commissioner, could you run that aberration thing past us one more time? Have we had one or not? And that task force appears to be giving him some questionable advice. Since 1989, Oakland, San Francisco, Cincinnati, Minnesota, and San Diego have all been in the World Series. The Florida Marlins and the Toronto Blue Jays, neither of them truly large-market teams, have not only been to the World Series, they have each won it twice. And again, neither the Cleveland Indians nor the Atlanta Braves, who have appeared in five World Series since 1995, are large-market teams. On the other hand, the Los Angeles Dodgers, Anaheim Angels, New York Mets, Baltimore Orioles, Chicago Cubs, and the Chicago White Sox, all among the likely candidates for Selig's unnamed four or five teams playing by a different set of rules, appeared in zero

World Series between 1989 and 1999, although the Mets did make it in 2000, the Angels won their first in 2002, and the White Sox won in 2005 after an 88-year drought.

So aberrations do occur. They occur so often, in fact, that you can't really call them aberrations. Now Selig might respond that all of the non-large-market World Series participants mentioned above had relatively large payrolls. However, small-market teams with high payrolls undercut his basic argument. If they are at such a competitive disadvantage, how did their payrolls get so high? Moreover, the evidence in Chapter 1 indicates strongly that teams tend to become good *before* they get paid large sums. And many small-market teams have gone through that process in the 1990s. Because salaries lag rather than lead performance and because the draft allows teams to accumulate players at relatively low salaries, all teams, no matter the size of their market, have an opportunity to get a good group of young players together and keep them for some time.

But the commissioner would probably say that, no, many teams really can't afford to pay even young players because they are already going broke:

> There are over 22 clubs losing money. And a lot of them very significant (money). There's not doubt about that. The industry as a whole is in a loss position. And if those numbers aren't right, that means every major accountancy agency in America and Canada is in some conspiracy, and that obviously isn't true [*Baseball Weekly*, February 9, 2000, 8–10].

And this is where it becomes exceedingly difficult to believe Bud Selig. For the most part, his "aw shucks" simplicity could almost be considered endearing, but on this point he's either a fool or is being incredibly disingenuous. And it's doubtful he's that foolish.

Zimbalist (1992) has analyzed franchise profitability and explained the reasons why accounting losses are *not* reflective of economic losses to major league owners. The main insight hinges on rising franchise values:

> If measured profits of a franchise are negative, the team is not necessarily a bad investment. Indeed, if one considers only the negative book profits reported by Major League Baseball for practically every year between 1974 and 1985, it would be impossible to explain the eruption of franchise values that took place over this period. The value of a franchise will approximate the discounted value of future estimated profits, where profits are conceived broadly to include all forms of return. If these values are high and rising, there must be (an expectation of) a significant and growing return. The value of companies in an unprofitable industry simply does not rise over time [Zimbalist, 1992, p. 62].

So why don't operating profits tell the same story that franchise values do? Zimbalist quotes Paul Beeston, former vice president of baseball operations for the Toronto Blue Jays: "Anyone who quotes profits of a baseball club is missing the point. Under generally accepted accounting principles, I can turn a $4 million profit into a $2 million loss, and I can get every national accounting firm

7—Conclusions

to agree with me."[6] And from a tax perspective, those losses can be very valuable. So yes, Mr. Commissioner, in a sense the accounting firms are in a sort of conspiracy.[7]

Accounting chicanery or no, Zimbalist also points out that from 1986 to 1990 Major League Baseball reported sizable operating profits. So even their own figures undercut Selig's remarks to some extent. But the most damning information is still the franchise values. Economists James Quirk and Lance Davis offer evidence that average franchise values increased steadily between 1910 and 1970.[8] In separate research, Quirk also estimated that the 1980s values were 69.6 times greater than they were in the 1910s. As of 1990, an equity investment in every U.S. professional sport at its inception would have yielded a rate of return three times as high as that of the S&P 500.[9] Zimbalist offers additional evidence that franchise values were increasing even more rapidly in the early 1990s than they had in the past.

So Commissioner Selig starts from the unfounded propositions that most teams are losing money and that there is severe competitive imbalance in baseball, and concludes therefore that something must be done about disparity:

> I have a lot of things I'm already talking to clubs about. I don't feel I have a lot of time to waste on this issue. I think it needs to be dealt with directly and as expeditiously as possible. I can't give you a specific time because there are so many variables, but it's something I don't think I have a lot of time to fiddle with. When I say expeditiously, I am not kidding. I do think this problem is so significant, and disruptive, and clearly not in the best interest of the game or the fans [*Baseball Weekly*, February 9, 2000, p 10].

Is he so confused that he doesn't know what strategy to pursue, or does he actually have a strategy, and is trying to be evasive when talking to the press? Hard to say, but you can rest assured that he will pursue increased revenue sharing in some form. When asked by *Baseball Weekly* whether the current revenue sharing through the so-called luxury tax had been a waste of time, Selig responded that "We've still come a long way. We do a lot more revenue sharing than ever before. This year, we're going to transfer $140 million from top to bottom. Remember, six years ago people said we couldn't do any of that. Do we need more? Of course, we do" (*Baseball Weekly*, February 9, 2000, p. 10).

He'll likely introduce additional forms of revenue sharing, and then rediscover how much competitive balance there is in baseball. He'll ascribe that balance to revenue sharing, but you'll know better. Pitching variability, the amateur draft, a salary system that rewards past rather than future performance — these are the main reasons that baseball continues to enjoy competitive balance. Is it bothersome that Selig will take credit where it is not due? A little, but eminent baseball historian John Thorn, speaking in the Ken Burns documentary *Baseball*, offers some reassurance:

Nothing worries me about the future of baseball. I worry about any number of things, but this is one thing I never, ever worry about. When I read in the papers that escalating salaries or gambling are going to be the end of baseball, I love it because we've been hearing this, or reading about this, for 130 years.

Epilogue

As this book goes to print, the Chicago White Sox are the reigning World Series champions—and, to the author's knowledge, hell has not frozen over. And as predicted by this author, Commissioner Selig is now discovering the parity that has existed for some time in baseball and, of course, claiming credit for it. When asked by *Sports Illustrated* to comment about 17 of the 30 teams being within five games of first place on July 5, 2004, he noted:

> This is exactly the way I dreamed about it in the 1990s.... Without revenue-sharing, [baseball] wouldn't look like it does today. San Diego, Detroit, Cincinnati, Milwaukee, Minnesota, Oakland, Florida ... without revenue sharing they are nowhere.

Read Zimbalist (2004) for a balanced assessment of the new revenue sharing plan and its potential impact on team finances. At this point no evidence exists to suggest that the teams that receive such revenues have used them to sign free agents. Only time will tell, but the suspicion here is that those teams won't do so unless they are compelled to under a minimum payroll rule. And yet baseball will continue to be competitively balanced for the reasons laid out here, with or without such a rule.

Appendix A
Market Size Population of Metropolitan Statistical Areas

Team	(1) Metropolitan Area Population	Team	(2) Population Divided by Teams in Market
1. New York Yankees	19,876,488	1. New York Yankees	9,938,244
1. New York Mets	19,876,488	1. New York Mets	9,938,244
3. Anaheim Angels	15,608,886	3. Anaheim Angels	7,804,443
3. Los Angeles Dodgers	15,608,886	3. Los Angeles Dodgers	7,804,443
5. Chicago White Sox	8,642,175	5. Baltimore Orioles	7,206,517
5. Chicago Cubs	8,642,175	6. Philadelphia Phillies	5,971,860
7. Baltimore Orioles	7,206,517	7. Boston Red Sox	5,827,654
8. Oakland A's	6,700,753	8. Detroit Tigers	5,438,756
8. San Francisco Giants	6,700,753	9. Texas Rangers	4,683,013
10. Philadelphia Phillies	5,971,860	10. Toronto Blue Jays	4,682,897
11. Boston Red Sox	5,827,654	11. Chicago White Sox	4,321,088
12. Detroit Tigers	5,438,756	11. Chicago Cubs	4,321,088
13. Texas Rangers	4,683,013	13. Houston Astros	4,320,041
14. Toronto Blue Jays	4,682,897	14. Atlanta Braves	3,627,184
15. Houston Astros	4,320,041	15. Florida Marlins	3,515,358
16. Atlanta Braves	3,627,184	16. Montreal Expos	3,426,350
17. Florida Marlins	3,515,358	17. Seattle Mariners	3,367,872
18. Montreal Expos	3,426,350	18. Oakland A's	3,350,377
19. Seattle Mariners	3,367,872	18. San Francisco Giants	3,350,377
20. Cleveland Indians	2,908,439	20. Cleveland Indians	2,908,439
21. Arizona Diamondbacks	2,839,539	21. Arizona Diamondbacks	2,839,539
22. Minnesota Twins	2,792,137	22. Minnesota Twins	2,792,137
23. San Diego Padres	2,722,650	23. San Diego Padres	2,722,650
24. St. Louis Cardinals	2,557,806	24. St. Louis Cardinals	2,557,806
25. Pittsburgh Pirates	2,361,019	25. Pittsburgh Pirates	2,361,019
26. Colorado Rockies	2,318,355	26. Colorado Rockies	2,318,355
27. Tampa Bay Devil Rays	2,227,000	27. Tampa Bay Devil Rays	2,227,000
28. Cincinnati Reds	1,934,145	28. Cincinnati Reds	1,934,145
29. Kansas City Royals	1,709,273	29. Kansas City Royals	1,709,273
30. Milwaukee Brewers	1,636,572	30. Milwaukee Brewers	1,636,572

Appendix B

Major League Attendance Regressions, 1945–1996

Team (Dependent Var: Attendance)	Current Winning Percentage	Last Year's Winning Percentage	Real Income (constant $)	MSA Population	Constant	Observations	Adjusted R-squared
AL East							
Baltimore	730,572.3	-4,184,930.0†	-39.99	2.542†	-926,482.9	43	0.62
	(0.57)	(3.39)	(0.84)	(4.17)	(1.33)		
Boston	3,309,919†	2,580,911†	68.93†	0.142†	-3,028,981†	51	0.82
	(5.28)	(4.18)	(6.43)	(2.71)	(7.25)		
New York	3,339,286†	199,026.3	20.52	0.063†	-1,385,162	51	0.31
	(2.74)	(0.17)	(0.86)	(2.97)	(1.56)		
Milwaukee	1,585,138	3,994,702†	95.41*	-0.07	-2752,564†	27	0.65
	(1.52)	(3.94)	(1.75)	(0.10)	(3.30)		
Toronto	Insufficient Data						
AL Central							
Chicago	1,828,811†	673,260.3	-81.00*	0.453†	-1,625,737†	51	0.51
	(2.09)	(0.82)	(1.97)	(3.66)	(3.18)		
Cleveland	4,913,269†	2,554,940†	68.93†	0.436†	-4,612,779†	46	0.69
	(6.69)	(3.28)	(2.26)	(2.88)	(7.30)		
Detroit	2,943,257†	882,702.2	78.83†	-0.148	-1,055,684†	51	0.53
	(4.78)	(1.36)	(3.17)	(1.39)	(2.61)		
Kansas City	1,900,330	626,639.6	127.52*	-0.331	-1,269,211†	40	0.55
	(1.30)	(0.44)	(1.94)	(0.50)	(2.07)		
Minnesota	5,457,986†	1,669,922	15.92	0.855†	-4,157,384†	36	0.37
	(3.96)	(1.24)	(0.38)	(2.37)	(3.56)		
AL West							
Anaheim	4,346,447†	4,247,943†	130.67†	0.089†	-5,747,967†	32	0.74
	(3.15)	(3.00)	(3.39)	(3.78)	(5.93)		
Oakland	3,040,752†	2,030,467†	38.32	0.328†	-3,482,898	29	0.74
	(3.18)	(2.22)	(1.15)	(5.56)	(4.88)		
Seattle	4,276,568†	2,793,523	62.94	0.254	-3,601,426†	19	0.63
	(2.17)	(1.33)	(0.74)	(0.99)	(2.33)		
Texas	2,442,502†	1,035,470	81.86	0.622	-3,349,965†	25	0.75
	(2.34)	(0.97)	(1.10)	(6.32)	(3.18)		

Team (Dependent Var: Attendance)	Current Winning Percentage	Last Year's Winning Percentage	Real Income (constant $)	MSA Population	Constant	Observations	Adjusted R-squared
NL East							
Atlanta	5,878,372† (4.04)	2,561,331* (1.92)	73.18 (0.87)	0.289 (0.90)	-4,352,658† (2.83)	31	0.80
Montreal	Insufficient data						
New York	2,390,968† (2.30)	640,923.4 (0.66)	111.63† (4.51)	-0.019 (0.74)	-1,500,609† (3.04)	46	0.50
Philadelphia	3,999,431† (4.50)	281,160.9 (0.31)	159.74 (4.19)	-0.089 (0.58)	-2,482,740† (5.61)	51	0.75
NL Central							
Chicago	3,436,744† (3.55)	2,340,361† (2.68)	-15.63 (0.44)	0.292† (2.76)	-3,004,064† (5.45)	51	0.63
Cincinnati	1,996,678† (2.45)	1,057,012 (1.28)	180.10† (5.25)	-0.078 (0.25)	-2,704,556† (5.18)	46	0.74
Houston	2,964,258* (1.77)	671,764.5 (0.42)	-17.72 (0.35)	0.048 (0.39)	-184,073.3 (0.24)	34	0.06
Pittsburgh	2,738,455† (5.23)	554,863.6 (1.07)	77.59† (5.39)	-2.273† (5.52)	3,711,588† (4.73)	51	0.62
St. Louis	3,371,033† (3.98)	639,115.2 (0.75)	308.24† (8.65)	-1,613 (4.45)	-1,239,291 (1.51)	51	0.78
AL West							
Los Angeles	3,835,589† (3.17)	1,831,820 (1.52)	66.80† (2.16)	0.080† (2.89)	-2,374,231† (2.20)	39	0.53
San Diego	4,828,195† (6.25)	3,081,192† (3.76)	30.98 (1.06)	-0.043 (0.41)	-2,716,467† (5.43)	27	0.82
San Francisco	5,061,444† (4.66)	1,250,131 (1.15)	-9.96 (0.34)	0.203† (3.56)	-2,547,250† (2.74)	39	0.45

*indicates significantly different from zero at the p = 0.10 level. †at the p = 0.05 level.

Notes

Preface

1. Book jacket to Jack Sands and Peter Gammons, *Coming Apart at the Seams: How Baseball Owners, Players and Television Executives Have Led Our National Pastime to the Brink of Disaster* (New York: Macmillan, 1993).
2. In his PBS series *Baseball*, Ken Burns also noted the lack of competitive balance that frequently ended the season by July for followers of the Washington Senators and St. Louis Browns in the 1940s and 1950s.

Introduction

1. It is no coincidence that the drop coincided with the arrival of the amateur draft, which is discussed in a subsequent chapter.
2. See Andrew Zimbalist, *May the Best Team Win: Baseball Economics and Public Policy* (Washington: Brookings Institution Press, 2003).
3. Of course, by splitting the last period in that way the share of sub–.400 teams from 1996 to 2000 would have been 4.1% (3.4% if expansion year 1998 is ignored), the lowest figures for any five-year period.
4. The Blue Jays were actually slightly worse in their third year (1979) than in their inaugural season (1977) when their winning percentage was .335.
5. Similar results obtain when the standard is teams within five, seven, or 12 games of a championship.
6. Other variations of the model produce similar qualitative results. Also, replacing the dependent variable (attendance) with per team attendance produces similar results.
7. Taking the natural log of a variable is a standard transformation in empirical research. It is often done to test whether the variable might be related to another in a nonlinear fashion. For example, the function $y = \log x$ is the inverse of the exponential function $e^x = y$. Thus x is the exponent that indicates the power to which e must be raised to equal y.
8. Mantle did come back to have a great 1964: .313 BA, 35 HR, 111 RBI. He did, however, have only six stolen bases and 465 at-bats, indicating perhaps that both his speed and durability were in decline. Between 1952 and 1962 *Total Baseball* ranked Mantle among the top five position players in the American League in every year but 1953. He fell out of the top five in 1963 and never returned.
9. There is also a more practical reason to exclude 1963–4 from the first era — to do otherwise would make the second era much smaller than the others, which could make some of the statistical analysis that follows less reliable.
10. It is interesting to note that the Orioles became dominant after Frank Robinson, a black player, came over from the National League. And it was almost universally acknowledged that Robinson's leadership skills were as important as his on-field exploits for his team's success.
11. In 1963, for example, he led the league in runs scored (121), RBI (130), home runs (44), total bases, slugging percentage, total average and runs produced. He was fourth in batting, second in both on base percentage and stolen bases, and third in both walks and hits (201). Sandy Koufax, who won the award, also had an outstanding year. He led the league in wins (25), opponents' batting average, opponents' on base average, ERA (1.88), shutouts, and strikeouts. He was second in winning percentage. He certainly deserved the Cy Young Award, but the MVP should have gone to Aaron. Not only didn't Aaron win the award, he finished only *third* in the balloting, behind Koufax and Dick Groat. Groat's 1963 stat line: .319 batting average, 201 hits, .380 on base percentage, six HR,

73 RBI, 85 runs scored, 56 walks, and three stolen bases. Aaron had the same batting average and the same number of hits; he had a higher on base percentage (.394), 38 more homers, 57 more RBI, 36 more runs scored, 22 additional bases on balls, and 28 more stolen bases. It is true that Koufax's Dodgers and Groat's Cardinals finished first and second in the National League while Aaron's Braves finished sixth, but that hardly seems enough to justify Aaron's third-place finish.

12. Again, a part of the motivation for excluding 1976 from the third era is to expand the size of the Aaron era for statistical purposes.

Chapter 1

1. These salary totals include prorated shares of signing bonuses and earned incentive bonuses.

2. *Baseball Weekly*, November 18–24, 1998: 5.

3. Although bonuses for appearing in the postseason were not included in Table 1.1, other incentive bonuses were included.

4. Special thanks to Kari Labrie for doing the lion's share of the work in creating the salary database. When these data were originally collected, the SABR Web site offered two types of salary estimates: one with an estimate for bonuses, one without. For the reasons already outlined, the salary estimates without bonuses are more relevant for this analysis. The SABR Web site did not make clear whether salary estimates were for the beginning or the end of a season. If they were for the end of a season, they would reflect the late-season acquisitions that inflate the payrolls of winning teams. Perusal of the data indicates, however, that SABR used beginning of season data. For example, in 1996 Cecil Fielder was acquired by the Yankees from the Tigers in the middle of the season. SABR credits his $9.2 million salary to the Tigers. Similarly, in the aforementioned Guzman trade, the Orioles, not the Reds, are credited with paying Juan's 1999 salary of $5.25 million.

5. Doug also maintained these data on his own Web site, *http://www.roadsidephotos.com/baseball/1999.htm*, but that source is also no longer available.

6. As an aside, neither Cleveland nor Atlanta are large-markets in any obvious statistical sense, a point elaborated upon in the next chapter.

7. Note that simply converting the payrolls into real terms to adjust for inflation does not accomplish this objective. Multiyear correlations with inflation-adjusted data were very similar to the simple multiyear correlations that appear in the tables.

8. Maddux led major league pitchers in the 1990s in wins (157) and ERA (2.44). *Baseball Weekly*, January 19, 2000:20.

9. In footnote 83 of his revised edition, Zimbalist mentions that the correlation between payroll and winning percentage is also positive and significant for 2002, though he does not report a figure. He also notes that he used forty-man season-ending payrolls for his calculation.

10. Results are very similar if we use the adjusted population measure, that is, MSA population divided by the number of teams located in the market.

11. Unlike Cleveland and Seattle, Florida relied more on high-salary veteran acquisitions than on their own development of young players to achieve their success. And as a result, their success was short lived. They dismantled their lineup, casting off almost all of their high-priced veterans, in 1998.

12. This excludes 1994, when the Braves trailed the Expos when the strike came.

13. Full regression results for each team are presented in Appendix B.

14. Assuming, of course, that they can also get a stadium.

15. Because the regressions run only through 1996, the Brewers are placed with the American League in Table 1.8. They did not switch to the National League until 1998.

16. Admittedly, the high share of sub-.400 teams in the NFL is due in part to fewer games played per season.

Chapter 2

1. To avoid repetition, those results are not reported.

2. Quirk and Fort (1992) were the first to demonstrate theoretically that the switch from the player reserve system to free agency need not have any effect on competitive balance.

3. To compute the median, all free agent transactions during a given period were ordered by market size (MSA population), and the one in the middle of the list was reported in Table 2.3. So, no matter what the size of the largest MSA in any given list, the size of the median market is not altered.

4. In many cases, sources listed the

amount but not the duration of the contract. The figures in Table 2.4 are for the full amount of the contract regardless of its duration. Salary per year would have been a better indicator, but the total contract data are sufficient to highlight a number of important points.

5. No relationship, that is, since the inception of free agency. As noted above, prior to the amateur draft, there was a positive correlation between city size and winning percentage.

6. This type of estimation does result in just one a2 for all teams, which some readers might find troubling. However, if the X's are chosen well, much of the team-specific variation in revenues is controlled for, and thus it may not be too great a stretch to rely on the estimated a2.

7. Some teams also bought and sold a lot of players. Since that type of player movement is much less common today, no attention is devoted to it here.

Chapter 3

1. Admittedly, given the lack of a farm system in basketball, high school draftees are the exception and not the rule.

2. On June 3, 2000, Peter Gammons put forth some evidence on the ESPN Web site about the importance of the draft's first round in producing major league players. He reported that 67.1% of the first-round picks from 1986 to 1995 played in the major leagues. Of the major league players signed out of those drafts, 28.3% came from the first round (including "sandwich" picks between the first two rounds), 7.9% from the second round, 8.5% from the third, 5% from the fourth, 4.6% from the fifth, 19% from the sixth through 10th, 15.7% from the 11th through 20th, and 11% from the 21st round and up. Based on those figures, the choice to analyze the careers of first-round choices was a sound one.

3. Allan Simpson, ed., *The Baseball Draft: The First 25 Years* (Durham, NC: American Sports, 1990), p. 10.

4. Neil J. Sullivan, *The Minors: The Struggles and the Triumph of Baseball's Poor Relation from 1876 to the Present*, (New York: St. Martin's Press, 1990). On the impact of televising major league games on minor league attendance, see pp. 237–41. On the resurgence of the minors and their differentiation from the major league product, see pp. 261–4. On the somewhat adversarial relationship between major and minor league owners, see, e.g., pp. 264–5. Another good example of this relationship is covered in Sullivan's discussion of the Pacific Coast League's attempts to merge with the major leagues. See pp. 208–29.

5. Buzzie Bavasi, Dodger general manager, 1964. Quoted in Simpson, *The Baseball Draft*, p. 10.

6. Simpson, *The Baseball Draft*, pp. 10–19.

7. Ibid., p. 19.

8. Note, however, that a team selecting in the first half of the draft rotation cannot lose its first-round pick. If such a team signs a Type A or B player, it forfeits its next-highest pick.

9. For a complete discussion of rule changes and the draft see, Simpson, *The Baseball Draft*, pp. 19, and the recent follow-up to that publication, Will Lingo and Allan Simpson, eds., *Baseball America Draft Almanac 1965–2003* (Durham, NC: Baseball Almanac, 2003).

10. Players selected from junior colleges are a problem for these calculations—they have attended a college, but most are probably closer in age to the high schoolers. They are left out of the percent high school and percent college calculations, so the numbers in the last two columns of Table 3.3 don't always sum to 100%. Of the players selected in the first round from 1965 to 2003, only 12 have come from junior colleges.

11. This figure excludes the drafts of 1988 and 1989. When Baseball America published its study in 1992, many players from those drafts had not yet reached their peak levels.

12. Only those first-round draftees that made it to the major leagues are included in the calculations in Table 3.5.

13. It is true, however, that many Latin American players do not enter organized baseball in the United States through the draft. This is discussed later in this chapter and in Chapter 7.

14. See, e.g., Sands and Gammons, *Coming Apart at the Seams*, p. 2.

15. Bill James, who looks at this issue more systematically, also has trouble coming to definitive conclusions regarding changes in the talent pool. James, *Whatever Happened to the Hall of Fame?*, pp. 230–42.

16. However, first-round draft choices have become increasingly apt to demand more money or even sit out if those demands aren't met. This topic is also covered in Chapter 7. Based on the historical evidence presented in this chapter, such salary demands would appear to be a potentially serious threat to competitive balance.

17. Midway through the season, Bones's 1996 record was 6–10, with an ugly 5.80 earned run average. Mieske had become an effective, if part-time, outfielder, hitting .278 with 14 home runs and 64 RBI in 1996. Valentin became the Brewers' everyday shortstop and hit .259 in 1996 while displaying some power (24 HR, 95 RBI). Valentin was also a major cog on the White Sox' 2000 playoff team.

18. Casual baseball fans appear to be far more forgiving about a bad first-round choice than is the average football or basketball fan. My friend Stan Engerman, an economist at the University of Rochester, points outs that the average baseball fan knows less about who draft choices were because there is a longer lag between the time of selection and the time when they appear in the major leagues than in other sports.

19. *Baseball America Draft Almanac* (2003), p. 76.

20. Gohr was traded to the California Angels in late 1996.

21. Actually, eight of the 15 pitchers selected in the '70 and '73 drafts made the majors. Randy Scarbery was selected in both years, but did not sign with the Astros in 1970. In Table 3.9, Scarbery's starts and appearances are counted for both the '70 and '73 drafts. Had Scarbery been included in only the '73 figures, the '70 draft would have appeared even weaker. The other seven major league pitchers from the 1970 and 1973 drafts were Steve Dunning, Dave Cheadle, John D'Acquisto, David Clyde, Eddie Bane, Mike Parrott, and Joe Edelen.

22. *The Baseball Draft*, p. 19.

23. *The Baseball Draft*, p. 19.

24. Teams that are unable to sign a second-round pick receive a so-called sandwich pick between the second and third round in the next draft.

Chapter 4

1. Source: *The Baseball Encyclopedia*, Ninth Edition, Home/Road Performance, pp. 523–555.

2. Because it is based on runs allowed instead of earned runs, the park-adjusted figure summarizes overall defensive performance — both pitching and fielding. As a result, the figure may slightly understate the quality of the pitching staff by assigning to the staff all responsibility for opponent runs scored. Any possible skewing of results, however, is mitigated by the fact that all league pitching staffs are affected by this facet of the park-adjustment factor.

3. Viola was the World Series MVP.

4. Thomas Boswell, *Cracking the Show* (New York: Doubleday, 1994), p. 213.

5. The Twins did, however, beat the Tigers in Detroit in games four and five of the AL championship series.

6. Frank Viola had a very good year (17–10, 2.90 ERA), but the rest of the staff was unimpressive — not one had an ERA under 3.94.

7. For that matter, the Dodgers also played their home games in a relatively large park.

8. My friend Tim Sloan notes that the 1974 Orioles were seen as a radical departure from the 1969–71 dynasty. They were understood as an anomalous team because they relied so much on speed to generate runs. They led the American League in stolen bases in 1973 and finished a close third on that measure in 1974. No Baltimore team before or since has finished higher than fourth in stolen bases.

9. The park-adjustment also hurts the Red Sox. They ranked 5th in the AL East in runs per game and 6th in park-adjusted runs per game. Clearly, however, they are listed among the low-scoring champions not solely because of the park adjustment, but because they were a truly weak offensive team.

10. Only full seasons are included in the calculations in Table 4.12. Because 1994 and 1995 were strike-shortened seasons, they are excluded.

11. All statements about ballparks favoring hitters or pitchers are based on the park factors reported at *www.baseballreference.com*.

12. For those interested in the intricacies of the park adjustment factors presented here, see the description at *www.baseballreference.com*.

Chapter 5

1. A .600 winning percentage is a somewhat arbitrary definition of a dominant team. It is, however, as good a benchmark as any to determine whether strong teams generally have balanced pitching attacks. The 12 teams with zero or one pitcher among the top 25% in wins are the '49 Cardinals, '56 and '62 Dodgers, '57 and '58 Yankees, '70 Twins, '72 and '76 Reds, '79 Pirates, '85 Blue Jays, '94 Yankees, and '03 Giants.

2. Those nine teams are the '64 White Sox, '64 Yankees, '65 and '70 Twins, '66 Orioles, '68 Tigers, and the '71, '72 and '75 A's.

3. Messersmith would also become one of

the important test cases that brought about free agency.

4. Andrew Torrez has a nice discussion of why additional pitching, because it is the rarer input and more highly variable, contributes more to a team's marginal utility than does additional hitting. See Torrez, *Off Base: New Insights into an Old Game* (San Francisco: Woodford, 1999), pp. 107–109.

5. Arroyo's numbers in 1961 (15 wins and 29 saves in 65 games) seem to be a fluke akin to Phil Regan's 14 wins and 21 saves in 1966 and Roy Face's 18 wins and 10 saves in 1960.

6. Making the cutoff at 10 appearances is somewhat arbitrary. Two very good pitchers, Bob Gibson and Bob Lemon, appeared nine times. Juan Marichal, Billy Pierce, Jim Bunning, Mickey Lolich, Ron Guidry, Orel Hershiser, and Chuck Finley appeared eight times; Don Drysdale, Jamie Moyer, and David Wells seven. However, to make the point that even among the best, pitching consistency is not easily achieved requires only the 19 pitchers in Table 5.6. Note that over 48 years there were about 2,700 starting pitching slots (536 team seasons times five starters per team). Even if one assumes that starters averaged 10-year careers, which is an overestimate, only 19 of 270 (7%) potential starters appeared in the top 25% in wins 10 or more times.

7. "Steve Carlton had big seasons, and because of this he found the Hall of Fame door as open as Madonna's . . . uh, arms. He was elected on the first ballot when he became eligible in 1993. Sutton, who plodded along at a pace of 17 or 18 wins, will still provoke an argument despite his overwhelming credentials." Bill James, *Whatever Happened to the Hall of Fame?* p. 80.

8. James conducted some interesting statistical simulations in which he placed a consistent "Sutton-like" pitcher on various simulated teams and an erratic "Drysdale-like" pitcher on the same teams to demonstrate that the addition of an erratic pitcher capable of having 20-some wins was slightly more likely to produce a championship than the addition of a Sutton. See Bill James, *Whatever Happened to the Hall of Fame?* pp. 82–87. Note that Drysdale wasn't that erratic in that he won at least 12 games in every season from 1957 to 1968. However, it wasn't unusual for him to win 13 in one year (1961) and 25 the next. He won 23 in 1965 and 13 in 1966.

James's analysis did, however, seem a bit backward. He assumed a winning percentage (or a distribution of winning percentages) for the team, and then added his hypothetical pitcher to determine the team's performance. The variance in the simulated team's performance, therefore, was generated almost entirely by the additional pitcher (Sutton or Drysdale). In practice, the team's success would depend not only on the variance of the additional pitcher, but also on the variances of the other pitchers on the staff. One wonders how the analysis would have turned out if James had added a "Drysdale-like" pitcher to a team of Suttons; or vice versa. In assessing the value of each of these types of pitchers, it would be helpful to know which type is more rare. If the league is comprised mainly of erratic pitchers, the Sutton type may be more highly prized. If the league has mostly plodding Sutton-type pitchers, the addition of a Drysdale may be especially valued. The suspicion here is that Suttons are more rare than Drysdales.

9. Outraged Texans are still hunting down the four sportswriters who dared to vote against Ryan.

10. One author used regression analysis to predict the performance of other great pitchers had they replaced Ryan. His methodology controlled for both the quality of Ryan's teams (generally poor), and the size of his home ballpark (generally spacious). The results indicate that most great pitchers would have performed better than Nolan did. Sutton is among the group that would have outperformed Ryan. Tim Sloan, *The Ryan Express: Fast and Powerful, But Can it Get You to Cooperstown?* (unpublished manuscript).

11. This excludes his brief stint with the Boston Braves in 1942. He appeared in four games, had an 0–0 record, and a 5.28 ERA.

12. Actually, in 1969, Carew only batted 458 times, and was therefore ineligible for the batting title. He did, however, bat .332 and have 152 hits. In the hits race Frank Howard finished fourth at only 175; the league leader in batting, Reggie Smith, batted only .309. It seems fair to include Carew among the batting leaders in 1969. In 1970, however, he probably shouldn't be included. He did hit .366, far ahead of league leaders Carl Yastrzemski and Alex Johnson at .329, but he played in only 51 games and batted only 191 times. Excluding 1970, he still had 13 consecutive years among the top 10 in batting average.

13. This includes 1969, but excludes 1970.

14. Unfortunately, a serious eye condition spelled the end of his career in 1996.

15. David Lamb, *Stolen Season: A Journey Through America and Baseball's Minor Leagues*

(New York: Warner Books, 1991), pp. 99–100. Lamb went on a Steinbeck-like RV tour through the minor leagues and, at the same time, tracked down ex-players from his favorite team, the Milwaukee Braves. It's a good read.

16. It's difficult to know whether the changing role of relief pitchers has had an impact on these numbers. In the Mantle Era, pitchers were expected to do more than get their teams through the sixth inning. Perhaps the additional strain associated with trying to finish games landed more pitchers on the disabled list, and made for larger swings in yearly pitching performance. On the other hand, the 162-game season faced by pitchers in the latter eras imposed additional strain on them. It seems unlikely that either effect had that great an impact on the results in Table 5.8.

17. A player's age is computed by subtracting the year of his birth from the year of his appearance among the victory leaders. Because the calculations do not include months, some ages may be off, but by no more than a year. The methodology should not introduce any bias in favor of concluding that pitchers from the recent years were as old as those from past eras.

18. In comparing the youngest pitchers across eras, the methodology does introduce a subtle bias against Spahn's immediate contemporaries. The database begins in 1945, well after many of Spahn's cohorts had begun their careers. It includes only those pitchers whose earliest appearance among victory leaders occurred after World War II. If, for some reason, the vast majority of pre–World War II pitchers reached the victory leader list before age 20, the conclusions drawn here are undermined. This seems highly doubtful. In any event, it is safe to conclude that of those pitchers who made their first appearance among victory leaders after the war, those who were 20 years old (or younger) were sprinkled pretty evenly across the Aaron and Miller eras.

19. The relatively low average for the Miller Era was also not caused by the strike-shortened 1981 season, as that year was excluded from the analysis.

20. David Halberstam, *October 1964*, p. 41. Halberstam suggests that Weiss had a very personal stake in keeping Yankees salaries low:

Weiss firmly believed that a well paid-athlete was a lazy one. That gave him the philosophical justification to be penurious, but unbeknownst to the players he had a more basic motive: The lower the sum of all the players' salaries, the greater the additional bonus he received from the owners. The owners gave Weiss a budget, say, $1 million a year. If Weiss kept the salaries down to, say, a total of $600,000 a year, he took home 10% of the remaining $400,000 [Halberstam, *Summer of '49*, pp. 193–4].

21. To some extent, Raschi's 1949 and 1951 statistics also undermine this hypothesis. In each of those years he won 21 games and led the league in games started (37 in 1949 and 34 in 1951).

Chapter 6

1. Under the wild-card format, the champions of each division (East, Central, and West) make the playoffs along with the wild card—the team with the best record that is not a division winner.

2. *Washington Post*, September 8, 1996, Section D, p. 3.

3. The true purist would argue that the divisional format was just as egregious an innovation as the wild card. However, as the number of teams in the major leagues has nearly doubled since 1945 (from 16 to 30 teams), league playoffs are a necessity, unless one wants to inflict incredibly boring baseball summers on most cities. In any event, eliminating the playoffs was never going to happen. To judge the wild card relative to the pre-'69 format is, therefore, pointless.

4. It would be a lot trickier in the National League. Because the Rockies and the Marlins did not begin play until 1993, guessing what the three divisions would have looked like from 1977 to 1992 under the wild-card format would be difficult. If those two teams were simply taken out of the existing (1996) divisional structure, that would leave three teams in the NL West, four in the East, and five in the Central. Obviously, some juggling would have had to occur, but who knows how it would have turned out? Fortunately, the American League data afford a sufficient examination of the issues.

5. Similar qualitative results obtain when considering the number of teams within five or seven games of a playoff berth.

6. Hargrove was, however, third in the American League in on base percentage (.424). Harrah's on base percentage (.397) was also impressive.

7. The 27.4% figure understates the improvement, moreover, because the Red Sox

showed a 4.5% dip in attendance (relative to their season average) due to bad weather that eventually resulted in a rainout on one of the September days in question. To be fair, however, because the Red Sox tend to fill Fenway most of the time, any correction for the rainout would have little effect on the attendance improvement figures.

8. Additional details are provided in the notes to Table 6.23.

9. Again, format comparisons for the National League are more difficult to do because, in the years when the old divisional format was in force, the league had only twelve teams. With the arrival of the Florida Marlins, Colorado Rockies, Arizona Diamondbacks, and the Milwaukee Brewers, the league now has sixteen teams. Dividing those sixteen teams into two divisions would be subject to a lot of guesswork on my part, and thus would not constitute as clean a test of the two formats as that afforded by the American League.

Chapter 7

1. In 1961, when the American League expanded by two teams, the worst record was found in the National League. Because players from both leagues are eligible in an expansion draft, it is valid to look at the Phillies' winning percentage in 1961 as an indication of how overmatched was the weakest team in baseball.

2. By 2000, the Marlins were hovering around .500 and in 2003 they were World Series champions, which reinforces that 1998 was an aberration.

3. Bob Costas, *Fair Ball: A Fan's Case for Baseball* (New York: Broadway Books, 2000).

4. Because there were no playoffs in 1994, Costas includes the two teams that would have qualified for the wild card if the season ended at the point at which the strike occurred.

5. Seattle, Oakland, and San Francisco all made the playoffs in 2000, just months after Selig made the remarks printed here.

6. For tax purposes, teams can treat players as assets that depreciate in value. Player salaries, therefore, can be converted readily into a paper loss that reduces a club's tax bill.

7. Based on a thorough analysis of all sources of franchise revenues (and costs), economist Roger Noll came to the conclusion that MLB was not in the financial trouble that it claimed to be, and that "everybody (each franchise) is just fine as far as I'm concerned." See Roger Noll, "The Economic Viability of Baseball." Report to the Major League Players Association, July 1985.

8. Lance Davis, and James Quirk. "The Ownership and Valuation of Professional Sports Franchises." Social Science Working Paper No. 79, California Institute of Technology, Pasadena, CA, April 1975. Davis was the author's Ph.D. thesis advisor and coauthor.

9. Reported in Zimbalist (1992).

Bibliography

Aaron, Henry, with Lonnie Wheeler. *I Had a Hammer: The Hank Aaron Story*, New York: HarperCollins, 1991.
Bernstein, Peter L. *Against the Gods: The Remarkable Story of Risk*. New York: Wiley, 1996.
Boswell, Thomas. *Cracking the Show*. New York: Doubleday, 1994.
Costas, Bob. *Fair Ball: A Fan's Case for Baseball*. New York: Broadway, 2000.
Davis, Lance, and James Quirk. "The Ownership and Valuation of Professional Sports Franchises," Social Science Working Paper No. 79, California Institute of Technology, Pasadena, CA.
Gorman, Jerry, and Kirk Calhoun, with Skip Rozin. *The Name of the Game: The Business of Sports*. New York: Wiley, 1994.
Halberstam, David. *Summer of '49*. New York: Avon, 1989.
_____. *October 1964*. New York: Villard, 1994.
Helyar, John. *Lords of the Realm: The Real History of Baseball*. New York: Villard, 1994.
James, Bill. *Whatever Happened to the Hall of Fame? Baseball, Cooperstown, and the Politics of Glory*. New York: Simon & Schuster, 1994.
Kahn, Roger. *The Boys of Summer*. New York: Harper & Row, 1972.
Krautmann, Anthony C. "What's Wrong with Scully-Estimates of a Player's Marginal Revenue Product." *Economic Inquiry* 37, no. 2 (1999) 369–381.
Lamb, David. *Stolen Season: A Journey Through America and Baseball's Minor Leagues*. New York: Warner, 1991.
Lewis, Michael, *Moneyball: The Art of Winning an Unfair Game*. New York: Norton, 2003.
Lingo, Will and Allan Simpson. *Baseball America Draft Almanac 1965–2003*. Durham, NC: Baseball America, 2003.
Miller, Marvin. *A Whole Different Ballgame: The Inside Story of Baseball's New Deal*. New York: Simon & Schuster, 1991.
Noll, Roger. "The Economic Viability of Professional Baseball." Report to the Major League Players Association, July 1985.
Parkin, Michael. *Microeconomics*. Reading, MA: Addison-Wesley; 1994.
Quirk, James, and Rodney D. Fort. *Pay Dirt: The Business of Professional Team Sports*. Princeton, NJ: Princeton University Press, 1992.
Sands, Jack, and Peter Gammons. *Coming Apart at the Seams: How Baseball Owners, Players, and Television Executives Led Our National Pastime to the Brink of Disaster*. New York: Macmillan, 1993.
Scully, Gerald. "Pay and Performance in Major League Baseball." *American Economic Review* 64 (December 1974).
_____. *The Business of Baseball*. Chicago: University of Chicago Press, 1989.
Simpson, Allan, ed. *The Baseball Draft: The First 25 Years*. Durham, NC: American Sports, 1990.

Sullivan, Neil J. *The Minors: The Struggles and the Triumph of Baseball's Poor Relation from 1876 to the Present.* New York: St. Martin's Press, 1990.
____. *The Diamond Revolution: The Prospects for Baseball After the Collapse of its Ruling Class.* New York: St. Martin's Press, 1992.
Thorn, John, and Peter Palmer, eds. *Total Baseball.* New York: HarperCollins, 1993.
Torrez, Andrew. *Off Base: New Insights into an Old Game.* San Francisco: Woodford Press, 1999.
Weiss, Peter. *Longshots: The Most Unlikely Championship Teams in Baseball History.* Holbrook, MA: Bob Adams, 1992.
Will, George F. *Men at Work: The Craft of Baseball.* New York: Macmillan, 1990.
Wolff, Rick, ed. director. *The Baseball Encyclopedia: The Complete and Definitive Record of Major League Baseball.* 9th ed. New York: Macmillan, 1993.
Zimbalist, Andrew. *Baseball and Billions: A Probing Look Inside the Big Business of Our National Pastime.* New York: Basic Books, 1992.
____. *May the Best Team Win: Baseball Economics and Public Policy.* Washington, DC: Brookings Institution Press, 2003.
____. *May the Best Team Win: Baseball Economics and Public Policy.* Washington, DC: Brookings Institution Press, 2004.

Index

Aaron, Henry 10, 141, 210, 223–224
Abbott, Jim 99
Abbott, Kyle 99
Abbott, Paul 136
above .600 teams 128, 131–132, 136, 204–205, 226
Alexander, Doyle 56, 149, 167
Alexander, Grover Cleveland 142
Allen, Dick 1, 52
Almon, Billy 91
Alomar, Robby 65–66
Alomar, Sandy, Jr. 35
Alou, Moises 2, 206
amateur draft: and competitive balance 77–78, 80–81, 88, 94, 97, 99, 100, 201, 205, 207–208, 210, 225; early drafts 81–82, 96–97, 100; foreign players 101–103, 206–207, 210, 212–213, 225; Juan Nieves rule 101–102; NBA 77; NFL 77; 1998 first round 100–102; rules changes 81–82, 101–102; shift to college players 78, 82–84, 86, 94, 101–102, 104–105, 225; shift to pitchers 93–102, 105, 126
American League attendance 38–41
Andujar, Joaquin 53
Angelos, Peter 16, 21
Aparicio, Luis 1
Appier, Kevin 99
Arizona Diamondbacks 13, 22, 46, 203
Armstrong, Jack 99
Arrojo, Rolando 103
Arroyo, Luis 136, 227
Astacio, Pedro 101
Atlanta Braves 13, 22, 26–27, 33–36, 39–40, 49, 63, 89, 97, 107, 116, 119, 120, 121–122, 125, 132–135, 153–154, 164, 166, 198, 211, 224
Avery, Steve 27, 99

Backman, Wally 91
Baines, Harold 91
Ball Four 10
ballpark at Arlington 121
Baltimore Orioles 2, 10, 13–18, 21–22, 38, 46, 67–68, 80–81, 111–113, 115, 117–118, 123, 125–126, 132–135, 152–153, 161, 163–167, 169, 171–174, 183–185, 189–190, 192, 198, 211, 223–224, 226
Bane, Eddie 226
Banks, Ernie 10
Banks, Willie 99
Bannister, Floyd 137
Barber, Steve 136
Barr, Jim 56
Baseball (by Ken Burns), 213, 223
Baseball America 78, 81, 85, 97, 104, 225
Baseball America Draft Almanac 85, 226
The Baseball Draft 78, 225–226
Baseball Encyclopedia 42, 48, 52, 55, 58, 61, 69, 226
Baseball Weekly 13–15, 191–192, 194, 196, 198, 211–213, 224
Baseball Writers of America 138
Bavasi, Buzzie 80–81, 103, 208, 225
Beeston, Paul 212–213
Bell, Buddy 175
Belle, Albert 35, 58
Bench, Johnny 130
Benes, Andy 99
Bernazard, Tony 179
Bernstein, Peter L. 66–67
Berra, Dale 91
Biancalana, Buddy 90
Bibby, Jim 56
Big Red Machine 128–131
Billingham, Jack 128–131
Blue, Vida 131
Blyleven, Bert 108, 140, 144–145, 167
Boggs, Tommy 96
Boggs, Wade 141–142
Bonds, Barry 2, 66, 85
Bones, Ricky 89, 226
Bonilla, Bobby 66, 206
Bonus babies 78, 80
Boras, Scott 207
Borbon, Pedro 128–129
Boston Braves 227

233

Boston Celtics 151
Boston Red Sox 2, 13, 18, 26, 37, 39–40, 53, 80, 106–107, 111–113, 115, 116–117, 121–122, 134, 152, 161, 165, 167–169, 172, 178–179, 181, 183–187, 199, 226, 229
Boswell, Tom 108, 226
Bouton, Jim 10, 148
Bowden, Jim 211
Branch, Roy 96
Brennan, Tom 96–97
Brett, George 66, 167
Brett, Ken 100
Broberg, Pete 97
Brock, Lou 141
Brooklyn Dodgers 9
Brown, Kevin 99, 133, 206
Bruton, Bill 141
Bryant, Kobe 77, 126
Buehrle, Mark 136
Buhl, Bob 134
Buhner, Jay 34
Bumbry, Al 52
Bunker, Wally 146
Bunning, Jim 136, 227
Burdette, Lew 134, 210
Burks, Ellis 66
Burns, Ken 2, 213, 223
Busch Stadium 109
Business of Baseball Research Committee 17–18
Byrd, Paul 63

Caldwell, Mike 110
California (Anaheim) Angels 2, 37, 40, 56, 63, 97, 99, 130, 138, 168–170, 172, 175–177, 183–184, 199, 211–212, 226
Camden Yards 21
Caminiti, Ken 27, 36
Camp, Rick 107
Campaneris, Bert 167
Campbell, Bill 53, 56
Candiotti, Tom 179
Capilla, Doug 131
Carew, Rod 140–142, 227
Carlton, Steve 138, 140, 142, 144–145, 227
Carroll, Clay 128–129
Carter, Joe 179
Casey, Sean 36
Castro, Fidel 207
Chalk, Dave 91
championship teams: home-away run differentials 111–112, 115; pitching quality on 106; with below-average offensive performance 111–117; with below-average pitching 106–111, 116–117
Charlton, Norm 123
Chass, Murray 204–205

Chavez Ravine 114
Cheadle, Dave 226
Chicago Bulls 150–151
Chicago Cubs 2, 18, 36–37, 39–40, 49, 51, 63, 107, 116–118, 122, 125, 153–154, 198, 205, 211
Chicago White Sox: attendance 39–40; Black Sox scandal 1; draft choices 89; futility of 1–2, 18, 58, 211; new ballpark 36; playoff races under wild-card format 152, 165, 167, 172, 174–175, 180, 186–190; World Series (1959) 5, 111–114, 117–118, 204; (1983) 137, 174–175; (1994) 35; (2000) 226; (2005) 1, 212, 215
Christenson, Larry 100
Cincinnati Reds 9–10, 15, 17, 22, 33, 36–37, 40, 51, 81, 99, 101, 113–115, 128–131, 134–135, 153, 195, 198, 209, 211, 224, 226
Clark, Will 77, 85
Clemens, Roger 58, 77, 126, 133, 136, 142, 144–146, 179, 181, 185
Clemente, Roberto 10, 141, 142
Cleveland Indians 6, 13, 22, 34–36, 39–40, 101, 116, 121–123, 125–126, 132, 134–135, 137, 152–153, 166, 178–180, 199, 211, 224
Clyde, David 226
Cobb, Ty 142
Colborn, Jim 167
Coles, Darnell 91
college baseball, quality of play 86–87, 104
College World Series 77
Colon, Bartolo 136
Colorado Rockies 3, 101, 153–154, 195, 228
common value auction 66–67
Contreras, Jose 103
Cooper, Cecil 110
Costas, Bob 32, 76, 164–165, 168, 171, 177, 189, 208–210, 229
County Stadium 110
Cruz, Jose 52
Cuban National Team 88, 103
Cubas, Joe 103, 207
Cuellar, Mike 132–133
Curtis, John 56, 100

D'Acquisto, John 56, 100, 226
Darling, Ron 128
Davis, Chili 59
Davis, Lance 213, 229
Davis, Storm 135
Davis, Tommy 142
Dawson, Andre 66
Dent, Bucky 168
designated hitter rule 88
Detroit Pistons 150
Detroit Tigers 2, 6, 18, 37, 39–40, 80, 99, 101, 113, 115–116, 138, 169, 172, 174–175, 178, 180–181, 187, 200, 204, 209, 211, 224, 226

Index

DiMaggio, Dom 134
DiMaggio, Joe 210
Dobson, Chuck 131
Dobson, Pat 132–133
Doerr, Bobby 134
Dotson, Richard 137
Downing, Al 135
Dressler, Rob 100
Drew, J.D. 207–208
Driessen, Dan 130
Drysdale, Don 111, 227
Dunning, Steve 100, 226
Durham, Leon 91

Edelen, Joe 226
Edge, Butch 96
Eldred, Cal 99
Ellis, Doc 167
Engerman, Stan 226
Esasky, Nick 91
ESPN 77, 207, 225
Espy, Cecil 91
Estrada, Chuck 136

Fassero, Jeff 123
Feller, Bob 132, 137, 142, 148
Fenway Park 106, 111, 122, 229
Fernandez, Alex 89, 99
Fernandez, Sid 128
Fielder, Cecil 224
Fingers, Rollie 110, 131
Finley, Chuck 227
Finley, Steve 27
first round draftees busts 83, 85–86, 90; 1998 100–102; percent reaching major leagues 83, 86, 90; quality of careers 87, 90–92, 94–100, 104; time to reach major leagues 87–88
Fisk, Carlton 66
Florida Marlins 3, 36, 89, 103, 116–117, 121–122, 126, 201, 203–204, 206, 211, 224, 228, 229
Ford, Dave 100
Ford, Whitey 10, 131, 136, 142, 144
Fort, Rodney 224
Foster, George 130
Franco, Julio 179
Franklin, Jay 96
Fraser, Willie 97–99
free agents 42, 46–55, 61–62, 149, 206, 215, 224–225; compensation 82, 208, 225, 226; and competitive balance 149, 151, 201–202, 203, 205, 224, 225; overpaying for 63–67, 201–202, 206, 208, 212, 213; pitcher performance 53–58; position player performance 58–63
Fulton County Stadium 106

Gammons, Peter 1, 223, 225
Garcia, Freddy 136
Garcia, Mike 132, 137, 148
Garnett, Kevin 77
Giambi, Jason 2
Gibson, Bob 107, 142, 227
Gibson, Kirk 37
Gideon, Jim 100
Gillick, Pat 104
Glavine, Tom 27, 132, 134, 138, 143–144
Gohr, Greg 99, 226
Gonzalez, Juan 66–67
Gooden, Dwight 128, 146
Goodwin, Danny 90
Granger, Clive 32
Grant, Mudcat 136
Greene, Tommy 97–99
Griffey, Ken, Jr. 34, 36–37, 51, 89
Griffey, Ken, Sr. 130
Grim, Bob 131
Grimsley, Ross 130
Groat, Dick 223–224
Gruber, Kelly 91
Guerrero, Pedro 114
Guidry, Ron 142, 167, 227
Gullett, Don 128–131, 146
Guzman, Juan 17, 224
Gwynn, Tony 27, 141–142

Haas, Moose 110
Halberstam, David 2, 134, 147, 227
Hall, Mel 179
Hanna, Preston 100
Hargrove, Mike 167, 228
Harkey, Mike 99
Harrah, Toby 167, 228
Hazewood, Drungo 90
Hentgen, Pat 195
Hernandez, Livan 103, 206, 208
Hernandez, Orlando 103, 206–208
Hernandez, Roberto 99
Hershiser, Orel 227
hitting variability 140–142
Honeycutt, Rick 175
Hooten, Burt 97
Hornsby, Rogers 142
Hough, Charlie 135, 145, 175
Houk, Ralph 147
Houston Astros 13, 15, 37, 39, 53, 107, 111–112, 119, 138, 153–154, 192, 211, 226
Houtteman, Art 132
Howard, Frank 80, 227
Howell, Roy 91
Hoyt, La Marr 137
Hudson, Tim 134, 136
Huizinga, Wayne 203, 206
Hunter, Jim "Catfish" 10, 131

Hurdle, Clint 91
Hurst, Bruce 181

Irabu, Hideki 206, 208

Jack Murphy Stadium 166
Jackson, Reggie 10, 167
Jacobs Field 36, 123
Jacoby, Brooks 179
James, Bill 138, 205, 227
James, Dion 91
James, LeBron 77
Jay, Joey 134
Jenkins, Ferguson 144, 169
John, Tommy 134
Johnson, Alex 227
Johnson, Randy 34, 36, 51, 58, 123, 126, 133, 142, 144
Johnson, Walter 142
Jones, Chipper 63
Jordan, Michael 126
Juden, Jeff 99

Kaline, Al 80
Kansas City Royals 38, 40, 101, 108–109, 111–113, 115, 163, 165, 167, -169, 171–172, 175–177, 182–185, 197, 204, 209
Kellogg, Geoff 89
Keough, Matt 172
Kirby, Clay 128, 130
Klesko, Ryan 63
Knapp, Chris 100
Knowles, Darold 131
Komminsk, Brad 90
Koosman, Jerry 111, 145
Koufax, Sandy 111, 142, 223
Kraich, Norbert 155–157
Krautmann, Anthony 65

Lamb, David 228
Langford, Rick 172
Larkin, Barry 36, 85
Larsen, Don 131
Larson, Dan 100
Lary, Frank 136
Lee, Bill 107
Lemon, Bob 132, 137, 148, 227
Lemon, Chet 91
Leonard, Dennis 167
Lewis, Michael 3
Lidle, Cory 136
Linares, Omar 103
Lingo, Will 225
Locker, Bob 131
Lofton, Kenny 35
Lolich, Mickey 227
Lonborg, Jim 107

Long Beach State University 77
Lopat, Eddie 134
Los Angeles Angels 78
Los Angeles Dodgers 2, 9–10, 13, 21, 26, 37, 40, 63, 77–81, 89, 96–97, 101, 103, 107, 111–115, 117, 131, 134–135, 138, 153–154, 156, 159, 164, 166, 175, 195, 207, 211, 216, 223
Los Angeles Lakers 150–151
Lynn, Fred 167

MacPhail, Lee 81
Maddux, Greg 27, 49, 132, 134, 137–144, 224
Madlock, Bill 142
Magrane, Joe 97–99
Mahler, Rick 107
Major League Baseball amateur draft 11, 42, 45, 77–105, 126, 201, 205–207, 210, 212–213, 225; attendance 2–3, 7–9, 38–41, 44, 156–157, 211, 223; attendance and income per capita 38, 40–41; attendance and winning percentages 38–41; Blue Ribbon Panel and competitive balance 102; champions 1977–2003 150–151; competitive balance in 2–3, 7, 9–11, 41, 44, 61, 64, 68, 76, 79, 102–103, 105, 116, 126, 132, 134, 142–143, 149–151, 191, 201, 203–205, 207–208, 210–211, 213, 215; expansion years 202–204, 229; franchise values and profitability 212–213, 229; Hall of Fame 138–139; market size and payrolls 33–34, 41, 48–51; market size and winning percentages 43–46, 61, 64, 210, 225; minimum payroll 215; player development 63; player transactions 42–43, 225; Players' Association 10, 102; Players' Strike 1–2, 152, 191–192, 198, 226–227; revenue sharing 213, 215; team payrolls 13–17, 26–27, 36–37, 64, 215, 224; team winning percentages and payrolls 14, 17–18, 20–32, 35, 41, 64, 68, 210, 212; team winning percentages and revenues 64–65; veterans' salaries 42, 46, 201–202, 206, 208, 212, 213
Manning, Eli 77
Manning, Rick 91
Mantilla, Felix 141
Mantle, Mickey 1, 9–10, 223
Marichal, Juan 107–108, 227
Marshall, Mike 135
Martin, Billy 167, 172
Martinez, Dennis 144–145
Martinez, Edgar 141
Martinez, Pedro 2, 58, 126, 133, 142, 144
Martinez, Ramon 101
Martinez, Tino 34, 36, 51
Mathewson, Christy 142
Matlack, Jon 111
Matthews, Eddie 141, 210
Mays, Joe 136

Mays, Willie 10, 141
Mazzilli, Lee 91
McCatty, Steve 172
McClure, Bob 110
McCovey, Willie 10
McDaniel, Von 80
McDonald, Ben 99
McDonald, Stew 80
McDowell, Jack 89, 99
McDowell, Roger 128
McGregor, Scott 100
McGriff, Fred 63
McLaughlin, Bo 100
McNally, Dave 132–133, 135
McRae, Hal 167
Mercker, Kent 99
Messersmith, Andy 135, 226–227
Metrodome 37, 106, 138
Metropolitan Statistical Area Populations 13, 33, 43–47, 55, 224
Miami-Dade Community College 89
Mieske, Matt 89, 226
Miller, Marvin 10, 151, 202
Millwood, Kevin 134
Milton, Eric 136
Milwaukee Braves 9, 134, 150, 210, 224, 228
Milwaukee Brewers 3, 40, 78, 88–89, 99, 101, 103, 110, 152, 168–169, 171–172, 174, 180–183, 189–190, 199, 209, 224, 226
Minnesota Twins 3, 14, 32, 36–37, 39–40, 46, 59, 61, 80, 101, 103, 108–109, 111–113, 115–119, 138, 152, 159, 169, 179–180, 182–183, 187, 189–190, 204, 211, 215, 226
Minor leagues 78–79, 80, 225
Minoso, Minnie 1
Molitor, Paul 78, 91
Moneyball 3
Monroe, Larry 96
Montreal Expos 2–3, 6, 14, 21, 99, 101–102, 154, 194, 198, 203, 209, 224
Moore, Mike 135
Morgan, Joe 130
Morris, Jack 37, 138–139, 144
Moskau, Paul 131
Mossi, Don 136
Moyer, Jamie 123, 136, 145, 227
Mulder, Mark 134, 136
Murphy, Dale 73, 91, 97
Musial, Stan 141–142
Mussina, Mike 92, 133, 136, 143–144

Nagy, Charles 99, 133
National League attendance 38–41
NBA champions 1977–2003, 150–151
NBA playoffs 157
Neagle, Denny 134
New York Giants 9

New York Mets 6, 13, 36–37, 39–40, 80, 108, 111–113, 115, 128, 159, 203, 206, 208, 211, 212
New York Times 18, 204
New York Yankees 1–3, 6–7, 9–10, 13–14, 16, 18, 20–24, 26, 34, 36–37, 39–40, 43–44, 52, 63, 78–81, 89, 103, 107, 109, 116–117, 121–122, 125–126, 130–131, 134, 147–151, 153, 161, 163–170, 172, 174, 177–178, 181, 185, 195, 199, 206–207, 210, 224, 226
Newhouser, Hal 148
Neyer, Rob 205
NFL champions, 1977–2003 150–151
NFL playoffs 157
NHL playoffs 155–157
Nicosia, Steve 90
Niekro, Joe 145
Niekro, Phil 107, 144–146, 179
Nolan, Gary 100, 129–131, 146
Noll, Roger 229
Nomo, Hideo 101
Norman, Fred 128, 130

Oakland A's 3, 10, 14, 22, 32, 40, 45, 52, 61, 81, 101, 113, 115–116, 119, 121–122, 124–125, 131, 134–135, 152, 160, 163, 171–172, 175, 180–183, 185–186, 189, 204, 209, 211, 215, 229
Oakland Raiders 151
O'Dell, Billy 107
Odom, John "Blue Moon" 131
Oglivie, Ben 110
Ojeda, Bob 128
Oliva, Tony 142
Olson, Gregg 99
O'Toole, Jim 134

Pacific Coast League 225
Page, Joe 134
Palmeiro, Rafael 85
Palmer, Jim 132–133, 135, 140, 142, 144, 167
Pappas, Doug 17–18, 224
Park, Chan Ho 101
park-adjusted runs allowed 107–111, 116–119, 123–124, 226
park-adjusted runs scored 111–119, 121
park adjustment factors 120–121, 226
Parrett, Jeff 97
Parrish, Lance 91
Parrott, Mike 226
Pascual, Camilo 136
Pepitone, Joe 10
Perry, Gaylord 108, 138, 144–145, 167
Pesky, Johnny 134
Pettitte, Andy 132, 136
Philadelphia Phillies 9, 18, 37, 63, 97, 99, 109, 125, 130, 194, 196, 198, 203, 205, 207, 209
Pierce, Billy 1, 107, 227

Index

pitching: age and tenure of victory leaders 145–146; and competitive balance 127, 142–143, 149–150, 201, 209–210; dominant staffs 127, 226; five-man rotation 127, 146; performance measures 127, 141–143; top 25% in wins 127–128, 131–133, 135–140, 145–149; variability 126, 132, 134–140, 141, 143–145, 150–151, 201, 208, 213, 227–228; variability on dominant teams 132–137, 226
Pittsburgh Pirates 2–3, 9, 40, 56, 101, 103, 109, 196, 209, 226
Pittsburgh Steelers 150
Pizarro, Juan 136
player trades: and competitive balance 68, 76; pitchers 69–73; position players 72–75
playoff teams: home-away runs allowed 122–125; home-away runs scored 121, 123–125; home-away winning percentage differentials 117–125; with below-average offensive performance 111–119, 121–122, 125–126; with below-average pitching 106–111, 116–119, 122–126
Powell, Jay 92
private value auction 67
Puckett, Kirby 141, 227
Purists 154–156, 160–161, 163, 200–201, 228
Purkey, Bob 134

Quirk, James 213, 224, 229
Quirk, Jamie 91

Radke, Brad 136
Ramirez, Manny 35
Raschi, Vic 134, 148, 228
Rau, Doug 135
Reardon, Jeff 108
Reese, Pokey 36
Reichardt, Rick 78
Reinsdorf, Jerry 58
reserve clause 69
Reuschel, Rick 145
Reynolds, Allie 134, 148
Reynolds, Bob 100
Rhoden, Rick 96–99
Riccelli, Frank 96
Rice, Jim 167
Rickey, Branch 9, 106
Ripken, Cal, Jr. 68, 143
Roberts, Dave 91
Roberts, Robin 144, 147
Robinson, Brooks 167
Robinson, Frank 10, 223
Robinson, Jackie 9
Rodriguez, Alex 36, 51
Roenicke, Gary 91
Rosario, Victor 97
Rose, Pete 130, 140–142

Ruthven, Dick 100
Ryan, Nolan 138–140, 142–146, 227

Sabathia, C.C. 136
Sadecki, Ray 107
Safeco Field 36
Saint Louis Browns 210
Saint Louis Cardinals 2, 9–10, 80–81, 97, 106–107, 109, 121, 153–154, 166, 195, 207, 224, 226
Salkeld, Roger 99
San Diego Chargers 167
San Diego Padres 3, 6, 13, 27, 33, 36, 39–40, 46, 52, 56, 89, 107, 154, 156, 159, 164, 166, 195–196, 203, 206, 209, 211
San Francisco 49ers 150–151
San Francisco Giants 39, 45, 101, 106–111, 113–117, 121–122, 124–125, 135, 194–195, 205, 211, 226, 229
Sands, Jack 223, 225
Sanford, Jack 107
Santorini, Al 100
Scarbery, Randy 226
Schilling, Curt 58
Schrom, Ken 179
Schwall, Don 136
Scudder, Scott 99
Scully, Gerald 38, 64–67, 208
Scurry, Rod 96
Seattle Mariners 3, 34–36, 39, 51, 89, 101, 116–117, 123, 152–153, 172, 192, 209, 211, 224, 229
Seaver, Tom 111, 130, 137, 140, 142, 144–145
Segui, Diego 131
Seilheimer, Rick 90
Sele, Aaron 136
Selig, Bud 11, 15, 52, 76, 78, 88, 150, 202, 205, 210–213, 215
Shantz, Bobby 131
Sheffield, Gary 89, 206
Shuey, Paul 92
Simmons, Curt 107
Simmons, Ted 110
Simpson, Allan 78, 225
Slaton, Jim 110
Sloan, Tim 226–227
Smith, Lonnie 91
Smith, Reggie 227
Smithson, Mike 175
Smoltz, John 27, 134
Snyder, Cory 179
Society for American Baseball Research 17–18, 106, 224
Spahn, Warren 134, 137–141, 143–146, 210, 228
Sparks, Steve 136
Speck, Cliff 96
Splittorff, Paul 167

Sports Illustrated 215
Sportsman's Park 107
Stafford, Bill 136
Staley, Gerry 145
Stearns, John 91
Stein, Randy 96
Steinbrenner, George 16, 24
Stengel, Casey 147
Stewart, Dave 135
Strawberry, Darryl 91
Sturdivant, Tom 131
sub-.400 teams 5–6, 9, 41, 61, 128, 151, 202–205, 211, 223–224
Sullivan, Neil J. 78, 225
Sundberg, Jim 167
Surhoff, B.J. 85
Sutcliffe, Rick 96–99, 107
Sutton, Don 134, 138–139, 144–146, 227
Swindell, Greg 99
Swisher, Steve 91

Tabb, Jerry 90
Tabler, Pat 179
Tampa Bay Devil Rays 22, 46, 199, 203, 209
Tanana, Frank 96–99, 169
Taylor, Bob "Hawk" 80
TBS 27
Templeton, Garry 91
Terry, Ralph 136
Texas Rangers 13, 36, 39, 51, 56, 97, 109, 119–120, 121–122, 125, 152, 160, 165–169, 171, 175, 178, 184–185, 187–189, 199
Thomas, Frank 58, 77, 89
Thomas, Gorman 110
Thomas, Roy 96
Thome, Jim 35
Thompson, Scot 91
Thorn, John 214
Thornton, Andre 179
Tiant, Luis 107, 167
Tiger Stadium 138
Toronto Blue Jays 3, 6, 15, 37, 104, 111–113, 115, 135, 138, 149–150, 174–178, 180–181, 183–189, 195–196, 199, 203, 209, 211–212, 223, 226
Torrez, Andrew 227
Total Baseball 79, 223
Trammel, Alan 37
Tribune Company 37
Turley, Bob 131
Turner, Ted 36
Turner Field 36
Twain, Mark 3
Twitchell, Wayne 100

U.S. census 43
University of Miami 89
USA Today 18

Valdes, Ismael 101
Valentin, Jose 89, 226
Vatcher, Jim 97
Vaughn, Greg 27, 36, 211
Ventura, Robin 89
Viola, Frank 108, 226
Vukovich, Pete 110

Wagner, Billy 92
Wagner, Honus 142
Wakefield, Dick 80
Walk, Bob 107
Walker, Larry 2
Wallach, Tim 91
Washington Post 228
Washington Redskins 151
Washington Senators 46, 204
Weaver, Earl 167, 172
Weaver, Jeff 77
Weaver, Jered 77
Weiss, George 147, 228
Welch, Bob 135
Wells, David 133, 145, 149, 227
Whitaker, Lou 37
White, Frank 167
wild-card playoff format 9, 116, 122, 125, 152–201, 208–210, 228; and competitive balance 152, 154, 191, 201; comparison with divisional playoff format 152–191, 198–201, 208, 228; fans' response to 152, 166, 191–200, 229; 1996 164; quality of playoff participants 155–163, 165–191, 200–201
Williams, Pete 15
Williams, Ted 134, 141–142
Wilson, Glenn 91
Wilson, James 149
Winfield, Dave 77, 91
Winner's Curse 66
Wise, Rick 107
Witt, Bobby 97–99
Wrigley Field 37, 106, 122
Wynn, Early 132, 137, 144–146

Yastrzemski, Carl 142, 167, 227
Young, Cy 96, 142
Yount, Robin 78, 91, 110

Zimbalist, Andrew 6, 23, 30, 32, 42, 65–67, 202, 208, 212–213, 215, 223–224, 229
Zito, Barry 134, 136

www.ingramcontent.com/pod-product-compliance
Ingram Content Group UK Ltd.
Pitfield, Milton Keynes, MK11 3LW, UK
UKHW041941140426
5217IPUK00014B/595